Enterprise Risk Management

Enterprise Risk Management
A Common Framework
for the Entire Organization

Philip E. J. Green

ELSEVIER

AMSTERDAM • BOSTON • HEIDELBERG • LONDON
NEW YORK • OXFORD • PARIS • SAN DIEGO
SAN FRANCISCO • SINGAPORE • SYDNEY • TOKYO
Butterworth-Heinemann is an imprint of Elsevier

Acquiring Editor: Tom Stover
Editorial Project Manager: Hilary Carr
Project Manager: Punithavathy Govindaradjane
Designer: Mark Rogers

Butterworth-Heinemann is an imprint of Elsevier
The Boulevard, Langford Lane, Kidlington, Oxford OX5 1GB, UK
225 Wyman Street, Waltham, MA 02451, USA

ISBN: 978-0-12-800633-7

British Library Cataloguing-in-Publication Data
A catalogue record for this book is available from the British Library

Library of Congress Cataloging-in-Publication Data
A catalog record for this book is available from the Library of Congress

For Information on all Butterworth-Heinemann publications
visit our website at http://store.elsevier.com/

Dedication

To my parents, Les and Marion Green

Contents

Part I Physical Risk Management

Part II Intangible Risk

Part III Financial Risk Management

Part IV Global and Strategic Risk

Author Biographies

Chapter 1: Philip E. J. Green

Philip Green is CEO of First Resource Management Group, Inc., which manages forests in Canada and provides forestry-related remote sensing data. Before this, he was president of Greenbridge Management, Inc., during which time he provided risk management, process management, continuous improvement, and statistical consulting services to industries in many sectors across North and South America, Europe, and Asia. He is coauthor of *misLeading Indicators: How to Reliably Measure Your Business* (with Professor George Gabor of Dalhousie University), published by Praeger. He has an M.Sc. in statistics from McMaster University.

Chapter 2: John Roberts, M.Eng., P.Eng., and Dr. Frank Frantisak

John Roberts is a professional engineer who has worked in the natural resource industries at their interface with their environment and society for more than thirty years. He was vice president of environment for Noranda Forest, Inc., and its successor company Nexfor. He subsequently became vice president of environment for Aurora Energy, a junior uranium mining company. Currently he is vice president of environmental affairs at TMAC Resources, a mineral exploration and development company.

Frank Frantisak was one of the first corporate environmental executives in Canada. Now retired, he was senior vice president of environment, health and hygiene at Noranda, Inc. He produced Canada's first standalone environmental report by a publicly traded corporation, developed the world's first air pollution index, for the province of Ontario, served on the technical committee to develop the ISO 14000 environmental standard, and was a corporate leader in developing environmental management systems. He has a Ph.D. in chemical engineering from Czech Technical University and is a member of the Order of Canada.

Chapter 3: Gaston Lafontaine, P.Eng.

Gaston Lafontaine is a graduate in mechanical engineering of Ecole Polytechnique, with a career of twenty-eight years in petroleum refining. After five years in the various functions of technical engineering, he became manager of maintenance and production departments and eventually became general manager of the Montreal-East Shell Refinery for five years. Now retired, he was coordinator of safety and health for all Shell installations in Canada. After his career with Shell, he worked for some fifteen years as a consultant in the field of risk management in various sectors of the industries in Canada, the United States, and Africa and taught engineering at Sherbrooke University.

Chapter 4: Mike Fontaine

Mike Fontaine has more than thirty years' project experience from the perspective of an engineering, procurement and construction, and project management firm, primarily in the metals and mining sector. His experience covers the entire project life cycle, from conceptual studies through to project execution, including plant startup. Mike's experience includes process engineering, project management, project controls, quality management, and, for more than twenty years, risk management. He is regional risk manager for central North America for Hatch, an engineering and multidisciplinary professional services firm employing more than 11,000 people in more than sixty-five, with more than $35 billion in projects currently under management.

Chapter 5: Steve Osselton and Emily Heuts

Steve Osselton is national practice leader for Marsh's Risk Consulting Practice (MRC), Marsh Canada's risk advisory group. In this capacity, he leads a multidisciplinary team of risk consultants specializing in a wide range of technical and industry specific disciplines in the commercial, manufacturing, resource, and government sectors. Steve has been with Marsh Canada Limited since 1985 and previously held risk control technical positions with AIG and FM Global. He has a bachelor's of applied science degree in civil engineering from the University of Waterloo (1980), is a registered professional engineer for the Province of Ontario, and has a Canadian risk management (CRM) designation.

Emily Heuts is assistant vice president of Marsh Risk Consulting for organizational risk and resilience with Marsh Risk Consulting in Toronto, specializing in enterprise risk management (ERM). Emily's ERM experience spans various industry sectors, most notably within the Canadian real estate, mining, and public entity sectors. Emily has helped numerous large Canadian private and public companies develop formalized risk management frameworks (including risk assessment, prioritization, reporting, and senior management training). Emily holds an MBA from Wilfrid Laurier University and an HBA from the University of Western Ontario.

Chapter 6: Nick Wildgoose, B.A. (Hons), FCA, FCIPS

Nick Wildgoose is a qualified accountant and supply chain professional and has held a variety of global financial, supply chain, and commercial positions in a number of industry sectors, working for companies such as PWC, BOC Group, the Virgin Group, and, currently, Zurich Insurance Group. He served on the board of the Chartered Institute of Purchasing and Supply, the largest professional body in the world, having around 70,000 members. He has also served as a specialist advisor to the World Economic Forum on the topic of systemic supply chain risk and is chairman of the Supply Chain Risk Leadership Council. He is currently leading the roll-out of innovative and award winning supply chain risk products for Zurich Insurance Group in London, which has given him the opportunity to interact with a large number of global companies and understand how they are addressing the real issues they are facing in terms of supply chain risk.

Chapter 7: Kevvie Fowler

Kevvie Fowler is a Partner in KPMG's Risk Consulting Practice and has over 19 years of security and forensics experience. Kevvie assists clients solve a variety of cyber security challenges ranging from defining key organizational assets to developing security assessment and governance strategies to protect them, and leads a team of cyber forensic investigators who assist clients in preparing for, responding to and recovering from cyber attacks. He is author of *Data Breach Response and Investigations* and *SQL Server Forensic Analysis*; he is a contributing author to several security and forensics books; is a frequent speaker at industry conferences and is a media resource for a number of industry publications. Kevvie also sits on the SANS Advisory Board where he guides the direction of emerging security and forensic research.

Chapter 8: Jonathan Copulsky and Chuck Saia

Jonathan Copulsky is a senior principal with Deloitte Consulting LLP, where he works with the world's best-known brands on their most challenging sales and marketing issues. In addition to his client work, Jonathan serves as chief content officer of Deloitte LLP and Chief Marketing Officer of Deloitte Consulting. His critically acclaimed book *Brand Resilience: Managing Risk and Recovery in a High-Speed World* was published by Palgrave Macmillan in May 2011. Jonathan holds a B.A. from Haverford College and an MBA from Stanford University.

Chuck Saia is the chief risk, reputation, and crisis officer of Deloitte LLP, responsible for overseeing firmwide reputation and risk governance practices and driving the firm's strategic risk management program. Chuck has more than twenty years' experience advising clients on corporate governance, regulatory issues, risk management, and internal controls. He currently serves as the advisory partner for BMO Harris and Credit Suisse and has previously been the lead client service partner and lead advisory partner for multiple multinational banking and financial services clients. He is a certified public accountant, has an MBA with a focus on internal controls, and has written numerous articles and white papers on internal control subject areas.

Chapter 9: Mitch Albinski

Mitch Albinski is principal of Blackhall River Security Associates in Old Lyne, Connecticut. He delivers services that enable clients to build operationally focused security programs grounded by industry standards and based on assessment of risk. Mitch has an engineering background. He has led security program integration teams during multiple corporate mergers and acquisitions and is an advisor to key executive management on subjects related to security risk and crisis management, activist and terrorist activities, and other threats affecting company business and research operations.

Chapter 10: Steven Miller, Ph.D., CPCU, ARM

Steven Miller is an assistant professor of finance at Saint Joseph's University and is currently serving as a Visiting Foreign Scholar at the Central University of Finance and Economics (CUFE) in Beijing, China. Prior to joining academia, Steve worked at Marsh as a consultant. Steve was based in Chicago, New York, and London and has extensive international experience, managing consulting engagements around the globe. In 2009, he joined St. Joseph's University to help launch their new major in risk management and insurance, and he has published articles in a number of academic journals, including the *Journal of Banking and Finance, Journal of Risk and Insurance, Journal of Insurance Issues*, and *Journal of Insurance Regulation*.

Chapter 11: Sibt-ul-Hasnain Kazmi, M.A., FRM

Sibt-ul-Hasnain Kazmi works for Agriculture and Agri-Food Canada as a Program officer. Before this, he worked as a data analyst at the Canadian Imperial Bank of Commerce in Toronto. Prior to this, he wrote research reports for a private equity firm. He was a senior economist at the International Monetary Fund and a risk analyst in the Treasury of the Central Bank of Pakistan. He has two master's degrees in economics (social statistics) from McGill University, Montreal, and York University, Toronto. He is a certified financial risk manager.

Chapter 12: Greg Niehaus

Greg Niehaus is a professor of finance and insurance at the University of South Carolina, where he served as finance department chair from 2001 to 2004 and as senior associate dean for research and academics from 2007 to 2011. He teaches and conducts research on risk management, insurance economics, and corporate finance. He is the coauthor, with Scott Harrington of the Wharton School, of the textbook *Risk Management and Insurance*, 2nd ed., published by Irwin/McGraw-Hill. He has published articles in a number of academic journals, including the *Journal of Financial Economics, Journal of Finance, Journal of Business, Accounting Review, Journal of Banking and Finance, Journal of Financial Intermediation*, and *Journal of Risk and Insurance*.

Chapter 13: Oliver Davidson, Patricia Mackenzie, Mike Wilkinson, and Ron Burke

Oliver Davidson is a Senior Consultant at Towers Watson, with a background in organizational psychology and works with clients to help them improve performance through measuring, understanding and changing employee attitudes and organizational culture. Over the years he has acted as a consultant to leading businesses globally across a wide range of sectors. In particular, he has worked with many organizations specifically on aspects of their risk culture. Oliver has a BSc and PhD from the University of Durham and an MSc from the Institute of Work Psychology at Sheffield University.

Patricia Mackenzie is a Senior Consultant at Towers Watson with over 15 years' experience as a management consultant, leading major performance improvement and implementation of ERM frameworks projects. Patricia leads the Internal Model Validation initiative for the Europe, Middle East, and Africa region. She has supported insurance companies in Europe and Mexico in implementing risk management frameworks, with particular emphasis in tailoring regulatory changes to the companies' business models and corporate governance. Patricia is a frequent conference speaker and contributing author to a number of risk related publications. She has a Business and Accounting Degrees from the Universidad del Pacifico and a specialization in Corporate Finance from the London Business School.

Mike Wilkinson is a Director in Towers Watson's Risk and Financial Services practice and leads Risk and Solvency II for the Europe, Middle East, and Africa region. He has over 25 years' experience of supporting strategic, regulatory, organizational and operational developments in the insurance and financial services sectors. He has worked extensively with insurers, reinsurers and regulatory bodies in Europe, Middle East, Asia and the Americas to plan, implement and embed ERM and regulatory driven change. Mike's principle focus is on implementing and integrating risk management and models in decision-making, business operations, governance and culture.

Ron Burke is a Director at Towers Watson and leads the firm's Sales Effectiveness & Rewards practice for the Europe, Middle East, and Africa region. Much of his work involves the design of incentive programmes – and the consideration of the various risks related to these plans – for a wide variety of customer facing sales and service roles spanning many different industries. He has over 20 years of consulting experience, is a frequent conference speaker and is also a contributing author to *The Sales Compensation Handbook* (2nd Edition). He earned a Master of International Affairs (M.I.A.) degree with a concentration in international banking and finance from Columbia University, and also holds a B.A. degree in development studies with a concentration in economic and political development from the University of California at Berkeley.

Chapter 14: Peter Whyntie

Peter Whyntie is an independent governance, risk management and compliance consultant, with thirty years' experience in management, consulting, and regulatory roles. He spent his career with a number of leading Australian financial services companies, including ANZ Funds Management, Prudential, Colonial, and Zurich; he was subsequently the national partner for compliance at KPMG. He is a member of the Governance Institute of Australia's Subject Advisory Committee for Advanced Risk Management. He is a regular presenter on compliance and risk management at industry seminars and professional association forums in both Australia and Asia.

Chapter 15: Elizabeth Stephens

Dr. Elizabeth Stephens is an investment and country risk advisor, political columnist, and university lecturer. For eight years she was head of credit and political risk advisory at JLT Specialty, where she worked with some of the world's largest commodity traders, energy companies, and financial institutions. While at JLT, she designed and built the World Risk Review, a country risk ratings tool that provides risk ratings and analysis for 198 territories. Elizabeth received a Ph.D. in international relations from the London School of Economics and Political Science and is a guest lecturer at the University of Birmingham. She is a regular conference speaker and is regularly quoted in the media, including in the *Financial Times* and the *Times*, and has recently appeared on Sky News, the BBC, and CNBC.

Chapter 16: Michael E. Raynor

Michael E. Raynor is a director at Deloitte Services LP; he is an advisor to senior executives in the world's leading corporations across a wide range of industries. Raynor has authored or co-authored four books, most recently *The Three Rules: How Exceptional Companies Think* (Portfolio), with Mumtaz Ahmed, which was named the Best Business Book of 2013 by the Toronto Globe & Mail.

He was coauthor, with Professor Clayton M. Christensen, of the New York Times bestseller *The Innovator's Solution*, and author of *The Innovator's Manifesto*, a Canadian #1 bestseller.

He was sole author of *The Strategy Paradox*, which was named by Strategy + Business as one of its top five picks in strategy, with BusinessWeek naming it one of that year's ten best business books. Michael has a doctorate from the Harvard Business School, a master's degree in business administration from the Ivey School of Business at the University of Western Ontario in London, Canada, and an undergraduate degree in philosophy from Harvard University.

1

Introduction to Risk Management Principles

Philip E. J. Green[*]

Ultimately it is the business manager, not the risk specialist, who is responsible when things go wrong. The challenge the manager faces is that the many fields of risk management are dominated by specialists and jargon. The insurance broker, the safety manager, the cybersecurity specialist, the financial risk manager, and the engineer all use different language to describe risk. Even within each specialty there are variations in the way language is used, making it hard for a generalist to distinguish between what is particular about risk management in one field versus another—say, cybersecurity versus safety—and what is common, and thus what should be done by the specialist and by the generalist.

Another challenge is the seemingly infinite variety of risk management *processes*. If you search the Internet for "risk management process," you will quickly see the wide variety of approaches favored by different consultants and experts. There are four-, five-, six-, and nine-step risk management processes. There are risk management cycles, flowcharts, pyramids, and decision trees. There is obviously value in the creativity of the human mind applied to risk. But there is also value in simplification and standardization.

This book aims to equip the reader to effectively manage an organization's risks, to provide the reader with a common vocabulary and process for managing all types of risk and to provide insights into each of the particularities of several critical types of risk. The idea is to help readers focus on the substantive aspects of several risk specialties, rather than on the semantic and procedural.

This chapter sets out a vocabulary and risk management process common to the remaining chapters of the book (terms commonly used throughout the book are underlined in this chapter). All the authors have contributed to this chapter. In their own chapters, they have applied its concepts to their specific field of risk management. The terminology and the risk management process we have adopted for the book are inspired from an international risk management standard.[1] This book is respectful toward, but does not take a position on, that standard; nor does it blindly adhere to it. We do not claim that the words and the risk management process are novel. But what is novel is our use of them as a common approach applicable to the entire enterprise as well as to multiple types of risk—hence the title. This book cannot

[*]With input from the other authors.

cover all types of risk that an enterprise faces. By showing that different experts use a similar thought process and language, but employed from different viewpoints, I hope that the common approach will be clear to readers, allowing them to extend principles covered in this and the other chapters to specialties not covered herein.

The idea of a risk specialty is somewhat fluid. A single event may have multiple consequences; sometimes they can escalate or cascade in a ripple effect. These consequences may even affect areas of the business considered to be under the domain of different risk specialties. For example, a pipeline spill may injure employees or the public (health and safety risk), kill fish and pollute a river (environment and sustainability risk), shut down operations (operational risk), harm a pipeline company's brand or reputation (brand risk), disrupt supply chains (supply chain risk), increase insurance premiums and cost billions to clean up, causing share prices to drop (financial risk), change the political context in which the pipeline company is hoping to gain approval for a new pipeline (political risk), and disrupt the company's growth strategy (strategic risk). Complicating matters, specialists often view risks through their own lenses: The safety manager might classify a pipeline spill as a safety risk, the marketing executive as a brand risk, and the loss control manager as a financial risk, and so on, all dealing with the risk with their own specialty's tools and jargon. It is much better to have a common approach and an enterprise-wide risk management system.

What is Risk?

What is <u>risk</u>? The word contains two key ideas: uncertainty and outcomes. In common usage, people associate risk with negative outcomes more than with positive ones, but usually both are present. The idea of outcomes can be broadened to think of goals or <u>objectives</u>. A jaywalker may have two objectives: to save time instead of waiting for a green traffic light, and to cross the street without being hit by a car. There is uncertainty about whether he can jaywalk and meet those objectives. The first objective relates to a positive outcome (saved time), the second to a negative outcome (injury).

Risk can thus be thought of as the *effect of uncertainty on objectives*. This book expresses risk as *the consequences of an event*, such as being hit by a car while jaywalking, *and the associated likelihood of that event*.

There are several ways that people commonly use the word risk. Some use it to refer to the likelihood of an event's happening, others to the consequences if it does happen. For example, when someone states that California has greater earthquake risk than New York, he or she could be saying that earthquakes are more likely in California. Or when someone states that XYZ Corp has greater risk, should a cyberattack occur, than another company does, he or she could mean that XYZ Corp would have a greater loss if a cyberattack were to occur. In fact, risk deals with both likelihood and consequences. People also commonly use the term *risk* to refer to unpredictability or variability in outcomes. For example, financial analysts will say that a high-tech stock has greater risk than a utility stock because the returns on the high-tech stock have greater variability or are thus more difficult to predict. In other words, there is greater uncertainty over the desired outcome of a return on the investment.

What is <u>enterprise risk management</u>? Enterprise risk management is a system in which managers are concerned with managing the risks of the entire enterprise. In a more traditional approach various specialists focus on specific or "pure" risks, which are not aggregated to provide a view of the risk the enterprise faces.

What is <u>risk management</u>? Risk management is the coordinated set of principles, processes, activities, roles and responsibilities, and infrastructure, combined into a system and used to control the actions of an organization in light of the risks it faces.

Enterprise risk management applies many of the fundamental principles of management; indeed, it is an integral part of management. The contributors to this book have emphasized these principles from different viewpoints, but two receive special attention: communication and accountability (or responsibility). The authors look at these issues through the perspective of their own risk specialty, but taken together, they provide useful insights that are applicable to other types of risk. For example, Chapter 5 discusses operational risk and describes a top-to-bottom communication process (illustrated by Figure 5–2 of that chapter) that melds nicely with the process described in Chapter 9 regarding the portfolio method of aggregating risks. A challenge with the portfolio risk approach is communication of the risks that should be included in the portfolio. It also melds nicely with the approach in Chapter 2 regarding internal communication processes of environmental risks. The principles outlined in these chapters apply to many other areas.

To manage the risks of the entire enterprise suggests that some individual, perhaps a chief risk officer or a group reporting to him or her, knows the risks of the entire enterprise. But this is impractical and bureaucratic. Or perhaps people on the top of the organization should manage the small number of large risks and the people on the bottom the large number of small risks. This has appeal, but because a small mishap, indiscretion, or malevolent act by a single employee can in some cases cause disaster for the entire enterprise, the top cannot just leave it up the bottom to deal with risk unsupervised.

The solution that emerges from the contributors is that communications is a mix. Top management must use its communications to set tone, direction, and policy for the enterprise in relation to risk. It should provide training about the risks the enterprise faces and how to manage them. It must seek out information to determine whether risks, big or small, are being managed systematically throughout the enterprise. And it must ensure that people know when to communicate significant risks they have identified to the top so that they can be aggregated and managed in an enterprise risk "portfolio." These ideas are brought together in Chapter 13, on risk culture.

The contributors have addressed the issue of accountability and employee involvement by examining several questions: What should be done by people dedicated to risk management? What should be done by line management as part of regular responsibilities? What is the responsibility of top management? What are the responsibilities of the line organization? How should employees be involved? What should they be responsible for? Chapter 14 discusses the role of the board of directors in risk management and, in particular, whether there should be a dedicated risk committee. Chapter 2, on environmental risks, describes how this split in responsibilities between line and staff environmental experts changes with context. Chapter 3, on health and safety risk, graphically describes the responsibilities of management and employees for safety. Chapter 6, on cybersecurity, describes how all employees should be aware of their responsibilities for cybersecurity. Chapter 7, on brand risk, describes how, in a viral world, to embed a brand risk intelligence mindset across the entire organization—in other words, it addresses the central problem of getting everyone involved in managing the risks over which they have some influence.

Risk Context

Risk changes with context. It may help to think of context in terms of external context and internal context. The external context includes business, infrastructural, economic, social, cultural, and political context and the trends affecting—or that could affect—the organization. In the case of a jaywalker, it includes such things as the volume of traffic and the weather. The internal context includes the organization's culture, processes, structure, strategy, policies and objectives, and methods. A jaywalker rushing to a hospital where his daughter is undergoing emergency surgery has a very different internal context than one who is trying to avoid a ten-minute wait for the next bus. Both share the objective of trying to save time, but understanding the context is vital to understanding the criteria they use to evaluate risk.

Part of internal context is risk tolerance and risk appetite. Risk appetite is the amount of risk that an organization is willing to assume in pursuit of its objectives. For example, a young startup company may be willing to "bet the farm" in its pursuit of growth, whereas a utility would have much less appetite for risk. Risk appetite is linked to an expected return, to moral values, or to business objectives. Not all forms of risk are equally appetizing. A company may have a large appetite for financial risks in its pursuit of profits. For risks that could harm or kill employees or members of the public, the same company could (and should) have a much smaller appetite. Shell, for example, says: "Goal Zero captures the belief that we can operate without fatalities or significant incidents despite the often difficult conditions in which we operate."[2]

Risk appetite depends on who eats the risk. The 2010 Deepwater Horizon drilling rig explosion and subsequent oil spill in the Gulf of Mexico was catastrophic for those who were killed and for their families. It was catastrophic for some small business owners, who lost tourism business along with a substantive amount of their own equity. It caused extensive damage to the environment. But was it a catastrophe for British Petroleum, who leased the rig? Even though BP suffered a huge financial loss and has paid billions of dollars in restitution and fines, it is still a large, viable business.

Risk Assessment

Risk assessment is the process of

1. Risk identification
2. Risk analysis
3. Risk prioritization

The risk profile is a description of the risks of an enterprise, resulting from the risk assessment.

Risk Identification

Risk identification is the process of identifying the sources of risk and the events that can occur, as well as the causes and potential consequences of such events. The sources of risk are those situations that may give rise to a risk. The traffic on the street is the source of risk to the jaywalker. Getting hit by a car while jaywalking is an event that could have potentially serious consequences.

The goal of risk identification is to create a list (or register) of risks that are based on events that could have significant consequences. This list should include risks that are under the control of the organization and those that are not, risks that are adequately controlled by the organization and those that are not, and risks that were previously known, as well as new risks uncovered during risk identification. Risk identification should identify the possible consequences, including cascading consequences, of the event.

Defining the "event" can be tricky, because events usually follow each other in a causal chain. Suppose a man jaywalks across a busy street and gets hit by a car. The impact breaks his leg. Is the event that the man jaywalked and the consequence that he was hit by a car? Or is the event that he was hit by a car and the consequence that he broke his leg? Reasonable people can view the same chain of events differently. The best guidance is to do what is reasonable and practical in your circumstances. For the zealous cop, the event is that a man jaywalked; for the ambulance driver, that he was hit by a car; for the orthopedic surgeon, that his leg was broken. In a general way, an event is some occurrence such as an "incident" or "accident," or a change in a particular set of circumstances that affect objectives. The change in circumstances that warrant being thought of as an event depends on an organization's context and objectives. An event can include something that does not happen (such as a new supplier failing to deliver). Or an event can have no consequences, such as in the case of a "close call" or a "near miss."

Another reason why defining the event can be tricky is because of the different perspectives created by the interplay of frequency, time and space. Volcanic eruptions are thought of as spectacular events if they happen in our own lifetime and vicinity, because on those scales they are rare. But on geological timescales, on the planet as a whole, they are a certainty—not so much "events" as a geological process. Jaywalking happens virtually all the time in large cities—it is thus highly likely that over the course of a statistical reporting year, several jaywalkers will be hit by cars. For city administrators, such occurrences become part of urban life. The likelihood of a particular jaywalker's getting hit on a particular street is much lower—so it is easier to see such a thing as an "event," especially if you are the jaywalker who gets hit.

Risk Analysis

The purpose of risk analysis is to understand the causes and sources of risk, the effectiveness of existing risk controls, the likelihood of the event, and the consequences—both negative and positive—of the event. The results of risk analysis are used for risk prioritization and risk treatment.

There are many ways to express the results of a risk analysis. Most typical is to rate a risk using a grid of likelihood and consequences. The 3 × 3 grid in Figure 1-1 is one such manifestation of a risk analysis grid.

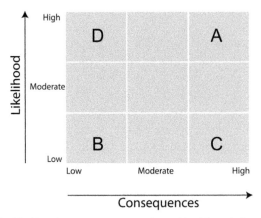

FIGURE 1–1 An example of the likelihood–consequences matrix used in risk analysis.

In such a grid, an event that has high consequences and high likelihood (A) is considered to be a greater risk than an event having low consequences and low likelihood (B). Depending on the criteria an organization or person uses to determine likelihood and consequences, a risk having high consequences and low likelihood (C) may or may not be considered to have the same risk as one having low consequences and high likelihood (D). For example, a parent may be less likely to worry about the likely but inconsequential cuts and scrapes that children get to their knees (D) than the less likely but very consequential risk of their child's being hit by a car (C). Similarly, a pipeline company may be less concerned about the relatively likely but minor oil spills that occur during vehicle maintenance (D) than about a single pipeline failure that spills large quantities of oil into a river in full view of the public (C).

Some organizations use risk analysis to *quantify* risks, others use a *qualitative* approach to risk analysis. For example, one organization may choose to classify risks as "high," "medium," and "low;" another to rank them from highest to lowest; and a third to assign a number, based on likelihood and consequences, to each. All are useful and valid approaches, depending on organizational context.

Ideally, two individuals or two groups within the same organization, provided they have the same information about a risk, should assign the same consequences and likelihood. If reasoning about risk were done by risk-management robots, programmed according to clear rules and having access to the same information, each robot would indeed assign the same likelihood and consequences. But in practice, people do not reason like robots about risk, and they do not always have access to—or pay attention to—the same information. There are also psychological aspects to how people perceive and reason about risk, likelihood, and consequences which are described later in this chapter (please see the description of "anchoring" and "availability" in the section Reasoning about Probability, Uncertainty and Likelihood) and in Chapter 11. Our goal, however, should be to achieve as high a degree of consistency as possible.

Some consistency can be achieved with well-defined risk criteria. Risk has two dimensions, likelihood and consequences, so it is useful to develop criteria for each. The criteria for evaluating consequences should describe what consequences are important, why they are important, specific things to be considered when determining consequences (such as the views or reactions of stakeholders), internal and external contexts, and thresholds for certain types of consequences (such as financial loss thresholds). The criteria should be based on the risk appetite. If a jaywalker is hit, fast traffic will do more damage than slow traffic, so the criteria for determining the consequences of a jaywalker's being hit by a car should include traffic speed.

Criteria for likelihood should consider both factors that make an event likely and factors that make an event less likely. Heavy traffic makes it more likely that a jaywalker will be hit by a car than light traffic; the criteria for determining the likelihood of a jaywalker's being hit by a car should include the traffic.

Consider the following examples of (cursory) risk analyses by three jaywalkers:

- Arnold defines the event as being hit by a car. At rush hour on a busy urban street, Arnold determines that there are high consequences (being seriously injured) and high likelihood of being hit by a car (A).
- Brett defines the event as jaywalking on his quiet residential street. He foresees two consequences: being hit by a car, which would lead to serious injury, and teaching unsafe practices to his children, which would put them at risk. He decides that the likelihood of being hit on his street is low. If he or his children were hit, traffic is slow, so serious injury is also unlikely. The consequences of having a bad influence on his children are minimal, for he teaches them to look both ways. The result of his risk analysis is both low likelihood and low consequences (B).
- Christine defines the event as being hit by a car. Late in the evening on the same stretch of road as Arnold, Christine determines that there are high consequences, but a low likelihood of being hit by a car (C).

Risk Prioritization

Risk prioritization[3] is the process of deciding which risks should be treated based on the risk analysis, as well as the priority for treatment. The likelihoods and consequences of the risks that have been analyzed are compared with each other and with the risk criteria. The purpose is to decide on possible treatments: implementing new or improved controls, continuing with existing controls, or analyzing controls further.

Risk prioritization can be done formally, by comparing the results with organizational guidelines, or informally, through discussion and consideration of the risk analysis. In either case, you should consider the internal and external context; the organization's objectives; views of stakeholders; and legal, contractual, and other requirements to determine high-, medium-, and low-priority risks. From this, one can determine which risks need to be communicated to more senior levels of management.

Risk Treatment

After a decision has been made that a risk is a priority, it should be treated. Risk treatment involves selecting options for modifying risks, implementing the options, and improving or modifying risk controls for each risk. When treatment addresses risks having negative consequences, people often use the terms "risk mitigation" or "risk reduction."

Risk controls are practices, devices, policies, and any other methods implemented by an organization or individual to modify risk. For example, an employee computer training program is meant to control some cybersecurity risks. During a risk assessment, it is determined that these cyberrisks are too high. The training was found to be inadequate. The treatment is to *improve* the training program.

Each option for risk treatment should be reviewed and considered through a cyclical process that considers the effectiveness of the risk treatment in controlling risk, the cost of the risk treatment, the benefits of taking the risk, the views of stakeholders, the residual risks that would remain after the controls are implemented, and whether the residual risk would meet the organization's risk criteria. If the residual risks do not satisfy the risk criteria, or if they do satisfy the criteria but the costs to meet them are too high, then other risk treatments should be devised.

The risk treatments can include many possibilities:

- Avoiding the risk altogether by not engaging in the activity that gives rise to the risk
- Taking, or even increasing, the risk to pursue some opportunity
- Changing the likelihood or the consequences or both
- Sharing the risk by means of contractual, insurance, financial, community, or governmental arrangements

To change likelihood and consequences, you can improve or implement controls that do the following:

- Aim to prevent the event from happening, thus reducing the likelihood (for example, keeping your home clear of combustible materials to prevent fire).
- Aim to detect the event if it happens, thus reducing the consequences (for example, a smoke detector).
- Aim to react (or respond) to it if it happens, thus reducing the consequences (for example, a fire extinguisher). Reaction (or response) means the actions taken immediately after an event to help contain it. Effective reaction will truncate many of the potential consequences. Reaction is related to recovery, the actions taken to return to the condition that existed before the event.

The three jaywalkers decide on the following treatments: Arnold decides to reduce the likelihood of being hit by a car by not jaywalking (avoidance). Brett decides that no treatments are necessary, the existing controls being adequate. Christine decides to reduce the likelihood by only jaywalking if she cannot see cars coming in either direction and she enjoys good visibility (prevention).

After a risk has been reduced (or changed) to its new residual risk, the residual risk becomes the risk for the next round of risk assessment. As an organization's context changes over time, the new residual risk, too, may be considered to be unacceptable. An example can be found in the case of seatbelts and other restraint systems in vehicles. The first cars had no seatbelts. Volvo was the first to introduce them as standard equipment, in 1959. By the 1970s, legislation began appearing making them mandatory. By the 1990s, automobile manufacturers were adding front air bags, and by the 2000s side and other airbags. At each juncture, the risk resulting from the existing restraint technology eventually became unacceptable to the public, legislators, and automobile manufacturers. The addition of new technology "treated" the previous risk and reduced it to a new level of residual risk.

Risk Monitoring and Review

The job of risk management does not stop after risk treatments have been implemented. Monitoring and review ensures that risk controls are effective, that lessons are learned from successes and failures, that trends are identified, and that changes in internal and external context are noticed. Risk monitoring and review also includes performing investigations into events (including near misses).

Key risk indicators (KRIs) are any indicators that an organization finds useful to monitor its enterprise risk management system, to monitor the effectiveness of a risk control, to monitor the effectiveness of the enterprise risk management system or some aspect of it, or to monitor or measure some variable that indicates potential likelihood or consequences (such as traffic speed or density).

Reasoning about Probability, Uncertainty, and Likelihood

What is probability, and can it be measured? There is a common misconception that probability can be measured. Some prominent authors on risk write about measuring probabilities from frequencies of past events.[4] This not only has caused confusion, but has caused people to draw mistaken, even dangerous conclusions about risk. I use the term "measurement" in the strict sense of objectively ascertaining and quantifying some property by comparison with a standard.

The words "likelihood" and "probability" have very specific meanings in statistical theory, but in common usage, they both refer to the chance that an event will happen or has happened or the chance that a statement is true. The need for probabilistic reasoning arises from the incomplete knowledge that results in uncertainty. It is thus central to risk, which is the effect of uncertainty on objectives.

Suppose someone holds up a coin in his right hand in front of you and then hides it in his fist, puts both hands behind his back, and shuffles the coin between the hands. He then brings both hands forward towards you, fists clenched, and asks you the probability that it is in his right hand. You would be uncertain whether it is still in his right hand, or whether he has switched it to his left.

Most people will answer that the probability of its being in his right hand is 0.5. Having no reason for thinking the coin is in one hand over another, they assign a probability of 50 percent to each. The coin-holder give the probability as 1 (or 100 percent) if it is in his right hand—0 if it is not. The observer is uncertain, the coin-holder certain. Because the observer and coin-holder do not have the same knowledge about the situation, they assign different probabilities. This is a key point: The probability you assign to a proposition (such as "the coin is in the right hand") describes your knowledge about it, as well as your degree of rational belief that it is true. Likewise, the probability that you assign to an event describes your degree of rational belief that the event will happen. And a probability is not just an opinion. Physicist E. T. Jaynes says that a probability assignment is "'subjective' in the sense that it describes only a state of knowledge, and not anything that could be measured in a physical experiment."[5]

In this sense, probability is a descriptive method that fills the gap left by missing information about some event or proposition. The event can be in the past or in the future. For example, one could say, "He'll probably get hit if he jaywalks across that street now," "The fire was probably caused by faulty wiring," or "Faulty wiring will probably cause a fire within a year."

Physicists and other scientists often express probability numerically as a number between 0 and 1 (or 100 percent). For example, in 2012 scientists trying to detect the Higgs boson announced that their experiment had detected a signal likely to be a Higgs boson. They said that there was a probability of only 1 in 3,000,000 that such a signal would be produced in a universe without a Higgs boson.[6] Such statements give the impression that probability can be measured in the same way as measuring properties such as temperature or speed or voltage. It cannot. When the physicists state a probability of 1 in 3,000,000, they are using their experimental data and their existing knowledge of the laws of physics to calculate it. In the same way, one would use one's knowledge about traffic in general, as well as traffic conditions at a specific time and place, to make a statement such as "He'll probably get hit if he jaywalks across that street now."

Just because some probabilities can be expressed quantitatively does not mean that all can, nor does it mean that a particular probability can or should be expressed quantitatively. John Maynard Keynes put it succinctly when he said, "[W]hether or not such as thing is theoretically conceivable, no exercise of the practical judgment is possible by which a numerical value can actually be given to the probability of every argument."[7]

There are many options for expressing degrees of likelihood or probability. Both qualitative scales (such as high, medium, and low) and quantitative scales are commonly used. Quantitative scales can include ordinal numbers (1, 2, 3) or percentages. Bond rating agencies use their own particular scale.

What is important to note is that these quantitative scales are not *measurements* of probability but *quantifications* of it. Measurements, such as key risk indicators, may form part of the body of knowledge used to assign a quantitative (or qualitative) value to a probability. For example, data on the number of jaywalkers who have been hit at a particular spot could form part of the knowledge needed to make the statement "He'll probably get hit if he jaywalks across that street now." But those data are not a measurement of the probability. The frequency of jaywalkers' being hit is related to the probability of being hit but does not tell you the probability. The frequency certainly provides useful background information in assigning probability, but that does mean that frequencies are probabilities—they are not.

In a very dramatic illustration of this, in 1992, the Westray mine in Nova Scotia, Canada, exploded, killing twenty-six miners. Just a few weeks earlier, it had been awarded an award for being the safest mine in Canada. This award is based on the frequency of accidents in mines. The Westray's frequency was the lowest in the country, with fewer workers were injured per hours worked than at any other mine. But the mine was very badly managed, as the subsequent inquiry showed.[8] The terrified workers knew that it was very likely to explode: The methanometers that measure methane concentrations at the mine face were frequently inoperable at a time when methane was "gassing out" of the coal face and mining equipment was causing sparks.

Coin flips are often (mis)used as an example of measuring probability from frequency. This notion can be dispelled using a simple thought experiment. Suppose you are told that a particular coin, which is bent, has been vigorously flipped hundreds of times. It came up roughly two-thirds of the time on one side (i.e., heads or tails) and one-third on the other side (i.e., tails or heads). But you do not know on which side it came up most frequently. That is all you know about this coin. What probability will you assign to flipping a head on the next flip? You have no choice but to assign a probability of one-half because of the missing information, even though you know this is not equal to the frequency. The frequency of heads, however, is either two-thirds or one-third. Thus frequency is not necessarily equal to probability—it is equal only in certain situations.

Often people will use the frequencies of events to help assign a probability. Such frequencies could include the percentage of bonds that default for each rating, the fatalities per million miles driven or the incidence of cancer per 100,000 people per year. These frequencies are part of the background information and are knowledge needed to determine probability, but they are not themselves measurements of probability.

These frequencies pose a similar problem as our bent coin when looking at specific circumstances. For example, the long-term frequency of defaults of AAA rated bonds will not match the probability at the onset of a severe economic crisis. In an economic crisis, when companies' finances may be under duress, the probability of default is higher than that suggested by the long-term default frequency.

Population frequencies are usually different from the probability of a particular individual event with its own circumstances. Suppose that on average 1 in a 100,000,000 people are killed by black bears every year in North America. The annual frequency of deaths by bear in the population in an entire continent is not a "measure" of the probability of getting killed by a black bear, but it is useful background information. If you suddenly see a hungry bear crawling into your individual tent, you will certainly not comfort yourself by thinking that there is only a one in a million chance of being killed! This new information will cause you to update your probability assignment from 1 in 100,000,000 per year to something much greater!

It is thus reasonable to speak of assigning, determining, or quantifying probability, but it is not correct to speak of measuring probability, and it is dangerous to act as if probability can be measured. Probability (or likelihood) is something that you should assign based on your knowledge about the things that make an event probable or improbable. This principle is illustrated in the descriptions of evaluating a health and safety event (Chapter 3) and a cybersecurity event (Chapter 6).

People reason about probability according to a small number of rules that simplify thinking. This makes the task easier, but it can also lead to severe and systematic errors and judgmental biases. An example of how such a rule can lead to errors is exemplified in how people judge and perceive distance. The sharper an object appears, such as a house on the other side of a lake, the closer it seems. This leads to an overestimation of distance when objects are blurred by haze and an underestimation when visibility is good and objects are seen sharply. Two such rules similarly used in evaluating probability are "anchoring" and "availability."[9]

Anchoring occurs when people are overly influenced by an initial observation or value. Anchoring may have occurred in how people perceived the probability of default of collateralized debt obligations (CDOs) before the 2008 financial crisis. CDOs contained many individual securities, some having high ratings (and thus low probabilities of default). If people "anchored" on these highly rated securities in a CDO, they could have easily assigned too low a probability of default for the entire CDO.

People tend to judge an event as being more likely if it is readily imagined or recalled and thus "available" to the imagination. They will tend to think airplanes are more likely to crash if there has recently been a crash in the news, or they may think that being hit by a car while jaywalking is more likely if they know someone who was so hit. Even talking about a low-probability event may cause people to think it more probable than they did before. It is because of the availability rule that people tend to think they are better drivers than average. If they themselves are accident-free and the media report accidents' happening to others, they think themselves unlikely to have an accident.

Structure of this Book

This book is organized into four somewhat arbitrary parts. Part 1 deals with risks that are roughly classified as physical in the sense that they deal with things that can go "boom" when something goes wrong. Part 2 deals with intangible and information risks. Part 3 deals with financial risks. Finally, Part 4 looks at the big picture, addressing culture, the role of the board of directors, politics, and—finally—strategy, which looks at the risks to the survival (or fortunes) of the entire enterprise when setting strategy. The final chapter, on strategic risk, goes right to the heart of the definition of risk: the *effect of uncertainty on objectives*. All chapters look at the effect of uncertainty on objectives, but this chapter also looks at the risks inherent in the objectives themselves.

Notes

1. International Organization for Standardization, *ISO 31000:2009: Risk Management—Principles and Guidelines* (Geneva, Switzerland: ISO, 2009).
2. www.shell.com/global/environment-society/safety/culture.html.

3. ISO 31000 calls this risk evaluation. Because *risk evaluation*, *risk assessment*, and *risk analysis* are terms so similar that they may lead to confusion, we have chosen *risk prioritization*.

4. For example, Peter Bernstein, *Against the Gods: The Remarkable Theory of Risk* (New York: Wiley, 1996).

5. E. T. Jaynes, *Probability Theory: The Logic of Science* (Cambridge, UK: Cambridge University Press, 2003), pp. 3, 17.

6. ATLAS Experiment, "Latest Results from ATLAS Higgs Search," July 4, 2012, www.atlas.ch/news/2012/latest-results-from-higgs-search.html.

7. John Maynard Keynes, *A Treatise on Probability* (New York: Cosimo, 2006/1920), p. 27.

8. Justice K. Peter Richard, Commissioner, *The Westray Story: A Predictable Path to Disaster; Report of the Westray Mine Public Inquiry* (1997).

9. For more on these rules, see Amos Tversky and Daniel Kahneman, "Judgment under Uncertainty: Heuristics and Biases," *Science* 185 (1974): 1124–1131.

Physical Risk Management

2

Environmental Risk

John Roberts and Frank Frantisak

Environmental risks arise from the relationships of corporations with the natural environment and with the entities that regulate, protect, and manage the environment. Sources of environmental risk include energy use and its effects, greenhouse gas emissions, water use and discharges, waste disposal, site contamination, and effects on biodiversity. Many corporate activities, such as manufacturing, mining, importing new materials, and selling automobiles, are the subject of environmental regulations developed to protect the environment. There is considerable risk in not achieving compliance with their requirements.

Environmental risks can be viewed through a social risk lens, and vice versa. Social risks arise when people react to corporate effects, whether actual or perceived, on the environment. The usual public reaction to industrial effects on the environment is ambivalence. But some effects, actual, proposed or perceived, can incite people to outrage, demonstrations, letters to the editor, boycotts, media campaigns, complaints to government officials, and lawsuits. Many such complaints will lead to investigations and even charges. There is political risk (see Chapter 15 on Political Risk), for companies can lose the support of political friends and elected officials such as a mayor or governor and even lose the support of industry groups. A company could wind up with disgruntled employees or have difficulty attracting employees because of its poor environmental reputation. This general sullying of personal and corporate reputations can affect a company's brand (see Chapter 8 on Brand Risk) and can have serious personal effects on managers who might be implicated.

Environmental Risks—the Social Dimension

Why do some members of the public get upset about environmental risks that experts are not concerned about? People often distrust experts, especially when they disagree with one another, and with good reason: In many high-profile cases, the experts have been wrong. Experts claimed PCBs[1] were inert and stable and thus ideal for use in electrical equipment. Years later, it was found they accumulate up the food chain and are persistent in nature. The U.S. Environmental Protection Agency describes their many toxic effects on humans and animals.[2] CFCs[3] were introduced because of their firefighting properties and because experts said that they were less dangerous than ammonia for refrigeration and air conditioning. After many years of use, it was discovered that they were burning a hole in the ozone layer of the atmosphere over Antarctica. Governments around the world have banned both chemicals.

People's reaction to environmental risk is strongly driven by the control (or lack thereof) that they can exert over the source of risk. People are more likely to get outraged if they feel that the company gets all the profits from taking a risk and the people get all the consequences—with little or no say in how the risk will be managed.

And not only exotic chemicals provoke this reaction: There were, and still are, major campaigns lead by public interest groups against forestry, energy, and mining operations. Some "outraged" people live near these operations, but many more are not directly affected. Their outrage is often driven by broader concerns about the environment. In 2005, TransCanada Corporation proposed the Keystone XL pipeline expansion, a 327-mile shortcut between existing pipelines that would shorten the distance between Canada's oil sands and the U.S. Gulf Coast refineries. Well-known climate scientists, environmental groups, newspapers, and celebrities opposed the project on environmental and climate grounds. Protests drew tens of thousands of people. The CEO of TransCanada called the pipeline "routine," saying that the company had been building pipelines for more than half a century and that 200,000 miles of similar pipeline already existed in the United States.[4] Yet at the time of writing, the project was still in limbo, with President Obama deferring a decision indefinitely.

When determining the consequences of environmental risks, you should determine the potential for community "outrage,"[5] because it is capable of halting a project or exaggerating a technically minor incident or project proposal. People often find many environmental effects outrageous even when technically informed people—experts—performing risk assessments judge the mechanical, physical or chemical or biological risks to be minimal. Thus environmental risks and social reaction to them must be considered together.

Consider the following example. Some of the world's best wood fiber for papermaking is made by a chemical process called the Kraft process. The Kraft pulp process emits a strong, pungent odor similar to that of rotten eggs. Though the smell is unpleasant, there are no known health effects at the usual concentrations. At a Kraft pulp mill in Thurso, Quebec, the odor had been prevalent for many years. The mill had been in the town for several decades, and many employees were residents of the town. Because of this, and perhaps because the nose becomes somewhat accustomed to the odor, this situation had been more or less tolerated over the years.

In the late 1980s and 1990s, the number of odor complaints increased. In addition, when there was an easterly wind, the odor would waft into downtown Ottawa, about 30 kilometers away, increasing the complaint halo. The managers of the mill did nothing for a while, as was often the case at that time. They believed the mill to be an important economic contributor to the community—and, in any case, it was not affecting public health. But complaints became increasingly frequent and vociferous. National political leaders in Ottawa joined in the fray. Eventually, to keep the peace, the company was obliged to implement a project in excess of $20 million to remove 90 percent of the odor. The complaints went away. To preserve the company's reputation, the company's board of directors had approved a zero-financial return project at a time when the pulp industry, and that mill, were not doing well.

Environmental Risk—the Legal Dimension

To ensure adherence to protection measures demanded by society, and to ensure that all actors are guided by the same standard, governments establish laws and regulations carrying financial sanctions for companies and personal sanctions for managers. Though fines and financial measures are criticized by some because they can be seen as a cost of doing business, personal charges against managers and directors are a different matter and necessitate clear actions by the directing minds of corporations. To protect their companies and themselves from prosecution directors and managers must install meaningful environmental policies that are implemented through an environmental management system. Then they must regularly follow up to ensure, through oversight visits and formal audits, that the system is working. In this manner, they will be preventing mishaps and will have a defense of due diligence in the event of mishap.

In the authors' experience, environmental charges laid against companies can have significant financial and legal implications. In the 1990s, a paper mill (we'll call it Mill 1) was charged with multiple contraventions of the effluent discharge regulations, and the mill manager was personally charged with many counts related to the same discharge contraventions. Potential fines for the charges amounted to $160 million, though legal precedent indicated clearly that fines were likely to be no more than $5 million—still a notable sum. The mill had had a history of overflows of untreated effluent from the mill sewer system during the previous several years. This had attracted the attention of the corporate environment department, which had been monitoring the mill's environmental compliance data every month and the mill had been through the regular corporate environmental audit program. The factors causing the overflows had been identified as risks of these processes. Risk management and reduction programs and projects were implemented, in response to the audit, to deal with the overflow situation. Overflow frequency had been greatly reduced over the prior two or three years and were rare at the time when the charges were laid. Nevertheless, the regulators laid charges for violations in previous years. In the words of one senior manager, "with that many charges, chances are we are guilty of something." Hence, the legal strategy was to have the charges against the mill manager dropped, and reduce the penalties to the corporation, by pleading guilty to a reduced number of infractions. Ultimately both of these objectives were achieved, and a modest fine was paid.

The lesson is that even though the risk of environmental harm can be identified and effectively reduced by risk assessment, oversight, auditing, and follow-up, past regulatory violations may be on the record, creating enhanced legal risk until the statute of limitations has run.

There is a personal side to this, too, for despite the best intentions of the company, the episode took a considerable personal toll on the mill manager and his family. Companies need, first and foremost, to ensure that they are in compliance with the rules and avoid charges. But in the case of charges, it is critical to consider very carefully how best to support and assist employees who are implicated, especially if they are charged personally. It is the right thing to do, and it will be noticed by other managers.

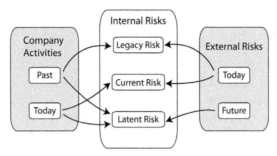

FIGURE 2–1 Different types of environmental risk.

Types of Environmental Risks

Environmental risks can originate from within the company or from outside; these are internal and external risks. There are three temporal categories of environmental risks: "present," "legacy," and "latent." (See Figure 2-1.)

Internal risks emerge from operations within the company's production facility fence line or at its other nonproduction activities. The effects of internal risks can be on the next street, fifteen miles downstream in another country, or thousands of miles away, in the case of large point-source air emissions, such as acidic emissions that cause acid precipitation. Internal risks can be classified by time frame as present, legacy, and latent.

Present risks are risks that stem from today's operations and can be subdivided into continuous and accidental risks. Continuous risks result from continuous activities such as discharging liquid effluents and air emissions as a result of routine production processes. Accidental risks occur suddenly, such as a tailings dam failure, pipeline rupture, and rail or road tanker accidents.

Legacy risks are those that exist today due to the practices of the past. These can include the leaks from an old underground storage tank or ecological damage to land or water resulting from historic emissions or discharges. Both present and legacy risks can be known or unknown, depending upon the degree of oversight and management applied. Legacy risks take a while to understand and develop plans to deal with.

Latent risks result from the practices of today but will not be evident until they are unearthed or realized at some future time. Today's leaking underground fuel tank is tomorrow's domestic contaminated well when the fuel migrates. Latent risk refers to situations that are developing now that will not be discovered, understood, or dealt with until sometime in the future. Historically such situations have resulted from practices that have left contamination in the soil and groundwater or that have resulted in contamination of sediments in receiving waters where effluents were discharged. Air, water, or soil contamination that becomes unacceptable after being discovered may have come from historic practices once considered acceptable.[6]

Of course it is not possible to predict changes in societal tolerance for industrial activities and their effects or what will be acceptable in the future. But such situations usually take a few years to develop, allowing risks to be identified, evaluated, and assessed, with treatments formulated in a timely manner—if one is watching. When such a situation is emerging, it may be important to modify production practices to accommodate the coming change.

Nonyl phenol ethoxylates, or NPEs, are endocrine-disrupting chemicals found in soaps and detergents and once used in the pulp and paper industry. They were entirely legal and acceptable at the time, but we became concerned about them and their potential to become an issue by watching the press and monitoring the activities of environmental groups. After investigating, it became clear that our suppliers had effective alternatives to these chemicals. We went forward with a program for all mills to eliminate their purchase, even though the science was somewhat equivocal on the strength of the effects. We took some corporate risk in asking the suppliers of important process control chemicals for new formulations of their products. Our assessment was that although the science was controversial, the reputational risk was significant, the cost was manageable, the effect on our production process was negligible, and it could prevent a protracted regulatory response in the future. Two or three years later, an environmental regulator called to inform me that there was now a regulation limiting the use of NPEs. It was a pleasure to tell him that we had already eliminated them.

Companies should regularly scan both internally and externally for emerging issues that can identify latent environmental risks to their operations. Matters that are identified as potential risks should be assessed to determine whether action is called for. Before acting, consider the potential effect on operations, the effort and cost required to "head things off" by changing current practice, the social risks, and the risk of diverging from industry practice, if applicable.

"External risks" come from outside the fence inward, sometimes even from other countries. In the 1990s, the Canadian government enacted regulations limiting dioxin emissions in pulp and paper mill effluent.[7] Though the toxicity of the dioxin and furan group of substances (here termed, collectively, dioxin) had been known for some decades, their occurrence in the pulp and paper industry was not observed until the 1980s in Sweden and the United States.[8,9] In relatively short order, an alarm was raised, and the research and regularity community identified dangers and acceptable limits. The regulations resulted in substantial spending by the industry to change pulp bleaching systems and reduce dioxin in effluent to meet the regulatory levels—no detectable dioxin in pulp mill effluents. (It is worth noting that the detection limits were in the part per quadrillion range, or 1 picogram per liter of water.) At the time, the rapidity with which the issue developed and resulted in regulation and process changes necessitated very quick, and expensive, responses from the industry.

External environmental risks might force changes to customers' requirements that do not relate specifically to the way they use the product. Many big-box building supply stores are under customer pressure to sell lumber that has been certified as coming from sustainably managed forests and that is labeled as such—the Forest Stewardship Council is an example of such a standard. These risks can also come in the form of new regulations, such as the dioxin regulations cited above. Companies, especially smaller ones, can rarely control the emergence or progression of external risks. Companies can only control how they respond to external risks, not control the risks themselves. To identify external risks requires taking a sweeping view of social, scientific, and regulatory trends around the world. A good way to do this is through industry associations that can pool resources to track issues that might affect its members. Members of the board of directors typically have a wide view of the world and can be a valuable source of ideas and insights on trends. A board member, having read that NPEs might become an issue, asked one of the authors what was known about them. And it was that question that initiated our proactive response to the issue, already described.

Identifying Environmental Risks

Suppose you were appointed as a new manager of some company or operation having a suite of environmental risks for which you are now responsible. How should you proceed? The first priority is to understand the processes of the company that are related to environmental risk at the appropriate level of detail for your new position. The precise position description for the new job will dictate whether the process understanding is at the production management level or the corporate strategic level. In either case, it is important to start by looking to the present risks, the legacy risks, and the latent risks, in that order.

A good first step is to perform a review of operations. The review should have the following elements:

- Document review
- Site review
- Formal risk assessments

Document Review

During the document review, you should review documentation describing present operations and the present risks that these operations entail, such as effluent exceedances or truck haulage accidents. Typical documents that offer a quick overview of the business are the permits and licenses under which it operates, design documents, and technical assessments of the operations, as well as environmental audits and regulatory reports. Legacy risks can be assessed by reviewing past practices and by accessing the corporate memory of these practices and the anecdotal evidence they generate. The corporate memory is the recollection and knowledge of operators and managers who are present or past employees of the operations. For latent risks, it is important to consider the known activities of the business in the context of emerging concerns in the press and among leading environmental groups.

Most production facilities require a variety of environmental permits. These cover limits placed on effluents to water, emissions to air, solid, and hazardous wastes disposed of on site or off site. It is critical to make sure all the necessary permits are in place, up to date, and complied with. Permit requirements often include more than simple limits on emissions quality or quantity. Permits often require detailed and frequent reporting of everything from emissions data to reports on management of wastes—and sometimes even products stored within a facility. The administrative compliance aspect of permits is often the source of minor violations when the inspector comes calling.

Site Review

Familiarity with the site is critical. Fortunately, a site review need not be overly formal. One of the authors, when a new environmental officer at Noranda, was sent to a paper mill for the first time. The first order of business was a brief meeting with the mill manager and the local environmental manager. Mill management described the operations and risks at the site, indicating that compliance with effluent discharge regulations was considerably less than 100 percent and that there was a hazardous waste storage facility on site. In less than an hour, without a formal risk assessment, a good view of the site's present environmental risks was gained. The types of risks one should look for in this initial review are related to

- permits
- effluent or emission compliance
- solid and hazardous waste management
- specific materials or operations that carry or increase risk

After the introductory meeting, we went on a site tour to look at the production operations and the various potential environmental risk locations. Such tours should follow the flow of the production process so that the origin of wastes and discharges is understood in the context of production. Eventually we visited the effluent treatment system and discharge point to get an understanding of the circumstances of effluent exceedance risks. Later we saw that the hazardous waste storage facility was unlocked and untidy, and located in an aging, repurposed building. The hazardous waste permit required that it be locked with access limited to designated personnel and that the contents be neatly stored and accessible. Clearly we were noncompliant on at least two counts and bore the risk of a charge and a fine, not to mention tampering by trespassers.

By the end of the meeting and site tour, we had thus quickly established the main present environmental risks to the operation: There was a need to manage hazardous waste properly, either by using a better storage facility or by removing the waste from the site, and a mechanism was needed to curtail the frequency of untreated effluent overflows and improve the mill's compliance with effluent limits.

After the main present risks are understood and being acted upon, the new manager must take stock of legacy risks. A good approach is to ask whether there are any cleanup programs currently under way, planned, or known to be required. If there are, they should be well characterized, be reported to the applicable government agencies, have strategic long term objectives for cleanup or containment designed by consulting experts in these fields, and be able to be executed with a minimum of disruption.

At one of Noranda's plants, copper metal was bent, welded, and worked into specialized heat exchange tubing. In the process, the metal was degreased using a solvent, trichlorethylene, so that it could be properly worked. The solvent is a handy degreaser that is nonflammable, reusable, and economical. It is also cancer-causing and denser than water, so when it gets into the environment it is very difficult to recover. The facility had been closed and put up for sale, but the buyer insisted on an environmental study of the site, including drilling holes to see whether there was contamination on the property. After years of managing the solvent in accordance with old practices, the site had nevertheless been contaminated and groundwater affected. The contamination was discovered, the sale fell through, and Noranda was stuck with this legacy. The result was an expensive assessment and cleanup program and a seriously degraded asset value. Evidence of these risks can often be found during corporate due diligence in advance of transactions. When this occurs, it is typical for the owner to implement and pay for a cleanup, reduce the price, or offer indemnity for the purchaser. Commonly, banks or other lenders are involved in business transactions, and they typically have high standards for reviewing site contamination risks.

The metalworks plant just described was a relatively small contamination event, but legacy risks can blossom into very large issues requiring multiyear and multi-million-dollar programs to mitigate. A good example is the Love Canal in Niagara Falls, New York, one of the earliest large historic contamination situations. In 1894, William T. Love started building a canal to connect the Niagara River with Lake Ontario for electric power production. The venture failed, but the excavation remained. Between 1942 and 1952, the Hooker Chemical Company used the old canal to dispose of wastes from their nearby manufacturing plant. When Hooker was finished, the waste was covered and the property was sold to the board of education of Niagara Falls, New York.[10,11] Subsequently, the area became the site of a new neighborhood, complete with schools. In the late 1970s, leaks from the site resulted in health effects and, eventually, the closure and remediation of the entire neighborhood. The events kicked off a level of concern for chemical wastes and disposal practices that eventually changed how the industry handled hazardous waste disposal.

Formal Environmental Risk Assessments in Operations

Most operations have present risks that are unknown or that are known by someone in the operation but without the knowledge being institutional—and thus the risks are not managed. Formal risk assessments are a useful way to identify these risks and develop plans for treating them.

At Noranda Forest, we encouraged operations managers to conduct formal risk assessments in their operations. These assessments followed the general outline described in Chapter 1. In each major operating area—for example, the paper machine, the wood room, the receiving area, or the waste water treatment plant—we established a risk assessment team. The teams always had one or two operators, preferably one of whom was an "old-timer" who had seen upset conditions over the years. They also had a process engineer, someone from maintenance—frequently an instrumentation technician—and the supervisor. A risk consultant was often engaged to facilitate the teams through the risk assessment process.

The criteria used to evaluate consequences were derived from the corporate environmental policy. This provided some standardization in how the risk assessment teams evaluated risks. Mostly these teams identified mundane but still important risks, such as lubricating or hydraulic oil leaks or spills that could get into the effluent. Occasionally they identified serious risks such as leaks of toxic gases that could have had very serious consequences in the mills and in surrounding communities. In all cases, the teams prioritized the risks and made recommendations for preventing, detecting, and reacting to them. Management reviewed and occasionally reprioritized the risks and included them in maintenance, capital, and training budgets. We followed up the implementation of treatments in our audit program. (See Section 5.)

Environmental Risk Management: The Noranda Model—and Beyond

Noranda, Inc., parent company of Noranda Forest, was a major Canadian natural resources company that owned assets in mining, forest products, energy, and manufacturing businesses, primarily in the Americas and Europe. The company understood the inherent intrusiveness of resource developments and installed an environmental management system in the 1980s. In the mid- to late 1980s, Noranda managed environmental risk using two basic tools—oversight and audits. Both were driven by a corporate environmental policy that was to be implemented in each operation. The corporation had installed a corporate environmental department charged to ensure that environmental risks were being identified and managed. As the system evolved, more familiar risk management steps of identification, assessment, analysis, prioritization, and treatment were employed. The corporate environmental staff were assigned to groups of similar operations and liaised closely with facility management to review present and legacy risks. The results of this oversight system were reported quarterly to the board of directors through the environmental committee of the board by the senior vice president of environment.[12]

Demonstrating effective policy implementation at each production facility is an exercise in long-term assessment of results. In the Noranda model, environmental staff members reported on the efforts and results of their assigned operations. This ensured day-to-day improvements and focus on improving operations and reducing risks within those operations. But with the financial, reputational, and personal risks involved in environmental matters, senior management and the board required greater assurance, so the company implemented an environmental auditing system both as an early risk identification tool and, ultimately, as a long-term continual improvement system. Environmental auditing had emerged as a corporate risk management approach in the early 1980s to fill this need. Noranda's corporate environmental audits started with emergency preparedness auditing and came to encompass industrial hygiene and occupational health. They grew from the aftermath of the tragic Bhopal incident in India, as a result of which several thousand people died from accidental emissions on the part of a chemical facility.

Audit teams were composed of trained staff members from different production facilities, often from different industrial groups within the company. The corporate audit manager assembled the teams under an experienced auditor and sent them to the subject site. Each audit typically took three to five days. Site operations and records were reviewed for compliance with regulations, adherence to corporate policy, and conformance to best practices. The final report of the audit presented a list of findings to the plant manager and their immediate superior. Action plans to resolve the findings (treat the risks) were developed by the facility based on the risk analysis and prioritization of each particular risk. These were vetted by corporate staff and the site implemented the actions on a schedule. The board of directors received quarterly reports on the performance of the audit program. Quarterly reports included the number of audits completed, the number of findings found, the action plans developed, and the rate of completion of the findings.

This cycle of audit findings established a de facto environmental management system (EMS) even before the named concept had become a widely understood system within corporate management. Noranda's system was adopted by its mining and forest product subsidiaries and was at the root of Noranda's improving environmental performance. The oversight provided by corporate environmental staff helped operations correct the findings and also identify new areas of focus. The combination of oversight and auditing does not ensure that legal risks from past noncompliances will not result in charges to the company, as discussed earlier, but it does reduce exposure by identifying and treating risks as well as offering a due diligence defense in cases in which "strict" legal liability permits it.

In the 1990s, the increased awareness of corporate environmental risks prompted the International Organization for Standardization (ISO) to establish a standard environmental management system template based on its successful quality management standard (ISO 9000). This system has widely acknowledged for including steps that identify, assess, analyze, and prioritize risks in a cyclical process designed to foster continual improvement. Accordingly, ISO 14000 has emerged as a useful overall framework for managing environmental risks. Companies using the ISO 14000 system have the opportunity to be registered by a third party as being ISO 14000 compliant and can then use this designation in their branding.

Subsequent the legal case related to above, Noranda Forest decided to ensure that a management system approach was in place at each operation but noted that the ISO approach had the potential to be overly bureaucratic and time-consuming in some implementations. Furthermore, the benefits of registration were not universally accepted as useful owing to the time consumed and the expense. In the end, the choice of management system (homegrown or ISO) and registration (if ISO) was left to the operations themselves. Corporate policy dictated that "systematic environmental management" be implemented. Operations could choose ISO or modifications thereof or their own systems. Operations were monitored in their implementation of systematic management using a measurement tool specifically designed by the environment department for the purpose and reported quarterly to the board of directors. After management systems had been implemented, the company environmental audit system monitored their operation on a two- to three-year cycle and also reported it to the environmental committee of the board.

Interestingly, most sites decided to use a modified ISO 14000 template, and few decided to be certified. At one of the sites that chose ISO 14000 registration, the manager, a man having a long and successful career in leadership, felt that certification was a useful discipline for the operation in the long term. He once commented, "I am more worried about losing a public certification than having the corporate office mad at me."

It is our experience that systematic environmental management systems are best put in place by line managers, meaning the people who manage the production facilities that carry the risks. They are best placed to understand the site's environmental risks and to be able to establish the best solutions for their reduction. Whether it be a homegrown system such as Noranda's oversight and audit system or an ISO template, so long as it is championed by senior corporate leadership and implemented by line and production managers, risk reductions should be achieved.

Approvals for Large Industrial Projects: The Environmental Risks

Chapter 4 of this book describes the management of project risks, beginning after a project has been given permission to proceed. Obtaining environmental permits for large industrial projects to proceed, however, cannot be taken for granted as a perfunctory process leading to assured approval. There is often substantial risk that permits will be denied. It is usual for major permits for a large project, or even a relatively small project, to be finally adjudicated in the political realm, further increasing risk. Clear assessments of environmental and social risk for projects in the permitting phase are required to reduce these risks and to successfully acquire the permits necessary to operate.

Minerals development projects are a case in point, for they follow a multistage path, including prospecting, exploration, and deposit delineation in the field. At that point, if there is the likelihood of a successful mine, the project moves toward environmental baseline studies, system design, permitting, construction, operation, and ultimately, closure and abandonment. At each stage financial resources must be acquired from investors or debt to advance the development of the project. Because of the high-risk nature of minerals projects, the industry has developed very detailed and sophisticated methods to evaluate, design, and assess projects so as to reduce risk to investors. A tremendous amount of effort is appropriately expended in delineating the area of the ore body during the exploration stage. This, along with very detailed engineering planning and design, is prepared so that financing can be acquired from investors or lenders who are comfortable with the geological, technical and financial risks of the project. Historically there has not been the same attention focused on the regulatory and social aspects of the project, and this has led to some significant difficulties. Acquiring the permissions to develop a project is an expensive and time-consuming activity that must be considered in the overall schedule, capital requirements, and design of a project. Typically in developed countries there exist regulations that require environmental assessments; licenses for exploration, production, and abandonment; and licensing to cover the uses of water for processing or waste discharge. In most countries these are subject to detailed evaluation, often in public fora, as well as to public input. These public processes afford a convenient avenue for public interest groups to provide input or opposition to a project. The level of public scrutiny on natural resource projects has grown in the face of large projects in remote areas and occasional spectacular failures, such as a major tailings dam failure at the Mount Polly mine in British Columbia on August 4, 2014.[13,14]

Who Does What?

Establishing an organizational structure that facilitates identification and mitigation of environmental risks necessitates attention at all levels of the company. Though it may not be absolutely necessary in smaller entities to have a dedicated department for the purpose, the responsibilities and actions need to be identified and delegated. In cases in which a corporate structure exists for several business units, leaders can consider implementing a corporate environmental management group. In any structured management system, it must be decided who does what. A guiding principle for developing this system is to have the decision making authority at the correct level of the organization for effective and efficient action.

Line versus Staff Roles

Although the environmental role must be carried out by someone in the organization, the scale of the entity makes a difference in how this function might be organized. In small organizations with minimal environmental risk, line operating personnel can complete these tasks as a part of their regular job description. This could apply for example to a small manufacturer that generates a small amount of hazardous waste—for example, paint booth waste. Because there is typically a highly regulated process for handling, shipping, and disposing of this material, a production manager could carry out the function.

In a large single manufacturing site or a medium-sized corporation having multiple sites, a dedicated environmental position is often preferable. In a single manufacturing facility, the role would be to carry out some of the functions but also serve as a source of new information on environmental risk from outside the company. The environmental position could be responsible for identifying risks and evaluating treatments to reduce them as well as having an operational role in managing a site waste management facility.

In large organizations, or even small or medium-sized companies in some high-risk industries, a dedicated environmental staff operating at a corporate level will serve to assess the risks of the operations and the industry as a whole and bring these to the operation side of the business for consideration. A healthy dialogue between the staff and line personnel will ensure that operational personnel can bring issues forward while being open to those brought by the environmental staff. The operational personnel should take the lead in implementing the necessary changes in operations to address the identified risks, because they know their facilities and processes better than anyone else. It is appropriate for environmental personnel to bring possible solutions for consideration and to coach, and occasionally even cajole, operators over the magnitude of the risk and the need to find solutions. If an impasse is reached, then the matter should be moved to the next corporate level for consideration and resolution. It is important to see this as a normal course of events and not a negative reflection on either party. A systemized environmental management approach, such as ISO, can foster good relations in these situations.

It is important that the environment department not be seen as a policing entity. Cooperation and joint objectives with operations are critical to the effective reduction of environmental risk. A policing demeanor on the part of environmental staff can lead to concealing important issues, which increases risk, confrontation, and in the event of an environmental failure, much acrimony and finger-pointing. This cooperative stance must be especially present in the environmental audit. Audits are an important aspect of providing assurance that management systems are functioning, but they should not be about catching someone out or inflicting maximum scrutiny on operations. The audit should be positioned and supported as a help to the site managers to continually improve their performance in measured and meaningful steps. Most audits generate a list of findings that need to be addressed. Our experience is that site managers are interested in improving their operations and find lists of things to do a helpful way to focus and delegate execution. This is especially true when they have the opportunity to schedule actions to meet their needs and even to contest findings with which they do not agree.

The Role of the Board of Directors and Senior Managers—Governance

The direction from senior management and the board of directors is critical to successful environmental risk management. For the board, the governance role should be to ensure that there is a corporate policy on environmental matters that improves environmental performance and reduces the risk to the corporation and to the interests of the shareholders. With the guidance of senior environmental staff and possibly eternal experts, and with an understanding of the company's environmental risks, the board can formulate a clear and concise policy. After this is done, the role should transition to monitoring the implementation of the policy and the quality of its operational results. Regular reports from management should demonstrate performance against achievement of the key environmental indicators and the objectives of the company. Indicators can be compliance measures, waste or emissions reduction objectives, or product initiatives. In some cases, the board may wish to install an environmental committee to more closely track some of the more technical or complex discussions necessary to set policy and evaluate progress. The role of the environment committee is not only risk reduction, but also to serve as a support to the executive team in culture building and policy setting. In other words, they aid in "directing" the company, not only protecting it from risks. Chapter 14 of this book discusses the role of the board of directors in risk management more generally.

Management Incentives

It is important to make clear to management through their remuneration that environmental performance and risk management are important. Frequently there are discussions about whether variable compensation (in the form of a bonus) should be linked positively or negatively to compliance with environmental regulatory standards. (Chapter 13 of this book discusses in more depth risk culture and the role of incentive plans on shaping it.) Should a manager receive a bonus for improving the compliance frequency of facility air emissions—or is meeting this standard part of the job and therefore reimbursed within the bounds of salary compensation? Similarly, consider whether bonuses are provided to financial staff for not filing illegal or erroneous tax submissions to the government. It may be that the "improvement" of a poor situation is a bonus-worthy objective in a particular context and incentive framework—or it may not be. It all depends on the structure and philosophy of the compensation program.

What is critically important is ensuring that achievement of environmental objectives is included in the variable compensation opportunities of relevant management (and other) personnel. Whether the KPIs in question are related to the reduction of risk or the improvement of environmental circumstances for the business, the increased acceptance of a company by stakeholders, supply chain management to reduce environmental footprint, or simply compliance with regulatory obligations, communicating their importance within the remuneration structure is good management.

The Importance of Corporate Culture—from the Board Room to the Shop Floor

Much has been said and written about corporate culture and its importance in achieving results. Indeed, Chapter 13 of this book covers the topic. Once again, leadership is important to environmental culture. If leadership does not ask environmental performance questions of operations, then little emphasis will be perceived. Leaders must send messages to the employees that demonstrate their own commitment to good performance and their willingness to commit the company as well. Early in Noranda's environmental management evolution, it was faced with a serious risk based on its contribution to acid rain degeneration of lakes and forests in the Canadian Shield. A senior leader of the company, after hearing the details of this risk, reportedly remarked, "We must not ruin the environment with acid rain."

That was a number of years ago and today a culture of environmental leadership is even more firmly installed in the new generation of corporate leaders. A generation of environmental regulation, media focus, societal reforms, and educational initiatives has raised the base knowledge and impetus for protecting and managing the environment. Thus many corporate environmental programs find fertile ground for implementation among the employees and leaders of today. However, companies are creations of humans, so continual vigilance is necessary to ensure that backsliding does not occur and that the great challenges of the present and future, such as climate change, resource depletion, and water quality are met by the creativity and focus that can be brought by corporations.

Notes

1. Polychlorinated biphenyls.
2. U.S. Environmental Protection Agency. Polychlorinated Biphenyls (PCBs): Health Effects of PCBs, www.epa.gov/osw/hazard/tsd/pcbs/pubs/effects.htm.
3. Chlorofluorocarbons.
4. Claudia Cattaneo, "TransCanada in Eye of the Storm," *Financial Post* (Toronto), September 8, 2011.
5. Peter Sandman, *Responding to Community Outrage: Strategies for Effective Risk Communication.* (Fairfax, VA: American Industrial Hygiene Association, 1996).
6. Editor's note: This is an example of acceptable residual risks' becoming new unacceptable risks, described in Chapter 1.
7. Pulp and Paper Mill Effluent Chlorinated Dioxins and Furans Regulations (SOR/92-267), Canadian Environmental Protection Act, 1999.
8. Ray C. Whittemore, LaFleur, L. E., Gillespie, W. J., Amendola, G. A., Helms, J., "USEPA/Paper Industry Cooperative Dioxin Study: The 104 Mill Study, Chemosphere, Vol. 20, Nos. 10–12 (1990): 1625–1632.

9. U.S. EPA/Paper Industry Cooperative Dioxin Screening Study, Office of Water, Office of Water Regulations and Standards, Washington, DC, EPA-440/I-88-025.

10. New York State Department of Health, "Love Canal: A Special Report to the Governor and Legislature: April 1981" (2005), http://www.health.ny.gov/environmental/investigations/love_canal/lcreport.htm#history.

11. *The Niagara Gazette*, "Love Canal Chronology, 1984–1980." http://library.buffalo.edu/libraries/specialcollections/lovecanal/about/chronology.php.

12. Both authors of this chapter worked at the Noranda Group of Companies.

13. Imperial Metals, Inc., "Tailings Breach Information." www.imperialmetals.com/s/Mt_Polley_Update.asp?ReportID=671041.

14. *The Globe and Mail*, "Waste Water from Central B.C. Mine Spills into Waterways, Prompting Water-Use Ban." August 5, 2014, www.theglobeandmail.com/news/british-columbia/water-use-ban-imposed-after-tailings-pond-breached-near-fraser-river/article19911069/.

3

Health and Safety Risk Management: Perspective of a Petroleum Refinery Manager

Gaston Lafontaine

I was superintendent of a major refinery when an employee of one of our contractors, a man aged 47 years, was killed in an unfortunate accident while working at our installations. As superintendent, I had overall responsibility for the operations of the refinery. I attended the funeral and personally witnessed the devastating human effect that this man's death had on his family, his friends, his working companions, his company, and our own personnel. I hope you will never have such an experience.

Why should you spend any time and effort on health and safety risk management? After all, isn't your job to "deliver the goods" and make money? But to reach this objective, you cannot ignore health and safety risk management. Just having insurance is not good enough. In this chapter, we will examine the important ramifications of health and safety in a successful business.

"Hey! You have to be more careful!" says a supervisor loudly to an employee. Will this approach significantly improve performance and the behavior of employees? Emphatically not! With human error the major cause of accidents and industrial health problems, managers and supervisors need a better way to manage health and safety risks.

Effects of Health and Safety on Organizations

You may be a board director, a field manager, or a production foreman. All these roles are crucial in the effective and successful management of health and safety. It is not a job that can be delegated to safety "experts." As a member of management, you are responsible for the safety of your employees, contractors and visitors. Their health and safety affect the overall performance of the organization in at least six important ways:

- Human effects
- Material effects
- Intangible effects
- Legal effects

- Personal effects
- Financial effects

Human Effects

Compared to materials and equipment, humans are vulnerable and delicate. Your employees and your contractors are critical assets in the success of your operation. Injuries or industrial diseases caused by your workplace will sometimes result in permanent incapacity—even death. In other words, unlike equipment, human beings cannot always be "fixed."

Workplace injuries and diseases can also have a tremendous psychological effect on all your personnel and anyone associated with your operation. The death of the contractor I referred to earlier had a disastrous effect on his family and his friends. It also had an important impact in the workplace: the news of the accident spread like wildfire. Our employees and contractors started wondering: "Can this happen to me? How can I now trust management to protect me?" Everybody at the refinery, including my supervisors, my managers, my union representatives, my superiors, even government officials, was in a questioning mode. Work had come to a standstill, and it took a long time to re-establish a climate of trust and confidence among all concerned. In other words, all these people had trusted management, and in their eyes, management had let them down. It took me a long time to rebuild that trust.

Material Effects

Accidents that affect humans often also damage equipment and materials. Damage to equipment that is critical for continuous operations may result in very serious financial losses, including cost of replacements, repairs, production losses, failure to meet contract obligations, increase in insurance premiums and increased workers compensation rates.

Intangible Effects

The feeling that your employees and contractors have about workplace safety is definitely an important contributor to their morale and loyalty to the company. Effective management of health and safety shows that management cares about employees and will boost both morale and loyalty. The news of an accident such as a serious injury can have a negative effect throughout the organization, right up to the board of directors (directors do not like bad news), shareholders (they do not want to be a party to an unreliable or irresponsible outfit), clients and suppliers (if you cannot manage risks, what else can you not manage?), community (they want a reliable employer and corporate citizen), government officials (they will be watching you more closely from now on), and creditors (they do not want to lose their money).

Legal Effects

If the fundamental cause of the accident was serious flaws in your risk management system, you may be held legally responsible, possibly criminally responsible.

In the United States, the Occupational Safety and Health Act defines the responsibility of the employer, saying that the employer

shall furnish to each of his employees employment and a place of employment which are free from recognized hazards that are causing or are likely to cause death or serious physical harm to his employees

and

shall comply with occupational safety and health standards promulgated under this Act.

In Canada, the federal government updated the criminal code in the aftermath of an explosion at the Westray Mine in 1992 that killed twenty-six. There was evidence of gross negligence, but charges could not be laid against the directors. The amendment to the Criminal Code[1] read, in part,

Every one who undertakes, or has the authority, to direct how another person does work or performs a task is under a legal duty to take reasonable steps to prevent bodily harm to that person, or any other person, arising from that work or task.

The amendments also imposed criminal liability on organizations and its representatives for negligence and other offenses.

In a Canadian court of law, if you are accused of criminal negligence, you have to prove that you were duly diligent, which means that you must demonstrate that you took all the necessary and reasonable measures to prevent the accident from happening. Ignorance of the law, or the absence of ill intent, are not admissible defenses.

The European Union also outlines the responsibilities of the employer for health and safety,[2] ordering that an employer must

implement measures which assure an improvement in the level of protection afforded to workers and are integrated into all the activities of the undertaking and/or establishment at all hierarchical levels

Personal Effects

If it is revealed that the accident was the result of your managerial negligence, not only will you be liable, but you are likely to lose your job and seriously compromise your chances of future employment in a management position. Ignorance of the law is not a valid defense. Claiming that you did not mean to harm will not help, either. You had a duty to prevent harm, and if you did not prevent harm, then you will have to live with your remorse and with the negative effects on your reputation.

Financial Effects

The financial effect cannot be overstated. Robert McKee, chairman of Conoco (UK) Ltd., said it well:

Safety is, without doubt, the most crucial investment we can make, and the question is not what it costs us, but what it saves.[3]

The U.S. Occupational Safety and Health Administration claims that the ratio of indirect cost to direct cost of accidents varies from 20:1 to 1:1 depending on the circumstances. The direct and indirect costs can be broken down as follows:[4]

- Direct:
  - Medical costs
  - Lost wages
- Indirect
  - Lost production
  - Rehiring
  - Retraining
  - Overtime
  - Fines
  - Litigation costs
  - Lost wages
  - Poor morale
  - Administration time

Safety Culture

The most important role of the manager is to establish a culture of safety.

A culture safety starts at the top! Every member of management, from the board of directors all the way down to the crew leaders and foremen, must preach by example to establish a safety culture. Some of the key things managers should do to establish a safety culture are now described.

Every employee in a supervisory function must have a basic knowledge of health and safety risk management. There are many approaches and techniques on this subject that are suitable to a wide variety of industries and contexts. This knowledge must be acquired through training in the same way as general management training. When health and safety issues, projects, or programs are discussed, supervisors must have sufficient knowledge to raise valid questions and judge their validity. A good starting point is knowledge of the basic principles of risk assessment, corporate and local safety rules, and legal requirements.

Set health and safety targets, and regularly review performance against those targets. On this subject, there are two schools of thought. Some people think that targets should reflect the probability that some accidents will occur, which are then "budgeted" for. A different approach is to aim for excellence and "target" zero accidents, much like the professional golfer who visualizes the ball in the cup when he drives on a par 3. This latter approach challenges people and aims for excellence.

Here is a personal example:

At our refinery, we set a target of target of zero loss-time accidents for a $50 million modification to a processing unit. There were over 150 construction tradesmen, and heavy equipment operated around the clock for an intense three week period. We achieved our target, even though the work crew was from the construction sector where accident statistics are somewhat high. Our success was due to intense application of all the components of risk management. We took into account the fact that contract employees are often unfamiliar with the workplace environment and rules. We required contractors to come up with a detailed health and safety program, and a strategy to ensure its application, that was reviewed and approved by management. Close coordination and monitoring of contractor activities was also maintained throughout the shutdown. An incredible achievement? Yes. Aim high, manage accordingly, and you get results.

Performance measurement or assessment systems must place importance on individual performance in health and safety to reflect your claim that it has a high priority. Promotions, raises, and bonuses must not be given to your staff if they do a poor job in managing risk in health and safety. And that applies as well to anyone who may be a "star performer" in other fields of operational efficiency. If exceptions are made, it will be a glaring example that it's acceptable to bend the rules out of expediency.

At regular operation meetings, the review of health and safety performance and associated issues must be an integral part of the agenda, the first item for discussion. This practice will demonstrate that risk management of health and safety is an integral part of the operation of the organization and that it contributes positively to its success.

When health and safety activities are planned, the resources required must not be "squeezed in" by scrounging funds and resources from other areas with their own specific plans and budgets, with corresponding allocation of material and human resources.

The organization chart must also reflect the priority you place on health and safety. Staff who provide support (audits, expertise and coordination) must report directly to the highest authority in an operation. Note that line supervision (directors, CEO, managers, supervisors) is solely responsible for health and safety of employees, contractors, and visitors. Line personnel are responsible for the operational administration of the health and safety program and are directly accountable for the safe conduct of the business.

Your employees are watching you to see whether you mean what you say. As a manager, you cannot allow yourself to "break the rules" because you are in a position of authority. If you detect unsafe acts, you must correct the situation regardless of the political fallout. Here is a personal example:

Once the company president was visiting the refinery when I was superintendent. A meeting with the employees was held in the cafeteria. The president was addressing the group, dealing with various topics, including safety. While he was speaking, he casually pulled out a cigarette and was about to light it with a butane lighter, not knowing that such an item was forbidden anywhere in the refinery. I was sitting next to him and realized that this was a crucial moment for my credibility and for the credibility of our safety program. I reached over and took the lighter from him. I told him that I had omitted to mention that lighters were not allowed anywhere in the refinery. In doing so, I realized that I had created a situation of potential embarrassment for the President, but at the risk of displeasing him, I could not let him do something that was breaking a safety rule of the refinery. I could see that the employees appreciated my action: the rule is the rule for everybody!

Verbal and written communications to employees must reflect the priority that you give to this subject. If employee communications and reports seldom mention anything about health and safety, a message will sent: This is not a very important issue.

Everyday language and behavior must reflect your convictions on the subject. If you review your personal agenda, can you identify many times when you personally devoted time to the management of health and safety? Health and safety are here and now; they cannot be delayed.

Here is a personal example:

Once I was accompanying one of my supervisors on a safety audit in the field. We came across a storage tank that had been emptied and opened for inspection and maintenance. Reservoirs, storage tanks and pressure vessels are equipped with manways, which are openings normally covered with bolted plate that can be removed to gain access to the inside for inspection and repair. Entry into these restricted areas has to be carefully controlled, since the inside atmosphere may present be hazardous to health and safety. On that day, the manways were open and there was nobody around. The safety procedure called for chains to be locked across the manways to prevent unauthorized entry. The supervisor noticed that we were in violation of the procedure, and suggested that he would get this situation corrected after we had finished our audit. Perhaps he did not want to take too much of my time? I insisted that he immediately get the local foreman to fix it while I would stood guard against the open manway. This was for me a good opportunity to illustrate that safety is here and now, and cannot be delayed to a more convenient time.

All employees (and contractors) must be encouraged to think and act safely by having their personal contribution and involvement invited. The approach of telling employees what to do and watching them to make sure that they are doing it will have very limited success. Lead them to arrive at the safe approach, thereby being personally convinced of the precautions to be taken for their own benefit.

Thinking ahead before acting is the way to prevent accidents. A master chess player stays ahead of the game by planning many moves in advance. The work force has to adopt a similar approach. Depending on the complexity of the task, many aspects of the activity have to be thoroughly examine for their possible interaction with other components.

Here is a personal example:

> *I was driving through the refinery when I noticed a contractor employee standing next to the open manway of a pressure vessel. I stopped to inquire what he was doing. He explained that there was an entry permit for the work inside, and that, according to the permit, he was standing outside the vessel with the task of detecting if "everything was normal." He told me that, should there be a problem, he was to call for help. When I questioned him about details of the safety measures taken for the workers inside the vessel, and his role as a stand-by sentinel, I realized that this overall arrangement had not been thought through. I immediately stopped the work. I rounded up the contractor employees and their supervisor, and our operator who had issued the permit and his supervisor. They were then asked together to redefine in details all the steps that each member of that working team had to take for a safe operation, and the work then resumed with the detailed safety approach. In a refinery, news travel fast: within a few hours, everybody knew that the refinery manager had stopped unsafe work, and that safety permits should not be issued as a routine but should be the result of a thorough planning, review and understanding by all concerned.*

Demonstrating pride in the performance and achievements of health and safety in your establishment is also a sign that you care. Use it as a positive lever with all your stakeholders. Whenever I was dealing with my boss, my company colleagues, government representatives, community officials, insurance company agents, or contractors, our expectations and performance in health and safety were a source of pride at the refinery.

Risk Assessment—Cornerstone of the Program

This section will outline some of the basic principles of risk management. If your organization does not have an in-house specialist to help you set this up, get outside help.

In health and safety management, we want to introduce the concept of "hazard," which was not mentioned in Chapter 1. Generally in the field of safety the term "hazard" is used rather than "source of risk" as it is defined in Chapter 1. A "hazard" is any source of energy that can negatively affect the health and safety of people. Here are a few examples of energies that present a hazard:

- Kinetic (risk of collision, cuts, or abrasions)
- Potential (risk of collapse or fall)
- Thermal (risk of burns; exhaustion)
- Chemical (risk of damage to human tissues and organs; explosions; fires)
- Biological (risk of contamination or poisoning)
- Radioactive (risk of damage to ears, eyes, organs, and human tissues)

Risk Identification

For each type of hazard, certain events may occur in a given installation. It is important to carefully identify all these events for risk identification.

Depending on the nature and complexity of the activity or installation, there are three different approaches to risk assessment, with corresponding degrees of management involvement:

<u>Individual awareness approach.</u> For simple daily activities, an individual who is part of a successful awareness and safety culture will recognize obvious risks and act accordingly even if the situation has not been covered by safety procedures and training. For example, a mechanic will avoid positioning a heavy piece of machinery near the edge of his workbench because he realizes the risk of it falling on his feet. This approach will be successful when management maintains a climate of safety awareness and constantly encourages safe behavior, relying on individuals to use their judgment in their simple activities. Many activities involving the use of hand tools fall in this category.

<u>The job approach.</u> In these situations, the nature and complexity of the activities, substances, and equipment require information, training, and procedures that are usually part of craft training. These situations often arise on particular jobs and involve such risks as the use of power equipment or machinery, handling of chemical substances, and being in presence of other sources of energy. In these instances, management must supply information, training, procedures and monitoring that were developed as a result of a formal risk analysis, taking into consideration all risks involved. Work will then be assigned only to those who are competent to perform the tasks involved. Such activities will normally take place at the craftsman and operator level, with assistance from supervisors for the more complex cases.

Here is a personal example:

Historically, in a petroleum refinery, work permits are issued by the processing unit operators after they have made the work site "safe" by isolating, draining and venting the equipment and locking it up. On this particular occasion, a work permit had been delivered to a worker for welding stainless steel strips on the inside wall of a small distillation column of about four feet in diameter. A stand-by person was posted outside the column, ready to intervene if something went wrong. After sometime, the welding operation had consumed some of the oxygen inside the column, the welder started to feel dizzy and barely made it outside the equipment. Although the area had been made safe for the work, the worker had made the area unsafe by his repair activities.

With the new approach, the issue of work permits addressed not only the safety of the work site itself, but also the prevention measures taken in view of the repair activities. From then on, work permits were issued with the full participation of both the process operator, and also the maintenance workers. This constituted an important departure from the historical responsibility of the process operator who was the only one taking the preventive measures to make the work site safe, but ignoring the events associated with the activities of the maintenance workers.

<u>The formal approach.</u> We are dealing here with complex situations that require a systematic risk assessment. These situations will often involve a process combined with equipment,

activities and their environment, or a major project involving multiple integrated operations, such as a shutdown or construction project. An integrated study is required here to arrive at a complete risk assessment and analysis. The result will be a complete set of prescribed actions such as information, procedures, training, preventive maintenance, equipment controls, alarms and lockups, means of detection, and emergency procedures. Such an integrated risk assessment must be initiated, reviewed, and approved by senior management, its results implemented and monitored by line management at all levels.

Risk Analysis

Take the event of an employee injured from falling from a scaffold. For this event, there are a number of possible scenarios: a defective scaffold, a faulty erection of the scaffold, overloading of the scaffold, worker overreach beyond the scaffold railing, a vehicle hitting the scaffold. Each of these scenarios may have a different likelihood of happening.

Following the outline of Chapter 1, for a given hazard, a certain number of events may affect health and safety. For each event, different scenarios are considered for their "likelihood" of occurring and the corresponding "consequences," which may vary with the circumstances. The combination of likelihood and consequences defines the risk.

Estimating likelihood is a challenge. For a given event, depending on the scenario, likelihood is influenced by the quality of existing prevention systems and the number of contributing factors required to produce an accident. Consider the quality of your existing prevention systems:

- Preventive maintenance and calibration on critical equipment.
- Operating procedures that enable workers to control the key process variables of a process, thereby preventing accidents.
- Training of people in positions who can have significant effects on health and safety to ensure that they are competent to perform their tasks.
- Warning systems to warn that abnormal conditions exist. This enables workers to recover from the abnormal conditions before an accident occurs.
- Evaluation and monitoring of procedures to ensure that they are being performed effectively and when needed.

The likelihood will also vary depending on the number of contributing factors that must come into play. For example, for someone to be injured by a falling object, the person must be in the trajectory of the falling object at the exact time when the object is falling. If everyone respects the barricaded area under an overhead work site, an object may fall without injuring anyone.

The estimate of likelihood is not necessarily an absolute number but rather is a relative likelihood compared to other risks in the establishment, for the purpose is to place a higher priority on the higher risks.

To ensure consistency of results within an organization, some criteria for evaluating likelihood should be defined by management and used by the team doing the risk analysis. The points shown above can be used to develop these criteria. For example, an accident is more likely to happen if there are obvious deficiencies in maintenance of equipment, operating procedures, training, and warning systems.

Estimating consequences is somewhat easier. To ensure consistency of approach for a given organization, criteria should be developed to assist risk analysis teams. The following criteria can be used to establish a method for the evaluation of consequences:

- Quality of existing systems for detection
- Quality of existing systems for reaction
- Number of people affected and severity of the harm to them
- Toxicity
- Costs
- Legal implications
- Sensitivity of the location
- Atmospheric conditions
- Public outrage

These criteria can be compared with potential accident scenarios to determine possible consequences. The following grid is an example for a medium-sized installation:

Category	Humans	Property	Environment
Catastrophic or high	Loss of life Permanent incapacity	>$1 M	Irreversible damages Violation of laws or regulations

Critical	Partial permanent incapacity
	Industrial illness with
	  hospitalization
		>$200 K, <$1 M	Reversible damages
			Minor violation of laws or
			  regulations

Marginal	Injury/industrial illness with lost
	  time >1 day
		>$10 K, <$200 K	Damage correctable without
			  violation of law or regulations

Negligible or low	Injury/industrial illness with no
	  lost time
		>$2 k, <$10 K	Minimal damage that can be
			  easily corrected

In the above example of a grid, the emphasis must be on the potential effect of an accident on humans, with added consideration for the physical or environmental effect that often accompanies a workplace accident or illness.

The estimate of likelihood and consequences for a given scenario associated with an identified hazard is based on prevention, detection, and reaction systems that are currently operational. Here the adjective "operational" is crucial: It means that there is evidence that the risk controls are implemented and are used effectively. A risk control that exists on paper but is ignored is equivalent to a non-existent risk control.

Risk Prioritization

As outlined in Chapter 1, combining the likelihood and consequences defines the dimension or level of risk.

The priority must be given to those risks judged as high (high likelihood and high consequences). After these high risks are adequately treated, the medium risks will be examined for improvements. When resources become available, low risks will be considered for improvements.

Risk Treatment

Treatment involves reducing either the probabilities, or the consequences, or both. Some examples for reducing probabilities follow:

- Enhance management values, expectations, and behavior
- Improve information, communications, awareness, and training
- Review articles of personal protective equipment and their use
- Institute or enforce preventive maintenance
- Establish or improve lockout procedures
- Upgrade standards of cleaning and housekeeping
- Monitor noise level and atmosphere quality
- Increase monitoring
- Establish additional rules
- Control temporary installations, new equipment and substances, and practices
- Provide redundancy of equipment and communication
- Update alerts and alarms triggered by abnormal operations
- Adjust coordination of the activities of contractors and visitors
- Upgrade automatic lockouts
- Institute "go-no-go" and fail-safe systems
- Abandon high-risk installations and practices in favor of safer ones

Some examples for reducing consequences follow:

- Institute or improve systems to detect faults
- Review and improve emergency plans, including defining roles, communications, intervention, and reestablishment activities, and perform frequent drills
- Install physical installations, such as sprinklers, barriers (such as firewalls, berms), and make sure that existing ones are functional

Although priority should be given to prevention to reduce the likelihood of accidents or industrial diseases, attention must also be given to detection and reaction systems. Companies are often judged by the media and the public for their ability to manage emergencies.

Here is a personal example:

Our refinery was operating a small installation for blending lube oils. It was located a few miles from the refinery. One day, at that installation, a malfunction of a limit switch on a storage tank heater caused an explosion and fire. Our refinery fire brigade was dispatched to extinguish the fire with the use of foam. This foam is produced with a chemical mixed with water in a special eductor driven by high water pressure. Our firemen had always made foam at the refinery where the fire water pressure was boosted to 150 psi at the hydrants each time there was a fire drill or a fire. Unfortunately, the water pressure at the hydrants of the lube blending installation was not sufficient to generate foam. By the time the firemen rerouted the hoses through the fire truck booster pump to generate foam, the fire had burned itself out! This embarrassing performance was witnessed by a crowd of nearby residents, media representatives, and by the employees. Needless to say that our reputation had taken a hit.… The questioning was not centered on the cause of the accident, but of our poor management of the emergency. In all the frequent fire drills, we had overlooked that we could be called to fight a fire at the lube blending installation, which had different conditions from the refinery infrastructure.

Risk Monitoring and Review

There is a recognized indicator of loss time accident severity in industry, which is the number of loss-time accidents per 200,000 work hours. This indicator is meant to enable comparison between other operations in a similar industry on the basis of 100 employees working full-time for one year. This indicator can, however, be misleading. A company having a workforce of 100 employees, will, with each accident, increase its lost-time accident rate by 1, whereas a small company having only 10 employees would see its rate increase by 10. More important, however, it is not a measure of the quality of the health and safety management system, even though it is often seen so. As mentioned in Chapter 1, the Westray mine won an award for safest mine in Canada based on its lowest lost-time accident rate—weeks before it exploded fatally.

Beyond the number of loss-time accidents, a meaningful measure is the quality of the program, based on the effectiveness of its application and corrective actions. To ensure that all prevention, detection, and reaction systems are operational, we need a program of frequent independent audits, publication of results, and corrective actions. The management of health and safety uses the same approach as the management of quality: Define what you have to do, do it, and prove (by regular audits) that you have done it.

Learn from your accidents and those of others. Understand the fundamental causes. Remember the potential negative effect that industrial installations can have on the surrounding population. The horrible Bophal disaster in India in 1984 is a grim reminder. The release of a highly toxic gas outside the confines of the industrial installation killed or severely and permanently affected the health of the neighboring population. It was a stark lesson in the importance of considering the possible negative effects on people beyond industrial property limits, as well as of the importance of applying risk assessment to such eventualities.

Near misses are learning opportunities. There should be a reporting system to identify and analyze them. A near miss is an indication that one or more of your systems has failed, even if—fortunately—there was no undesirable consequences.

Here is a personal example:

We had a serious near-miss at the refinery when a railroad locomotive hitched a tank car while it was being filled with propylene. Although there was an important release of explosive gas when the loading arm broke, it did not ignite, and nobody was hurt. This incident raised many questions about the precautions which should have been taken: had a derailer (this is a device installed on the track to physically prevent rail traffic from going beyond a given point) been installed on the tracks before the loading operation?

Was the loader on site during all the loading operation? Who notified the locomotive driver to come and hitch the tank car? Somewhere, our system had failed. Nobody got hurt this time. But ignoring the causes of such a serious near-miss would have been to invite a future catastrophe!

A complete review of the health and safety risk management system is necessary periodically (say, every five years) to ensure that the various changes have been captured and the shortfalls corrected.

Current Trends in Health and Safety Risk Management

The current trends are making management task increasingly challenging and should be taken into account in developing your company's health and safety risk management systems.

- The education level of employees is generally higher, and their expectations are different. No more do they want to only be told; they want to understand, to be convinced, to participate.
- Increasingly heterogeneous work forces. The difference in personal values and culture must be considered when creating health and safety awareness.
- Multitasking. This trend should not be encouraged at the expense of focusing on the application of adequate health and safety measures for the task at hand.
- Rapid and constant technological developments require constant update of knowledge and skills. This emphasizes the importance of training updates and refreshers.
- Computerized applications and robots are multiplying. Unless careful attention is given to their introduction, employees may come to think that they don't have to positively interact with their environment.
- Autonomous teams have diffuse authority and responsibilities. It is important to clearly define the responsibility of each team member for safety and health. Ultimately, there must be an identifiable and responsible person.
- New materials and chemical substances are developed and introduced in the workplace increasingly frequently. The task of reviewing them for their safe introduction is becoming more onerous.
- Machines are increasingly complex, large, and quick in their operation. This creates conditions that amplify the consequences should the prevention controls fail.
- The complexity of modern technology often requires the consultation of "experts." However, line management is still responsible for decisions and their outcomes.
- The increased introduction of round-the-clock work schedules (to increase return on investments) and longer shifts (for more time off) are creating more conditions that can induce fatigue and lack of concentration.
- New regulations and union demands create more manpower disruptions. We now have to manage disruptions such as parental leaves, sabbaticals, and absences due to stress and still ensure that work assignments are compatible with competence of temporarily assigned personnel.

- Higher expectations of clients, society, shareholders, employees, unions. All stakeholders must be convinced that management is in control at all times. Accidents don't just happen!
- Speed and quality of public information. Social network creates instantaneous information of questionable quality, and rumors abound.
- Portable electronic devices such as smartphones and tablets create, for many users, an irresistible urge to continually view the latest information and to text others. This detracts from the attention that must be given to work safely.
- Worldwide trade and competition, just-in-time provision, inventory reduction, and other supply chain changes increase the pressure to deliver and thus the temptation to improvise without adequate analysis of new risks.

Despite all this evolution, which seems to accelerate, management is, and will remain, directly responsible for the health and safety of personnel, contractors, and visitors. This responsibility must be addressed systematically to ensure success. All management personnel must have an intimate knowledge of health and safety principles to adequately fulfill their role.

Notes

1. Bill C-45 (Section 217.1 in Criminal Code), www.ccohs.ca/oshanswers/legisl/billc45.html.
2. Directive 89/391/EEC—OSH "Framework Directive," European Agency for Safety and Health at Work, https://osha.europa.eu/en/legislation/directives/the-osh-framework-directive/1.
3. Phil Hughes and Ed Ferret, *Introduction to International Health and Safety at Work* (New York: Routledge, 2013). Quote taken from "Editable PowerPoint slides for Lecturers," Chapter 4.
4. Occupational Safety and Health Administration, Safety and Health Management Systems eTool, https://www.osha.gov/SLTC/etools/safetyhealth/mod1_costs.html.

4

Project Risk Management

Mike Fontaine

Failure to deliver projects can significantly harm the engineering and construction firms that build them, as well as the clients who engage these firms. For example, in 1989, Davy Corporation, a British engineering and construction firm, secured a large fixed-price project to convert an exploration rig into a oil production platform. The terms were 25 percent down and 75 percent on first production of oil. Severe cost and schedule overruns resulted in serious losses for Davy. As a result, in 1991, Davy Corporation was bought by Trafalgar House, a British conglomerate, at a much diminished share price. Later in 1991, the oil production platform finally went into operation, about two years behind schedule and in a very different business environment. The client was not able to buy back the rig per the original agreement. Trafalgar House was forced to write down the book value of the rig and charter the rig to the client for about 50 percent of normal rates to generate some revenue. This project, plus losses from other parts of their operations, eventually resulted in Trafalgar House itself being purchased in 1996. So not only was poor management of project risks disastrous for Davy, but the client and Trafalgar House incurred large losses owing to the delays.

By definition, projects are temporary undertakings having start and finish dates (a schedule). In addition, projects must meet certain requirements that satisfy the objectives for which the project is being undertaken (project scope) while meeting a budget for the project.

Because the resources available for completing a project (i.e., time, money, and human resources) are limited, the often competing demands of project schedule, scope, and budget must be balanced to best meet the project objectives. Furthermore, a project must also satisfy the objectives of a number of different project stakeholders, including the project owner, government, local community, equipment vendors, and construction contractors.

A formal risk management program provides a sound basis for decision making on projects to balance all these competing demands. Although management of risks on projects shares a lot of the same fundamentals and elements as the management of risks for the normal operation of enterprises, the different context requires that the focus of risk management on projects be different.

One of the key risk mitigation strategies on projects is to undertake projects in phases, where incremental financial commitments are justified by increasing levels of project definition and development actually achieved. Different industries use different project life cycles with different terminology used to describe the various project phases. However, the underlying concept of a project being completed in phases is universal. Because of the author's experience in mining and metals, this chapter will be based on the typical project life cycle used in those industries. In this chapter, we will illustrate project risk management using the following project life cycle scheme:

1. Conceptual study
2. Prefeasibility study
3. Feasibility study
4. Project execution

This chapter focuses on managing risks during the execution of engineering and construction projects. Some of the principles described in this chapter would apply to other sorts of projects, such as large software engineering projects. This chapter describes the following:

- Types of risk on projects
- Risk management activities over the project life cycle
- Managing the risk of being on time and on budget

Background

Everyone has responsibility for risk management on a project, but common practice is to appoint a single project risk manager to coordinate risk management activities and to provide specialist expertise.

One of the first tasks of the project risk manager is to develop the following four key risk management documents:

- Project risk management policy
- Project risk management plan (part of the overall project plan)
- Risk management procedures
- Risk registers

These should be consistent with the analogous enterprise risk management documents. However, since the context of a project is very different from the context of the normal operations of an enterprise, the enterprise risk management documents have to be modified to suit project requirements to produce project-specific documents.

The risk management policy is usually the same as the corporate risk management policy.

Two project plans are prepared toward the end of each project phase. One plan documents the plan for completing the subsequent project phase, and the other documents the plan for executing the project. The project risk management plans are subsidiary plans of each of these project plans.

One risk management plan describes how the risk management process described in Chapter 1 will be implemented during that phase, whereas the other describes how the risk management process will be implemented during project execution. For example, the project risk management plan for the conceptual study phase describes how risks will be identified, analyzed, and prioritized during the conceptual study and can give general guidance for how risks should be mitigated. For example, one firm may emphasize transferring risks to other parties when practical, whereas another may emphasize mitigating them itself.

In a project, conditions change quickly. The risk register is where the risks identified during risk assessment are recorded. As a result, the risk register normally is updated monthly. During the update, the assessments of previously identified risks are reviewed, new risks identified and assessed, the status and effectiveness of existing risk treatment plans assessed, and new risk treatment plans developed as required for both existing and new risks. The result is an updated risk register.

The ongoing operations of an enterprise are relatively standard and stable. As a result, the tools and techniques used for assessing risks tend to be limited in number, standardized, and used across the entire organization. However, projects, by their very nature, are dynamic, and different tools and techniques are used to assess risks during different project phases to suit the specific requirements of a given project phase.

Enterprises define key performance indicators (KPIs) for assessing the health of their organizations. These KPIs are selected to suit ongoing operations of the enterprise. Projects may require different KPIs to assess project health. The main project-specific KPIs are capital cost and project schedule. In addition, the rating scales that many enterprises use for assessing the magnitude of the consequences of a given risk on a KPI must be modified to suit project-specific requirements. Depending on project size, a risk that is insignificant to the enterprise as a whole could be catastrophic to the project.

Types of Risks in Projects

Risks on projects can be roughly divided into project risks and technical risks.

- **Project risks** are those that occur during the execution or building of the project. For example, suppose a piece of equipment such as a specialized filter needed for a smelter can only be purchased from a limited number of suppliers. If there is high demand for this product and none of the suppliers can supply it on time, the timelines for completing the project will be threatened. Generally groups such as construction, purchasing, finance, and human resources are responsible for managing project risks.
- **Technical risks** are risks that occur during the operation of a project after it is completed. For example, a tank is designed and built in such a way as to create a risk of overflowing and spilling into a river during the operation of the plant. This type of risk should be identified during the design of the project and mitigated by modifying the design.

Sources of Project Risks

Project risks arise from such things as the following:

- **Project location:** This includes geopolitical conditions, legal/regulatory environment, and manmade or natural catastrophes. For example, the risks posed by severe weather events such as floods, hurricanes, tornadoes, or extreme temperature during project execution and subsequent operation of the facilities associated with the project must be addressed.

- **Economic, industry, and market environment:** This includes demographic trends, inflationary environment, business cycle, changes to the business structure, changes in the price of inputs (both for completion of the project and for subsequent ongoing operations), and changes in interest rates or foreign exchange rates. For example, some project proponents purposely proceed with projects when the overall business cycle is in a trough. Although a project proponent must have the necessary financial resources, this will reduce the likelihood of cost overruns, for the equipment, material, and human resources required to execute the project can likely be procured at lower prices. Conversely, severe cost overruns can result when projects are executed at a peak in the business cycle.
- **Project size, complexity, and uniqueness:** Large projects tend to be more complex than smaller projects, with increased numbers of communication channels and increased levels of project governance. This tends to make large projects riskier than small projects.
- **Financial strength of the project proponent:** It may be prudent for the project proponent to find a partner with whom to share financial risk. However, this will introduce new risks related to project governance, for there will now be two different entities involved in the project.
- **Technology:** Projects using leading-edge, state-of-the-art technology will require extensive bench scale, pilot scale, and demonstration scale testing to prove out the technology and develop the design criteria required to complete detailed design for a commercial facility. Projects using mature, well-established technology will not require this extensive testing.
- **Logistics:** The transport of equipment, material, and people to and from the project site can be a major undertaking. Planning for this transport must take into account the maximum load dimensions and load weights imposed by the transport route. For example, a plant located on the coast could take advantage of the cost savings resulting from pre-assembled units or modules and barge transport to the site. On the other hand, a plant located inland will be restricted in terms of load size by the dimensional and load limits of the access road or rail line. As a result, extensive pre-assembly would not be an option.
- **Communication:** Communication becomes more complicated as project size increases and on remote project sites. Satellite communication or the installation of fiber optic cables may be required for the communication system to provide the bandwidth required by the project.
- **Design:** It may be advantageous to use low-cost global execution centers to design the facilities. However, coordination with the global execution centers is more complicated than if a local execution center was used.
- **Procurement:** Procurement risks relate primarily to the availability and quality of equipment vendors and construction contractors. There is a risk that costs could be higher if vendor or contractor availability is low owing to lack of competition.
- **Construction:** Construction risks can be due to extreme weather, the layout of the overall plant site, or the skill and number of construction craft workers available. For example, qualified local construction craft labor may be in short supply, and an extensive

training program may be required if labor from outside the immediate plant area cannot be brought in.

- **Commissioning:** The simplicity of equipment and system commissioning will vary from project to project. This will affect commissioning duration and commissioning labor requirements.
- **Integration with existing operations:** If the project is an expansion to existing facilities, then integration of project execution and operation of the new facilities with the existing facilities must be addressed. For example, there is the risk that construction of the new facilities could affect operation of the existing facilities or that operation of the existing facilities could affect construction of the new facilities.
- **Human resources:** Human resources are frequently a major source of risks on projects. Project cost and schedule can be affected depending on how the project team works together as a team.
- **Sustainability:** Sustainability is becoming more of an issue on projects. Sustainability issues include community and heritage values, disease and health risks, potential releases of hazardous materials, high sound levels, the effects of an industrial or environmental disaster, and conservation and endangered species. (See the chapter on environmental risks for more.)

Sources of Technical Risks

Technical risks are normally managed separately from general project risks, being primarily associated with the design of the facilities. Assessment of technical risks is an integral part of the design of the facilities associated with the project. Early in the project life cycle, technical risk management is used to guide the design of the facilities. Later in the project life cycle, technical risk management is used to verify the design of the facilities.

Treatment plans must be developed for all of the intolerable technical risks. In addition, as a second priority, treatment plans are developed for technical risks falling in the tolerable category. Treatment plans for risks in this category are defined based on cost/benefit analysis, where the risk severity is reduced to a level as low as reasonably practical (ALARP). In most cases, the treatment plans are related to the design of the facilities, whereas in some cases, the treatment plans are related to standard operating or maintenance procedures.

Sources of technical risks include the following:

- Fires or explosions
- Chemicals
- Pressure extremes
- Temperature extremes
- Mechanical conditions
- Radiation
- Electrical conditions
- Physiological conditions
- Human factors

- Ergonomic factors
- Control systems
- Vibration
- Motion
- Operating mode
- Miscellaneous conditions

Managing Risks during the Project Life Cycle

The phased approach to project risk management is used when projects are executed in phases, with formal reviews at the end of each phase. The initial phases focus on conceptual and preliminary design of the product or service the project is to provide, whereas the later phases focus on detailed design and actual execution of the project.

A progressive and phased increase in investment in a project, in line with progressively decreasing risk and increasing clarification and certainty over time, is the key to the project life cycle. Each incremental investment is made when the level of risk and certainty justifies it, rather than committing large sums to an uncertain investment at the outset. In one project, a large mining company was interested in extracting magnesium from asbestos tailings. During the feasibility study, a pilot plant was built and tested and appeared to work. The project proceeded to construction and operations. The extraction plant failed very soon thereafter, at great cost to the mining company. A key was not identified: that impurities would build up inside the equipment during continuous operations, impeding production. Had this risk been identified during the feasibility study, the project might have been canceled or redesigned at that point.

Conceptual Study

The purpose of the conceptual study is to determine whether there is a viable business case for the project based on the product to be produced, the markets for the product to be produced, proposed plant capacity, and proposed plant location. In addition, a workable plan and associated schedule and cost are developed for completing the next phase of the project, the prefeasibility study. At the end of the conceptual study, a decision is made to commit funds for the prefeasibility study and on the alternatives that will be studied further during the prefeasibility study.

For project risks (those risks primarily associated with completion of a project phase or final project execution), the effort focuses on assessing the major risk issues, identifying any fatal flaws, and identifying any special treatment actions and determining if they are practical during the execution and operation phases. Normally brainstorming is used to identify risks, and qualitative likelihood of occurrence and consequence magnitude scales are used to assess risk severity. The major deliverable is a conceptual level project risk register. An example of a typical project risk that would be identified during this phase of a project would be competition from other similar projects with similar finish dates that would increase market supply, reduce product prices, and reduce revenue.

Allowances are made in the capital cost estimate for contingency (known unknowns; the amount of money needed above the estimate to reduce the risk of cost overruns to a level acceptable to the organization) and in the schedule for additional float (the amount of time that activities can be delayed from their earliest start dates without delaying the project finish date).

For technical risks (those risks related to the effect on people, the environment, and physical assets during construction, commissioning, operation, and maintenance), the effort is concentrated on understanding the project, the process, and the materials involved and on identifying major hazardous facilities (facilities posing intolerable risk to people, the environment or physical assets). This way, issues can be assessed in more detail during later phases. Brainstorming is normally used to identify technical risks using conceptual site layout drawings, process block diagrams, and Material Safety Data Sheets (MSDSs) as inputs. The principal deliverable is a conceptual level technical risk register and a list identifying major hazardous facilities that focuses on the most critical technical risks. An example of a major technical risk that could be identified during this phase of the project would be the risk from using a toxic raw material in the production process.

During the conceptual study, the treatment plans and actions can involve major changes to the plant design, site plot plan, or general arrangement of the facilities. These major changes can, in turn, significantly affect the capital cost of the new facilities and the project schedule.

Prefeasibility Study

The purpose of the prefeasibility study is to select the best alternative for producing the product in the quantities defined at the location selected and to more rigorously test the project's viability. Moreover, a workable plan and associated schedule and cost are developed for the next project phase, the feasibility study. At the end of the prefeasibility study, an alternative is selected and a decision made to commit funds for the feasibility study.

Project risks are assessed and risk treatments defined for each alternative studied for decision making. Then the risk register is finalized for the preferred alternative. Normally, a checklist is used to identify risks and the major deliverable is a preliminary project risk register. Monte Carlo simulations of the capital cost estimate and the project schedule are used to establish the contingency reserve to be included in the capital cost estimate and the additional float to be included in the project schedule. The Monte Carlo simulations incorporate the effect of risks from the risk register that would affect project cost and schedule, plus the effect of the imprecision associated in estimating capital cost and schedule. A typical project risk that would be identified during this phase of the project would be the risk from selecting a process requiring extensive bench scale and pilot scale testing before the plant could be designed and constructed.

For technical risks, significant and major risks and their causes and consequences are identified, and risk treatment actions for all of the intolerable risks and some of the tolerable risks are incorporated into the plant design. Normally, a checklist of generic technical risks is used to identify the technical risks using preliminary site plot plans, preliminary process flow diagrams and preliminary general arrangement drawings as inputs. The principal deliverables are a preliminary technical risk register for the preferred alternative and for each of the alternatives evaluated.

Treatment plans and actions defined during the prefeasibility study normally involve more moderate changes to the general arrangement of the facilities and provide guidance for the design of the facility process control system. An example of a technical risk that would be identified during this phase of a project would be the risk of a release of a toxic material from the plant resulting from the loss of control over plant operations. The mitigating action could be to add interlocks to the plant control system to shut down the plant and prevent the release of toxic material.

Feasibility Study

The purpose of the feasibility study is to more fully define the selected alternative and develop a detailed plan for executing the project during the final phase of the project. Particular emphasis is placed on aligning the project schedule, scope, and capital cost estimate to the project plan and establishing the performance measurement baselines against which performance will be measured during project execution. At the end of the feasibility study, a decision is made to commit the often large sums of money to actually build the facilities that will be the end product of the project.

In terms of project risks, a full risk assessment of the selected alternative is conducted and finalized. In addition, risk treatment plans are defined for all of the intolerable risks and the most serious of the tolerable risks. The key deliverable is an updated project risk register. An example of a project risk that would be identified during this phase of a project would be the risk of late equipment deliveries caused by a lack of suitably qualified equipment vendors and qualified vendors already having full order books.

In addition, any specific detailed risk assessments that may be required to understand key project uncertainties are completed. Finally, Monte Carlo simulations of the capital cost estimate and project schedule for the selected alternative are completed to establish the contingency reserve to be included in the capital cost estimate and the additional float to be included in the project schedule.

For technical risks, a more detailed qualitative assessment of risks and their causes and consequences is completed and risk treatment actions finalized for all intolerable risks and the most serious of the tolerable risks. Contrary to the technical risk assessments done during the conceptual study and prefeasibility study, the technical risk assessment done during the feasibility study is used to verify plant design, not guide plant design. In addition, special quantitative studies may be started for intolerable risks requiring further study. A typical technical risk identified during this phase of a project would be the risk of producing poor-quality product as the result of not having included adequate analysis equipment in the plant design.

The hazard and operability (HAZOP) study technique is used for identifying risks in the design of process plants. It involves a detailed examination of the piping and instrumentation diagrams (P&IDs) and the control system functional description. The P&IDs show all of the process lines in the facility and the associated control hardware, such as switches, measurement elements, and control valves, and the functional description describes all of the functions to be programmed into the control system.

The HAZOP study technique is a structured brainstorming technique that uses guidewords to identify deviations from the design intent. The technique was originally developed by Imperial Chemicals, Inc. (ICI), for continuous flow process plants but has been extended to cover batch-type operations having discrete, discontinuous steps.

In a HAZOP study, each guideword (i.e., no, more, less, as well as, part of, reverse, other than, early, late, before, after) is applied to each parameter (e.g., flow, temperature, or voltage) associated with a process line on a P&ID to identify potential deviations, such as high flow, high pressure, or high temperature. For example, high pressure could result in a process vessel because of a high temperature caused by inadequate cooling water flow. After a meaningful deviation from the design intent has been identified, the causes and consequences of the deviation are noted. In addition, any controls in the existing design that will prevent, detect, or react to the deviation are identified. In the example discussed above, perhaps the design already incorporates low exit cooling water flow alarms and interlocks and high exit cooling water temperature alarms and interlocks. Then taking into account the effect of the existing controls, the likelihood and consequences are rated. For intolerable risks above the tolerable threshold, additional controls are identified that must be incorporated into the design. Again in the example discussed above, perhaps a pressure relief device should be incorporated in the process vessel to prevent a dangerous buildup of pressure.

The principal deliverable is an updated technical risk register with a list of proposed treatment actions. Each of these actions must be formally approved by the client before the changes can be incorporated in the facility design.

In addition, specialized techniques such as fire/explosion/gas dispersion modeling, fault tree analysis, event tree analysis, bow-tie analysis, human reliability analysis, machinery safety studies, layer of protection analysis (LOPA), safety integrity level (SIL) determination, or control system hazard and operability (CHAZOP) analysis are used to analyze the most serious, intolerable technical risks.

During the feasibility study, the treatment plans and actions involve mainly minor changes to the control system. In a few instances, minor revisions to the layout of the facilities are required.

Project Execution

During this phase, the capital investment is made and all the goods and services required to construct the plant procured. Equipment is purchased from vendors, construction contractors are engaged to build facilities and install equipment, and the plant is commissioned and started up.

The project risks identified during earlier phases are monitored on an ongoing basis to assess the effectiveness of the risk treatments. In addition, earlier assessments of previously identified risks are updated based on new information, and new risks are identified. An example of a project risk that might be identified during this phase of a project would be the risk resulting from inadequate power being available for construction. Finally, periodic Monte Carlo simulation of the project cost and schedule are used for estimates at completion in terms of cost and project duration.

Similarly, the effort on technical risks focuses on ensuring that all previous treatment actions are incorporated into the design and on identifying any new risks that must be treated. Also, all special quantitative studies are completed. The treatment plans and actions almost exclusively relate to changes to the control system. Only in a few instances are changes made to the facility layout.

Managing the Risk of Being Late and Exceeding Budget

Two of the key activities during each of the four project phases are the development of a capital cost estimate and a project schedule. Initially, they are developed as a single estimate of the estimated cost and a single date estimating the project end date, without any estimate of the possible variation (higher or lower) around these estimates that may occur in the final project. How well these single point estimates actually represent the actual costs and project duration depends on the level of project definition and the uncertainty associated with the estimates. During the conceptual study, allowances based on percentages are added to the base capital cost estimate and project schedule to allow for uncertainties. During the prefeasibility study, feasibility study, and project execution, Monte Carlo simulation is used to establish the contingency reserve to be included in the capital cost estimate and the additional float to be included in the project schedule.

Technical risk management activities and project risk management activities have different effects on the capital cost estimate. The technical risk management activities completed during any given project phase allow the facility design to be completed. This mainly affects the direct costs associated with the final, permanent end product of the project, such as the purchase and installation of equipment. The project risk management activities completed during any given project phase primarily affect the project indirect costs incurred to complete the project that are only indirectly associated with the project's end product (e.g., temporary construction facilities, spare parts, and construction management).

Although the project schedule can be affected by technical and project risk management activities, the project risk management activities have a larger effect on the schedule than the technical risk management activities.

To determine the possible variation from the single estimates for budget and timing, the first step is to estimate ranges for the unit price and quantities for the major cost estimate elements and duration of the major project schedule elements and then to estimate the correlations among the major elements.

After these initial steps have been completed, a Monte Carlo simulation model of the schedule is developed. In the simulation, the project is "completed" numerous times. The result of the simulation is a distribution of project schedule outcomes in terms of project

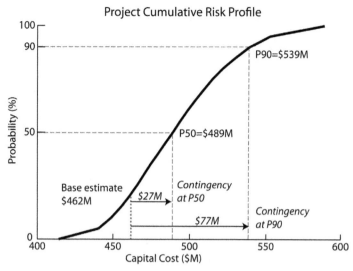

FIGURE 4–1 An example of the output from the Monte Carlo simulation of a capital cost estimate. *Source: Mike Fontaine.*

duration or end date. This analysis is used to establish the additional float to be included in the schedule based on the risk threshold established for the project (i.e., probability of meeting a certain project end date). The additional float is normally shown as a single activity at the end of the schedule.

The additional float to be included in the project schedule affects the capital cost estimate, because any increase in project duration will increase fixed overhead costs, such as project and construction management. After analysis of the schedule has been completed, similar analysis of the capital cost estimate can be done. The result is the contingency reserve to be included in the capital cost estimate (Figure 4-1).

Figure 4-1 plots the cumulative probability of not exceeding the estimated capital cost versus estimated capital cost. In this example, the base estimate, the total deterministic direct and indirect costs excluding contingency, is $462 million. The median value (P50, or probability of 50%) from the simulation is $489 million, or $27 million greater than the base estimate. This means that there is a 50 percent chance that the actual project cost will be less than $489 million. If the contingency reserve was selected on the basis of P90 (90% probability of not exceeding the estimated capital cost), one would expect the actual capital cost to be less than $539 million, $77 million greater than the base estimate, 90 percent of the time. Thus for the same project, the contingency reserve would be $27 million if based on P50 and $77 million if based on P90.

The probability used to establish the contingency reserve depends on the specific stakeholders involved in the project. A small company having only a single project in its portfolio, and for which the project represents a large part of the company assets, would tend to be more risk-averse and base the contingency on a probability closer to P90. The company would want increased cost certainty.

On the other hand, a large company having many projects in its portfolio, and for which a single project represents a small part of the company assets, would tend to be more risk-tolerant on any single project. A cost underrun on one project would offset a cost overrun on another project. This company would likely establish contingency based on a probability of P50.

During project execution, quantitative assessment is used to assess the estimated cost at completion and the estimated project completion date. As cost commitments are made, schedule activities completed, and purchase orders and contracts closed out, the ranges on those elements go to zero, for there is no uncertainty or risk on those elements. Normally, the cost and schedule simulations are run quarterly, during project execution.

5

Operational Risk: Building a Resilient Organization

Steve Osselton and Emily Heuts

All organizations have risk—both from within and from external sources. Many risks are known, fall within the organization's risk appetite, and are intentionally accepted—they're inherent to the business. But others, when manifested as unplanned and unwanted events, create deviations from the organization's strategic plan, and the inability to consistently deliver on their objectives. Operational risks typically disrupt the core value-creating assets, people, and business processes of the organization and, when they are not effectively anticipated and mitigated, create undue volatility for the organization and its earnings. To counter this, effective operational risk management programs help reduce volatility and create greater organizational resilience.

A strong operational risk management program builds resilience by minimizing both the likelihood and consequence of disruptions to the organization, thus helping do the following:

- Preserve the organization's capital
- Protect its people, processes and the environment
- Insulate customers and other stakeholders from shocks to operations
- Allow the organization to adapt to fluctuations to help ensure its sustainability
- Maintain a competitive advantage

This chapter examines operational risks—how they manifest and, subsequently, how they disrupt the organizational value chain. Supported by some brief illustrative case studies, the chapter explores common underlying drivers of failure and business upsets—"why things go wrong." These lessons from past events help to reinforce the importance of fundamental risk mitigation strategies that are essential to prevent, detect, and respond (or react) to hazard and operational risks and to drive continuous risk improvement.

Three themes in particular that, based on this author's experience, are foundational to effectively managing operational risk, and that percolate throughout this chapter, are:

- A focus on human factors
- Effective risk communication up and down the organization
- Building resilience capabilities

Operational Risk—Context

Never in all history have we harnessed such formidable technology. Every scientific advancement known to man has been incorporated into its design. The operational controls are sound and foolproof.

E. J. Smith *(captain of the Titanic)*

Other chapters in this section deal with environmental, health and safety, project risk, and supply chain, and "operational risk" can have specific connotations, depending on the industry segment—financial institutions in particular. So for clarity purposes, we're defining "operational risk," in the context of this chapter, as **the risk of unwanted events within an organization as a result of inadequate or failed processes, people and systems or from external events.** The consequences of these, in some way—from the trivial to the catastrophic—detract from the organization and its value, reputation, and abilities to operate effectively, meet its core goals and objectives, and satisfy key stakeholders' expectations.

Operational risks may be internal to the organization or due to externally driven events. At times the organization may feel itself the "victim," but at others times the "culprit"—where its actions (or lack of) were the direct cause of an unwanted event. Collectively, these risks can include the following:

- **Hazard Risks**—Fire, explosion, earthquake or other losses or impairments to physical assets. These "assets" are frequently the facilities, infrastructure, and investments housing, enabling, or driving the core value-generating processes and human capital of the organization.
- **Process or Systems Failures**—Breakdowns creating operational disruptions and impairment of the organization's value streams, diminishing efficiency and reducing capacity.
- **Legal and Compliance**—Noncompliance with laws or regulations, or prescribed organizational policies, procedures, or core values. These can result in diminished quality, increased costs, lost revenues, penalties, fines, and other sanctions—and certainly diminishment of the organization's reputation.
- **Illegal or Criminal Activity**—Theft, fraud, terrorism, or other illegal or criminal activity—by a range of potential internal or external perpetrators, with varying motivations (see Chapter 8, on human capital risk, for more on this aspect).
- **Human Factors**—Includes employee errors, or personnel responsible for management and control who do not possess the requisite knowledge, skills, and experience needed to ensure that operations are managed within an acceptable tolerance of risk.

Though operational risks can be grouped like this into a few categories, in reality the major challenge for organizations in successfully developing effective operational risk management processes is the myriad of sources of risk that can cause things to go off the rails. Hence it's helpful to understand some common sources of causation of operational failures.

Why Things Go Wrong

No organization wants or intends to have failures; and certainly never of the magnitude of tragedies such as the sinking of the *Titanic* after striking an iceberg or the fire and explosions on the Deepwater Horizon oil rig that caused catastrophic effects on life and the environment in the Gulf of Mexico. But even relatively small failures—a missed customer order, a vehicle collision, a dishonest employee making a false claim on an expense account, and so on, and particularly when considered in aggregation—erode organizational value. So why do things go wrong?

Research carried out at Leiden University and the University of Manchester during the 1980s and 1990s yielded the Tripod theory for understanding incidents and accidents. Its purpose was to understand and explain how and why incidents and business upsets happen, and allow the root causes and deficiencies to be uncovered and addressed. One of the interesting outcomes, still fully relevant today, was Tripod Delta[1]—which identified how individual acts are influenced by the operational environment through eleven basic risk factors within the operational workplace:

- **Design**—The design of installations, equipment, and instruments (Is it logical, fit for purpose and easy to use, having sufficient information for proper operation? Is it necessary to improvise to compensate for poor design?)
- **Tools/Equipment**—Required for a given job (Are they suitable and available when needed? Do supplies arrive at the right place at the right time? Do tools last as long as they should?)
- **Maintenance**—How maintenance is planned and organized (Is preventive maintenance structured, incidental, or prompted by failures?)
- **Housekeeping**—Order and cleanliness around workplace; systematic and appropriate cleaning and waste disposal
- **External Factors**—The extent to which external factors influence the operations (physical conditions: cold, heat, odor, darkness, noise, etc.; personal circumstances: motivation, boredom, abuse, addiction, illness, etc.)
- **Procedures**—The quality of operational procedures, manuals, and written instructions (clarity of application, language, legible, ready accessibility, updating to reflect change)
- **Training**—How people are trained for optimal performance of their jobs (enabled to attend courses and training sessions, putting learning into practice, with provision made for on-the-job training)
- **Communication**—The quality and effectiveness of communication between functions and/or individuals (doing the job properly and comprehending what's required)
- **Incompatible Goals**—How risk management is balanced against other organizational objectives (lack of encouragement, unrealistic time pressure, unsustainable working conditions, insufficient manpower and materials)
- **Organization**—The quality of the organizational structure (things' getting done how they are supposed to, effective coordination between groups or departments, people's willingness to take responsibility and be held accountable, ability to adapt and recover from unusual situations)

- **Defenses**—How people are protected against hazardous situations (e.g., quality and availability of personal protective equipment, measures to safeguard hazardous materials and processes, preparation for emergency situations)

The Tripod Delta basic risk factors provide in effect, a useful set of common denominators for risk such that (per Tripod's assertions) one or more of which can <u>always</u> be assigned as a contributing cause of an operational risk event.

A common "tension" in competitive business environments of financial performance versus operational safety illustrates the contribution of a number of these basic risk factors through the following situation. *A fast food restaurant chain's operational model is that stores are corporately owned, but their operations managers are incentivized financially through sharing their respective store's profits. At one particular store, an extended period of road construction restricted access and visibility of the restaurant so that sales diminished by 35 percent. To offset this, the manager took some cost-cutting measures, including reducing part-time help and working longer hours personally, reducing frequency of outside maintenance and cleaning services—one of which was the daily cleaning and monthly steam cleaning of the exhaust hood and ducts above the kitchen fryers. Just before the road work was complete, an exhausted manager working his tenth double shift in two weeks inadvertently left the oil on a high temperature. There was a fire that was detected automatically, interlocks shut down the exhaust system and triggered the extinguishing system in the hood. However, because of the residue buildup in the exhaust ducts, the fire spread too quickly through the ventilation system onto the roof, subsequently destroying the building (and ultimately the business at this location).* What happened?

- The risk profile changed. The road work was a new <u>external factor</u> to the business that ultimately challenged the economic model and subsequently affected revenues. This triggered some temporary changes in the operating model that compromised the normal risk management <u>procedures</u> in place.
- The required <u>procedures</u> for <u>housekeeping</u> and <u>maintenance</u> of the exhaust hoods were not adhered to, so despite the fire suppression system activating as intended, the fire challenge was beyond the scope of the systems range.
- The suppression system was an important <u>defense</u> against fire spreading in this high hazard area. Had its <u>design</u> incorporated additional discharge nozzles in the duct work, the fire might have been prevented from spreading to the roof of the building.
- The <u>organizational structure</u> and the manager's incentive formula created <u>incompatible goals</u>. Arguably the manager's financial incentives should have been independent of discretional cost components that could compromise aspects of the organization's broader business objectives (such as compliance, food safety, brand and reputation, and so on) by cutting back on processes that manage risk (including the increased fire hazard by not maintaining the cooking equipment).

Insights gained through concepts and research such as Tripod provide helpful guidance in planning operational risk management programs to ensure that they are comprehensive and systems-oriented—that is, the broad range of risks are anticipated, and a complete system of controls is in place and can be relied upon. Accepting that despite best efforts, some failures are inevitable, using basic risk factors as a post-event analysis tool helps analyze and understand the most common factors contributing to causation. This enables management to remedy deficiencies and "recalibrate" control systems to be to be more effective and efficient in future.

Operational risk events may result from changes in the risk environment, from unintended actions (a lapse or slip), or from intended actions that had unintended consequences (a bad plan, conflicting priorities). Ultimately bridging all the basic risk factors for operational risk is the human element. In our experience, the following are four underlying reasons why human factors typically enable or exacerbate almost all failures:

- Failure or breakdown of fundamental management and control systems. In essence, the presence of gaps in the assumed and accepted controls that results in their not addressing the full range of potential risks, not being contiguous or reliable in their application, being poorly executed, or simply being ignored. Particularly challenging is these may be latent failures wherein the breakdown or error occurs a long time before it is detected and the actual loss or upset occurs.
- Lack of recognition of potential threats. This can be because there is no structured risk identification/assessment process or through the failure of operational leaders to identify and address the basic causes of loss.
- No basis for risk management decision making. Too frequently, not making the "right" decisions around risk is a reflection of lack of organizational cognizance of the parameters and variants that should be part of any effective decision processes. This is particularly challenging for many decisions relating to risk—which typically have less tangible data available. This is also arguably influenced by the common human bias that "it won't happen to me."
- Ineffective communication around risk. The role of communication to operational risk management is addressed in subsequent pages.

Alignment Around Risk Communication

The single biggest problem in communication is the illusion that it has taken place.
George Bernard Shaw

One of the key challenges to effective operational risk management is the influence of organizational silos. Whether by business unit, functional areas, or aspects of individual responsibility, operational risk within an organization is frequently managed on a fragmented basis. Individual risk management programs are developed for specific purposes without a centralized strategy. This can result in competing priorities, a sometimes narrow "compliance approach" and lack of appropriate priorities for resources or funding for risk management initiatives. Ineffective communication is a common culprit in driving the failure of effective risk management. Conversely, effective communication can overcome the various silos of risk that exist to some degree within most organizations (see Chapter 10 for more on problems with the silo approach).

The following graphic represents the organization in layers, the associated operational focus, and how each layer is typically thought of and measured on a daily basis. Corporate and strategic leaders tend to focus on high-level macro issues of the company (e.g., new market initiatives, competitors, global market factors, and, as we saw in Chapters 10 and 12, earnings volatility), which can create "blind spots" to operational risks manifesting at lower levels. Middle managers often focus on unit or function revenue and cost centers to maximize profit. Front-line staff tend to focus on achieving day-to-day goals (e.g., processing information, building product components) (Figure 5–1).

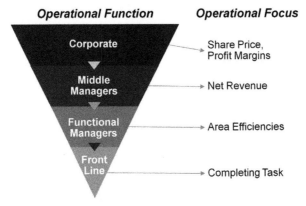

FIGURE 5–1 The relationship between operational function and breadth of focus. *Source: Marsh Risk Consulting.*

Breakdown in communication occurs in conjunction with misinformation, a failure in understanding, or simply disconnects between top-down and bottom-up processes. Consequently, failure to communicate and link operational implications of a major risk to the organization can create the potential for a material effect by a single front-line action (or inaction).

Ineffective communication in itself <u>creates</u> risk. There are numerous past examples of losses where a potential risk event had been identified at the front line, but concerns or early warnings were ignored and hence went un–acted-on by leadership. This may be caused by a lack of understanding of the potential consequences by leaders, but it can also result from ineffective communication. *A maintenance inspection at a utility detects a minor vibration anomaly on a large pump. The technician reports it via a memo to his supervisor. The memo is printed and sent inter-office mail to a department manager, and ends up in the inbox along with innumerable other reports, journals, and correspondence. Weeks pass with no action, and the vibration stresses materials, causing the pump structure to fail and explode. Several workers are killed and seriously injured, and the entire plant is shut down for several weeks.*

There are also innumerable instances of losses that occur as a result of communication failures during handover of responsibilities, at change of shift, and so on, whereby certain factors or conditions are not properly communicated or understood. This is why, for example, in clinical settings in which patient's lives are at stake, communication protocols for an assignment transfer at shift change are critical. A proven best practice technique in healthcare is the discipline for critical patient safety related information being provided by the outgoing practitioner to the incoming. The information recipient, coached in active listening, then is consciously required to reflect back the critical points to demonstrate their clear understanding of the message. As a proven communication technique, this method could be effectively deployed more broadly in other industry segments and applications, and would be valuable in reducing the responsibility "handover" risks.

Communication lapses also frequently occur in another common "handoff' of responsibilities—when organizations retain contracted services. Contracting operational functions to third-party specialists, may bring additional capacity and expertise, but without proper oversight can actually increase or create new risks. *A contractor doing maintenance work at a technology and infrastructure organization took an unauthorized shortcut to locking out electrical systems. In haste a tool was dropped onto a live electrical buss, causing an explosion and electrical system fire. This resulted in the evacuation of the facility and all equipment shutting down, which consequentially caused significant disruption and economic loss to the organization's client base—including hospitals and financial institutions. The contractor saw this as "routine" work and took a shortcut, but ultimately the communication around importance of procedures, the work planning, permitting and oversight of the job didn't reflect the extraordinary level of care that should have been in place to assure there were no interruptions to critical customer services.*

Given the organization's risk tolerance goals for system up-time were 99.999% (sometimes referred to as "five nine reliability") management should have initiated risk assessments to ensure any actions or activities that could potentially breach that standard were identified. It should have ensured that all risk control requirements were percolated down the chain to those overseeing the contracted work. This communication should—in front line procedural terms—stress the criticality of implementing all required controls and should reflect a commensurate "zero-tolerance" for deviation.

Leaders at the corporate level might agree that health and safety is a key operational risk priority, but developing the operational controls (policies, procedures, checks, employee training) occurs further down the organizational pyramid. Moreover, encouraging active communication of operational risks from the bottom up will leverage front-line observation, knowledge and insights and help functional and middle managers align their risk control priorities to those at the top and bottom of the pyramid. This communication helps drive operational awareness to enable informed and effective decision making at all levels of the organization.

Considering that "risk" is the uncertainty of outcomes against planned outcomes, the perception and comprehension of risk really depends on who you are and what your focus is within the organization. As reinforced in the introductory chapter, a common language around risk is one aim of this book. Having a common language around risk within an organization not only aids effective communication, but also fosters better engagement and buy-in at different levels, enables integration of the various layers of the risk management program, and, most important, creates the foundation for more effective and consistent risk management decisions.

The Elements of Operational Risk Resilience

Operational risk management is a function of a number of elements. Before an adverse event, it is risk-awareness—through risk identification and assessment—and preparation. Preparation can be looked at as prevention/mitigation, planning, and implementation. Following an adverse risk event, risk management programs focus on response and recovery. Then, importantly, it must include the ability of an organization to learn from the event and how effectively it was managed to subsequently adapt and adjust operations.

"Response" has the meaning of Chapter 1: the actions taken immediately after an event to contain it, as well as the capability to respond effectively. Effective response reduces the consequences of an event. "Recovery" means the actions taken after response to expedite a restoration to business as usual (or as close as possible).

This chapter looks at the following elements of operational risk resilience:

- Awareness and risk assessment
- Treatment through prevention and detection
- Treatment through response and recovery
- Adapt and operate in the face of change

It concludes with an operational risk resilience model.

The sheer number of risks at the front line of the operations can make it daunting to understand, prioritize, and effectively deal with every potential operational risk. If the triangle in Figure 5-2 actually represents a pyramid, and its base the vast number of risk issues at the front line of the organization, a small number of these—if not identified, communicated, and treated—potentially create a "crack" that reaches all the way up to create material consequences

FIGURE 5–2 The figure illustrates the importance of having an approach to operational risks communications that is understood at all levels of the organization. *Source: Marsh Risk Consulting.*

to the organization. Understanding the underlying causes, and more importantly the full extent of the "impact pathway" is an important discipline to help identify and prioritize risk issues.

Early signs of a small stress crack in a large piece of highly specialized production machinery are ignored because of production pressures and the cost effects of unscheduled shutdowns. The equipment is a process bottleneck with no alternatives, and the resulting catastrophic failure shuts down all production. A long-lead replacement time of 18 months results in financial losses of hundreds of times the cost of a pre-emptive repair, with customer contracts lost and staff laid off.

Resilience is the ability of an organization to withstand the effects of the material disruption to its operations. The goal of operational risk management is to minimize volatility and maintain an effective "business as usual" capability and the ability to change and adapt to the risk environment over the longer term. Hence, when effective, operational risk management programs build resilience.

Awareness and Risk Assessment

As described in Chapter 1, formalized identification and prioritization frameworks are essential stepping stones to developing effective risk management programs. Risk assessment includes risk identification of the source of risk, the events that can occur, and the causes and potential consequences and, combined, forms the basis of risk awareness; creating a better understanding as to operational risks that can surface—is a fundamental first important step toward preventing or managing a catastrophic event.

Operational risk requires broad-based awareness across the entire organization. Awareness starts with recognizing all credible uncertainties, evaluating and quantifying the potential effects on organizational KPIs, prioritizing the key threats, and identifying the needs and actions to manage the risks. The overarching objective is that everyone in the organization should have a high awareness of potential risks associated with their operational functions twenty-four hours a day, seven days a week.

The following are examples where lack of front-line risk awareness or recognition created significant operational effects:

- An operator at a water treatment system at a manufacturing facility inadvertently removed a screen while the system was running. This introduced contaminants and caused the unit, and consequently the factory, to be shut down for a protracted period. This resulted in millions of dollars of lost revenue for the organization.
- An organization, in search of operational savings, undertook a cost-cutting initiative. A finance analyst identified a mismatch between the number of phone numbers relative to head count. To save money, two "unused" lines were cancelled—including one that was part of the organization's emergency notification system. The analyst unwittingly, and without consultation, had impaired the organization's emergency management system—substantially increasing the firm's potential liabilities.
- Current building codes in a particular region require seismic valves on commercial natural gas systems that are designed to automatically shut off gas flows in the event of

an earthquake. Though this risk at one industrial facility was acknowledged, because of cost, disruption and the fact the regulation wasn't "grandfathered," no action was taken. Subsequently an earthquake occurred that initially caused minimal damage to the facility but that sheared a fitting in the gas line. The gas leaked until it interacted with an ignition source, and the resulting fire and explosion destroyed the building—and ultimately the business.

In such situations, focused risk assessment, involving direct stakeholders to the processes, could have pre-empted these types of actions and ensured that appropriate controls were implemented more reliably. After risk is understood, the organizational risk framework should work from bottom up and top down to create awareness and ensure consistent communications around all types of risk. The goal is for everyone in the organization to be sensitized to the risks that they in some way influence and that could cause an unwanted event. Optimally, a culture of intuitive risk thinking and behavior develops so that people are effective at managing risk when they don't consciously realize they're doing it.

From an operational perspective major or catastrophic risk events are rare—they have very low likelihood but threaten very severe consequences to an organization and its key stakeholders. These risks can be very difficult to effectively manage, for they can be viewed by organizational leadership as being so unlikely that they are not credible. But low risk is not no risk. To help counter this, and to avoid "blind spots," a good risk awareness exercise can be used to challenge leadership teams: "What's our *Titanic* (or *Deepwater Horizon*, or *World Trade Center*) catastrophe scenario?" These discussions can identify and acknowledge potential worst-case scenarios for the organization. Even if pragmatically there are limited opportunities to prevent an event, at least they can be acknowledged and contingencies planned for when feasible.

Treatment through Prevention and Detection ("Preparation")

A structured operational risk assessment process identifies and prioritizes risks and enables the organization to plan for managing risks. First and foremost the focus should be to reduce the likelihood of occurrence and ideally preempt the event manifesting. This is achieved by reducing the inherent threats or risk criteria and/or by improving the effectiveness of the risk control systems.

As a simple illustration, the first fundamental concept of fire protection is the fire triangle. This states that fire must have sufficient heat to raise the material to its ignition temperature, fuel in the form of some type of combustible material, and oxygen to sustain combustion. Remove one of the three, and the chemical reaction that is fire is not possible. Though a basic relationship, its principles are the foundation of all fire protection strategies. Effective fire prevention focuses on containing potential ignition sources. In an industrial setting, these commonly include high-voltage electrical equipment, friction, static charges, use of open flames, and use of cutting and welding equipment. All these are fully controllable. Should ignition of combustibles occur, water-based or other fire suppression systems are used to either cool the burning materials or diminish oxygen levels so that combustion isn't sustained.

Consider some space in an office building being renovated to accommodate a new tenant. The fire risk in the vacant space, with plain gypsum board walls, concrete floor, and no furniture or other contents is extremely low. Then:

1. A contractor on site prepares the floor by removing dried-on carpet adhesive. He brings a pail of solvent. A flammable material, with a low ignition temperature, has been introduced to the space. Fire risk increases.
2. The contractor removes the container lid. The risk has again increased, as flammable vapors at the surface of the liquid can mix with the oxygen in the air and now need only an energy source to create a fire.
3. An early delivery of wood paneling arrives. The fire risk has further increased with the additional combustible loading. More fuel equals more heat, more damage, and a greater challenge to extinguish.
4. The contractor pours a small amount of solvent from the pail onto the floor and begins to scrape. The risk has now increased very significantly as a highly flammable vapor/air mixture is created over a larger area, which even a relatively low energy source can ignite (for example, static while pouring out the liquid, a spark from the scraper, an electrical socket).

A system of controls at each step can manage this risk: (1) bring the minimal required quantity of solvent needed for the task, and have an appropriate fire extinguisher available and be trained on its use; (2) allow the pail to "rest" to dissipate static, and dispense into a smaller approved statically bonded safety container; (3) plan work to minimize unnecessary combustible loading; (4) use nonsparking tools—and so on.

The thought process through this example can be applied to any operational risk. The extent of controls should be commensurate with the risk—which isn't always readily apparent. Further, the apparent scope of the activity is not necessarily indicative of the potential effect, and the smallest breakdowns or lapses can have catastrophic consequences.

Meridian Plaza was one of the largest high-rise office buildings in Philadelphia. In 1991, a fire started in a vacant twenty-second floor office in a pile of linseed oil–soaked rags left by a contractor. The fire spread unchecked through nine unsprinklered floors. The fire claimed the lives of three firefighters. The building was ultimately deemed untenable and, after several years of legal arguments, was demolished in 1999. Litigation resulted in billions of dollars in civil damage liability claims.

A complete "system" of controls is important—controls to avoid or prevent the underlying causes of loss from manifesting, to monitor and minimize accepted ongoing operational risks, to detect at the earliest possible warning stage that something is not right, and to respond to any credible risk scenario. Training then helps continue to hone and improve overall organizational risk management capability.

A limestone and aggregates plant had natural gas–fired production equipment—including several continuously operating rotary kilns. Plant operations were such that there was never complete downtime for maintenance, there always being at least one kiln running. A fire broke out in an electrical motor control center near the head end of the gas kilns. The fire department responded but, because of safety concerns, required that electrical systems be de-energized in the area and all natural gas supplies shut off. Site personnel initiated this process, but when they attempted to shut down the main natural gas valve to the plant, it was seized open after many years of never being operated—or even lubricated. The utility was called and a technician dispatched to shut an isolation valve on their systems upstream of the plant. The fire continued to burn. The delay until the fire department could act resulted in extensive damage to the plant. The associated extended downtime to repair facilities and infrastructure resulted in significant loss of revenues—including at some unaffected interdependent operations that relied on this facility for materials. What could/should have happened?

- Awareness—The facility evolved over a period of time through expansions and modifications. An effective risk assessment or change management process could have identified the need for additional separation of fire hazard areas, better sealing of electrical cables and redundancy in the ability to isolate electrical and natural gas systems in an emergency.
- Preparation—The source of the fire was an electrical system. A risk-based infrared scanning program for all primary electrical systems was not in place; such programs have been proven to substantially reduce the potential for fires in electrical equipment.
- Preparation—Emergency response scenario planning and simulation exercises should have been conducted. This may not only have prepared responders for this type of event, it could have identified the main gas shut off valve as a critical mitigating control and subsequently been integrated into preventive maintenance programs.

Scenario planning can help organizations prepare by identifying points of failure and map out the full scale of the "impact pathways" that could result. These may be direct or indirect negative effects on functional goals and objectives or in some way affect stakeholders. This, in turn, enables an appropriate system of operational risk controls to be planned, implemented, and relied on to ensure critical business operations continue. Rigor and objectivity about "what can happen" can help avoid blind spots, and the organization needs to be comfortable with challenging itself and accepted norms to uncover and reveal previously unknown risks.

Captain Smith and the owners and designers of the *Titanic* tragically experienced the over-reliance on certain elements of control. This created "blind spots" to the actual risks and the need for a broader set of controls such as improved navigation systems, detective processes, and having lifeboat capacity for every passenger on board.

Response and Recovery

> *Everyone has a plan until they get punched in the face.*
>
> *Mike Tyson.*

It is illogical to contemplate or expect elimination of all potential failures. Notwithstanding the organization's risk tolerance, there may be a diminishing return threshold beyond which prevention is not pragmatic. In this case, the organization needs mechanisms for efficient and effective response. When "things go boom," normal operations cease, and response mode kicks in. Any complete system of controls includes policies, procedures, equipment, and other resources to both control the emergency situation at hand and expedite return to operations. For the organization to rely on them, they require the same rigorous "systems" approach to ensure effective response capability.

Response mechanisms may be physical in nature, aimed at containing or mitigating an event immediately when it occurs. Or they may be procedural, with formalized policies and procedures, education and training to ensure that required response protocols are followed to reduce the operational impact of the event. These may include, for example:

- Intervention by trained internal or external emergency responders to contain an incident at its incipient stage
- Emergency detection devices to trigger automatic response and shutdown of hazardous industrial processes
- Crisis management plans—including stakeholder communication to manage the organization's reputation
- Uninterruptible power supplies and disaster plans for critical technology and infrastructure systems to minimize operational disruptions caused by power outages

Vitally, these controls must work effectively when needed. History has provided a number of major loss events in which critical controls needed in the first vital minutes were impaired in some way—further exacerbating the loss. *In 1993, when terrorists exploded a bomb in the parking garage of the World Trade Center in New York, the blast damaged water lines. The building's emergency generators, essential for life safety systems to facilitate fire suppression and evacuation, were water-cooled and thus quickly overheated and shut down.*

An event with tragic consequences illustrates the consequences of ineffective response. *The Piper Alpha offshore rig fire in July 1988 killed 167 people. Postmortem analyses and investigations were damning. They showed an accumulation of errors, including informal communications, ineffective safety audits, inadequate training, and management decisions leading to tradeoff between productivity and safety. In addition, postevent flaws in design lead to the disabling of protective equipment by the initial explosion. One of these was the firewalls, which were not built to withstand explosion. The initial blast blew the firewalls down, and the subsequent fire spread unimpeded. The explosion damaged the control room and killed a number of employees who had the authority to order evacuation, all of which created a major void in postloss command and control.*

Leadership needs to be confident that the organization has strong situational awareness and the capability to respond quickly and effectively to ensure the seamless transition from normal operations to incident response and recovery.

Adapt and Operate in the Face of Change

We learn geology the morning after the earthquake.

Ralph Waldo Emerson

Organizations must be able to adapt to the prospect of continual changes in their risk profile, deal with new environments, and seek to continuously improve and learn from past experiences. The impetus to adapt could be a change in regulation, a loss event, an acquisition, or even a shift in competitive markets.

Certain events can put the entire organization at risk and can severely compromise it if the organization cannot effectively adapt to a new operating model.

Marsh & McLennan Companies was charged on October 14, 2004, by New York Attorney General Eliot Spitzer as part of his targeting certain alleged practices within the insurance industry. Even though subsequently all charges were dropped, and the practices challenged at the time continue to be industry norms and accepted by regulators, at the time it was a crisis of significant proportions. Marsh's stock plummeted, substantial fines were levied, revenues dropped, jobs were lost, and company reputation was damaged. Marsh needed to adapt—and quickly. It responded by putting in place new standard operating procedures that included industry-leading transparency models for clients, comprehensive training and education programs, and rigorous ongoing audit and validation processes—all of which continue today as part of the organizational fabric. And though there was pain during and after the crisis, Marsh's ability to respond and adapt allow the company to maintain its acknowledged industry-leading reputation ten years later.

Operational Risk Resilience Model

The operational risk resilience model is inherently, and of necessity, a dynamic process that recognizes that the organizational risk profile continually evolves to reflect external environmental and operational change. This, in turn, requires the organization to be nimble, to adjust, and to be rigorous in maintaining an effective and relevant system of controls. It requires a continuous readiness capability to mitigate and respond to a range of unwanted events that can affect the organization; the organization then must adapt and adjust to new operating models that frequently effect change in the risk profile—hence new preparation requirements—and so on (Figure 5-3).

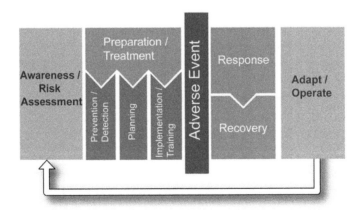

FIGURE 5–3 The relationship between the various operational risk management program elements outlined in this chapter that come together in an operational risk resiliency model. *Source: Marsh Risk Consulting.*

Perhaps, per the terms introduced in Chapter 1, if "likelihood" is the chance that an event will happen, resilience may be considered broadly as improving the chance the organization will meet its objectives—no matter what.

This chapter has shown how operational risk management processes build organizational resilience:

- Without effective communication, risks may not be understood or identified at various levels, which can have catastrophic implications.
- A strong risk assessment process promotes awareness, supports better decisions around risk, and is critical to avoiding operational risk gaps or blind spots.
- Rigorous systems of control are vital—particularly integrating human factors.
- Resilience includes effective preparation.
- How an organization responds and adapts after a risk event will determine how risk will affect that organization over the longer term.

Note

1. J. Groeneweg, V. Roggeveen (1998). Tripod: Controlling the Human Error Components in Accidents. In:Lydersen, Hansen, and Sandtorv (Eds), *Safety and Reliability*, pp. 809–816.

6

Supply Chain Risk Management

Nick Wildgoose

Supply Chain Risk Management for the Business Line Manager

It's widely recognized that global supply chains and transport networks form the backbone of the global economy, fueling trade, consumption, and economic growth. These include the food and pharmaceutical supply chains that are critical to human life itself. Trends such as outsourcing, globalization, lean processes, and the geographical concentration of production have made supply chain networks more efficient but have also changed, and increased, their risk profile. Many enterprises have risk management processes that can address local disruptions—for example, the nonarrival of trucks providing parts. However, recent high-profile events have highlighted how risks outside the control of individual enterprises can have cascading and unintended consequences that cannot be mitigated by one organization alone. And the damage to individual companies, nations, and the global economy can be significant. The leaders of corporate boards and governments are increasingly understanding, and being held accountable for, tackling supply chain risk.

As a general business manager, one of the most critical and complex risk areas you will face is that related to the supply chain of your organization. Many organizations are seeking to reduce costs and improve working capital management while at the same time relying increasingly on their supply chain in terms of the value that they add to customers. This reliance on suppliers is likely to involve a combination of some of the following aspects:

- Global sourcing
- Single sourcing
- Partnership approach
- Just-in-time (JIT) operations

Modern supply chains are operating against an economic background of increasing market shortages and complexities, driven by a growing population that has increased spending power—hence the actions you are taking to drive out short-term costs from a supply chain may be driving risk in. There is no point in saving a cent on a particular component from a supplier to then have the supplier fail to deliver and stop your production line, preventing you from delivering to your customer. The financial and reputational costs of such a disruption are nearly always very significant.

Main Causes of Supply Chain Disruption

It is worth understanding, initially, the main causes of supply chain disruption based on extensive analysis work carried by the Business Continuity Institute, which has worked with the Chartered Institute of Purchasing and Supply over the period since 2009 through a series of annual surveys.[1]

During this period, 70–85 percent of organizations reported experiencing at least one significant incident involving a supply chain in a given year. This is even though the majority of them did not have full visibility of supply chain disruption levels owing to a lack of firmwide reporting (Figure 6-1).

Many of the top causes are described in fuller detail in specific chapters of this book, including cyber attack in Chapter 7, new laws and regulations in Chapter 2, and healthy and safety incidents in Chapter 3.

The chart illustrates the wide range of causes that can lead to supply chain disruptions and thus shows the importance of having a comprehensive risk management approach. A number of other observations can also be made: Supply chain disruptions are not caused only by physical issues, but also by things such as lack of flow of critical information, insolvency, and loss of talent. In the chart, for 2013, unplanned IT and telecom outages, as well as adverse weather, continue to be among the top sources of supply chain disruption and were a significant cause of disruption over the research period. It is also interesting to note that supplier insolvency risk, which often receives substantial attention from organizations in terms of risk

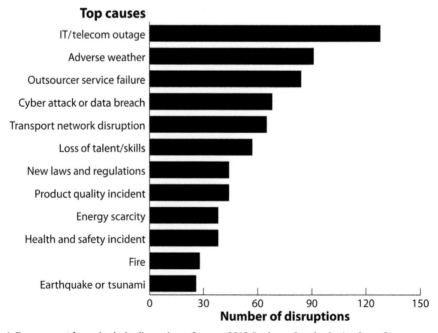

FIGURE 6-1 Top causes of supply chain disruptions. *Source: 2013 Business Continuity Institute Survey.*

management activity, is not, on a cross-industry basis, one of the top three causes of disruption. The chart also illustrates the interconnected aspect of risk in the context of the other areas covered in this book—for example, the importance of cybersecurity and information security (Chapter 6) and how these risks are managed throughout an organization's critical supply chains. We have also witnessed the increasing damage to brands that can be caused by environmental and sustainability issues; there are more details on these sources of risk and their effects in Chapter 2.

A further interesting finding of the research is that although most organizations focus on their tier 1 or direct suppliers, this is only the cause of around 60 percent of the disruptions that organizations face in their supply chains. Thus around 40 percent of disruptions are derived from failures occurring at the second or lower tier level in the supply chain. This needs to be considered in how you approach your supply chain risk management (Figure 6–2).

When considering sources of disruption by country and industry sector, some new sources are identified: Product quality incidents are prominent in manufacturing, whereas insolvency of a supplier is a leading concern in engineering and construction. An earthquake/tsunami ranks as one of the top issues in Asia, whereas adverse weather is a particular concern in the United States.

The consequences of these disruption events have typically involved the organizations in productivity losses, increased costs, and lost revenue. There is also growing concern around the effect that supply chain issues can have in terms of reputational damage on an organization. The issues in respect of brand risk are covered further in Chapter 7.

Though the losses from many supply chain disruptions are significant but not catastrophic, 2 percent of respondents recount losses of more than €50 million in a given year.

This background in terms of the nature, causes, and consequences of supply chain disruptions clearly indicates how important it is for a business manager to have a good awareness of these risks and how they are best mitigated.

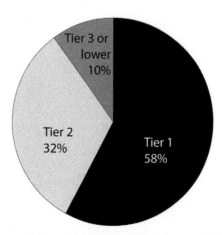

FIGURE 6–2 Chart showing where supply chain disruptions originate. *Source: 2013 Business Continuity Institute Survey.*

Risk Assessment

As defined in Chapter 1, risk assessment is the process of risk identification, risk analysis, and risk prioritization. In the context of the supply chain, the first thing to determine is which suppliers and supply should be focused on from a risk perspective.

The strategic importance of a given supplier and supply is related to its profit effect and the related internal and external context in terms of the risk faced. When value is added to a supply chain to drive business growth, there is also addition to the cost of potential failures and the likelihood of a business critical dependency (i.e., the effect of the failure of a particular node in the supply chain). A common mistake made is to focus on the cost of a particular part or service and only think about those suppliers that represent a high percentage of your spending. A supplier with whom you only spend a small amount of money can be providing a part that stops your production line or can keep you from being able to provide a key service. Suppliers that are difficult to replace represent a significant profit/revenue effect, because the failure of those suppliers will in turn affect an organization's performance over a longer period. A common metric that is used by organizations in this area is the use of a measure to look at the "time to recover"—i.e., if that supplier facility were to go down, how long before it can be replaced?

In identifying these critical suppliers, it may also be necessary to map out the relevant aspects of the supply chain so that key interdependencies are properly understood. For example, one of your critical suppliers might also supply another critical supplier. There are a number of software solutions now available to help you map out what can be quite complex networks.

When critical suppliers and supplies have been identified, the next step is to focus on assessing the degree and scale of both the operational and the financial disruption that the failure of these suppliers can cause to a business.

The supply chain risk identification process evaluates procurement and interdependency information to calculate specific potential loss scenarios—e.g., a fire at a key supplier location. A brainstorming session over what might go wrong can help developing such scenarios. Information such as locations, transport details, business terms, and even financial statements can be key inputs into this analysis.

Any supply chain risk identification will provide vital insights into an overall business effect analysis. Not only will it promote a better understanding of total cost of ownership for goods and services, but it can help with risk prioritization (as defined in Chapter 1) and quantify mitigation strategies and solutions that can protect a supplier network and profitability in terms of disruption effect.

Having identified the particular supplier and supplies to focus on in terms of potential profit or service/delivery effect, this then provides the foundation for carrying out the appropriate level of risk analysis. The key in this risk analysis is to look to make it as comprehensive as possible: There is limited value for example, in carrying out a very diligent financial appraisal on a supplier without even considering whether its key location is in a flood zone.

For ease of understanding, the sources of risk that can drive supply chain risk events have been grouped into five categories. In looking at these factors, consider not just the physical flows, but also the information and financial flows associated with the relevant supply chain:

1. The first area to consider is the industry-specific exposures relevant to the supply of that product or service from a
   - geographical/economic/political perspective—e.g. regulatory/fiscal, trade (embargo), raw material dependencies, pollution, natural catastrophe
   - structural perspective—e.g., generic sensitivity disruptions, product/supply chain maturity, supply concentration/complexity, merger and acquisition activity, inventory/capacity levels, demand patterns (reliability, variability, life cycles, competition)
2. The second area is the supplier-specific exposures relevant to the production of that product or service from a
   - geographical/economic/political perspective
   - structural perspective—e.g., source of supply/routing, regulatory/fiscal changes, trade (embargo), raw material dependencies, pollution, natural catastrophe
3. The third area is how well risk management is embedded into relevant supplier management processes, such as
   - supplier management selection and monitoring, supply chain management (inventory, key performance indicators), infrastructure
4. The fourth area is how well risk management is integrated into the various critical aspects of supply chain exposure, such as
   - enterprise risk management, business continuity management (BCM), commercial risk, personnel risk (intellectual property, skills, labor availability, industrial relations), vulnerability to accidents/errors, vulnerability to malicious intervention, obsolescence/legacy issues
5. The fifth area is ensuring that for critical suppliers and supply chains you have a good understanding of selected suppliers' own supply chain risk management approach, including
   - management issues (suppliers, including relationship in terms of both influence and maturity), BCM evaluation, capacity/capability, financial strength, health safety and environment, corporate social responsibility (CSR), supplier's supplier management, cybersecurity, sustainability[2]

To illustrate how this approach has been used in practice, let us take a key supplier of tires for excavation equipment. This is quite a specialist market. Initially we must ask, per step 1, what the overall supply chain market looks like. Are there clusters of production? What are margins like in the industry? Then, in step 2, we look at the specific supplier of excavation tires and where its production sites are based, within the context of various potential risk event exposures. In steps 3 and 4, we assess to what extent risk management forms an integrated part of the supplier management process in respect to assessment of the supplier and supply. In step 5, we consider how the relevant direct or tier 1 suppliers are managing their own supplier base.

Risk Assessment Challenges

Many challenges may need overcoming to achieve the best result when assessing supply chain risks. Often it is hard to correctly assess and document the risks and interdependencies involved. The completeness and transparency of information from suppliers about their own business systems, control processes, and operational activities will go a long way toward improving the effectiveness of a risk assessment. The following checklist will help in identifying and approaching these potential challenges.

Any successful assessment requires the following:

- Senior management support in terms of resources and objective setting
- The right skills and tools on the team and experience in applying them
- A cross-functional approach ensuring that appropriate individual objectives are aligned
- Mapping the interdependencies between strategic suppliers and their suppliers
- In respect of the critical supply chains, the ability to model the financial effects of various scenarios (in complex supply chains, this is likely to require an IT solution)
- A comprehensive approach that identifies problems and issues

In my experience having worked with a large number of companies to help them protect their supply chains, there are always significant risk mitigation opportunities provided by the exercise. In one particular example, two key suppliers at the secondary tier (i.e., the next level in the supply chain below the suppliers directly supplying the customer) were found to be in significant financial trouble, unknown to the product manufacturer. This discovery allowed the customer to take relevant follow-up actions.

In another example, thanks to the mapping out of a supply chain, overreliance on one supplier was discovered. The actual dependency on a single point of the supply chain was greater than presumed. When the assessment mapped out the flow of critical goods and components, the customer found that it was not 20 percent reliant on one supplier, but 70 percent, because further key subcomponents from this supplier were going to another tier 1 supplier. The company was thus able to address this problem, not an uncommon one in a number of industrial supply chains.

Another frequent finding is that the actual financial exposure posed by potential failure of a key supplier may be much higher than estimated. This is often because of the insufficient depth of the initial analysis. In one recent example, the actual exposure was US$10 million, compared with the US$1 million originally estimated. This can significant affect the risk mitigation actions that are appropriate.

Many companies are ignorant of the actual location of their suppliers and the potential risk they thus face. One company discovered that its key component supplier and its alternative source supplier were both located in the same earthquake/windstorm zone. Consequently, an effect on one supplier would also lead to a loss of the alternative source. Frequently, companies do not perform checks on the supplier's production facilities in terms of their exposure to natural catastrophes; the recent Thai floods have shown how geographic concentrations can quickly occur in manufacturing, having an effect on overall financial exposure.

Risk Analysis and Prioritization

We need to understand the consequences of losing a critical process or supplier. This deals with two very important factors having an effect on both the magnitude and the effects of loss: likelihood and consequences. Consequences deal with the magnitude of an event, whereas likelihood is a measure of how likely the event is to recur in any given period. Consequences also have a time element. The 2011 Japan earthquake and tsunami were severe events causing immediate loss of life, infrastructure, and property. The associated damage and interruption to key sectors of the Japanese economy has significantly influenced the financial performance of business all around the world.

Understanding an outcome in terms of both likelihood and consequences is not easy. For example, if there are two sites, one supplying the other, they may be exposed to different likelihood of interruptions and different severities, but if it is not known or understood how the production processes between these sites are interconnected or codependent, then any individual score is invalid. It might be necessary to go into more detail, analyzing and factoring risks for each site, then aggregating those scores up to the "receiving" site.

Scenarios encompass many kinds of risk, from internal ones such as fires or machinery breakdowns to external ones, such as geopolitical risk, natural catastrophes, or economic problems such as high inflation or the loss of exclusive markets. Another key resiliency measure that needs to be factored into any decision is measure of the "time to recover." When this is understood for a particular supplier site, it can be used as one metric in overall prioritization.[3]

A simple supply chain health check that you may find useful in challenging your organization's current position follows:

Basic Supply Chain Health Check Questions

Do you know who your critical suppliers are and how much their failure would have affect your company's profits?	Yes/No
Have you fully mapped your critical supply chains upstream to the raw material level and downstream to the customer level?	Yes/No
Have you integrated risk management processes into your supply chain management approaches?	Yes/No
Do you have routine, timely systems for measuring the financial stability of critical suppliers?	Yes/No
Do you understand your Tier 1 production facilities and logistic hub exposures to natural catastrophes?	Yes/No
Is supply chain risk management integrated into your enterprise risk management approach?	Yes/No
Do you record the details of supply chain incidents and the actions you have put in place to avoid future incidents?	Yes/No
Do your tier 1 suppliers have business continuity plans that have been tested in terms of their viability?	Yes/No
Have you provided risk training to your supply chain management team?	Yes/No
Is risk on the agenda at performance meetings with your strategic suppliers?	Yes/No

Risk Treatment

Risk treatment or mitigation as has been defined in Chapter 1 refers to selecting options for modifying risks, implementing the options, and improving risk controls for each risk.

The supply chain risk treatments involve many possibilities:

- Avoiding the risk by not engaging in an activity that gives rise to the risk in the context of a supply chain—e.g., by not sourcing from a particular country.
- Changing the likelihood or the consequences of a supply chain event, or both:
  - Aim to prevent an event from happening—e.g., ensuring that a key supplier site has not been built in a flood zone.
  - Aim to detect the event if it happens and thus reduce the consequences—e.g., a number of leading companies have mapped out critical supplier locations and the status of their business continuity plans.
  - Aim to react to an event if it happens and thus reduce consequences—e.g., a company that has mapped out its key supplier sites, because it gets regular status reports on whether they have been affected, is more quickly able to bring in alternatives.
- Selective increase in the use of inventory:
  - Improvements in the risk controls through increased of IT tools enabling supply chain transparency and the use of data analytics, such as financial health indicators: There are various financial measures, including the use of Z scores (which measure the likelihood of financial failure), payment records, and credit scores from a variety of third-party providers. These are now even able to start to look at the financial exposure of the whole chain.
  - Exposure to natural catastrophe (Nat Cat) risk: Many map-based incident dashboards and real-time data services can be used to monitor events in real time and identify exposure and risk concentrations.
  - Supplier databases can indicate whether suppliers have been the subject of legal action—for example, over intellectual property/employee/environmental issues. This is also a useful risk treatment in respect of brand risk, as discussed in Chapter 6.
  - Supplier and subtier risk management: A supplier and subtier risk management tool starts by mapping production site locations for an organization's suppliers and suppliers' supply chains ("subtiers"). It then, through risk assessment of each site, enables risk prioritization of treatment actions, such as changing to another supplier or a new production location.
  - Supplier and subtier crisis response: A supplier and subtier crisis response tool starts by alerting customers that a crisis event has taken place in the customer's supply chain—in other words, near the customer's supplier production sites or the sites of the suppliers' supply chains. It then contacts the emergency contacts in the supply chain to determine which supplier and subtier sites are affected by the crisis event.
  - Improve critical supplier/customer relationships: A number of metrics and assessment best practices frameworks can quantify the dependencies and relationships that exist between a customer and the supplier staff to understand and improve the approach at an individual level.
  - Supplier performance: There are many tools to record and measure the quality, delivery capability, and capacity of suppliers, and these can provide key insights into potential disruptions.

- Country exposure: A wide range of tools, services, and online resources can help in understanding the relative risk of doing business in different countries. They include a variety of risk factors and are often updated frequently, with alerts and warnings included as part of the service. For more details on the monitoring of political risk, see Chapter 14.
- Cost of risk in selecting suppliers and supplies: It is important when choosing between different suppliers that the cost of risk be taken into account in the overall decision making. Insurance premium pricing models can provide valuable input.
- Industry/country supply chain disruption risk data: These look at the causes of supply chain disruptions, analyzed by industry and location, to help you understand where you need to focus your efforts in terms of treatment activity

There are also an increasing number of options to treat risk through how contracts are structured, insurance coverage, and government and financial arrangements. A variety of innovative insurance models are even now entering the marketplace.

Risk Monitoring and Review

As already indicated above, there are an increasing number of service providers who, having helped you map out your supply chain, will then provide monitoring services. These can be used to drive ongoing improvements in the resilience of the supply chain and/or provide support for dealing with crisis events.

There are also service providers, as also already indicated, who provide ongoing country risk monitoring, financial risk monitoring, regulatory monitoring, and the like. In this age of big data, many information sources will provide you with relevant alerting services. The key is to ensure that you are only receiving the information you require, as well as which of these data sources can act as a source of predictive analytics around supply chain disruption.

Emerging Risks in Supply Chains

The frequency and scale of major supply chain effects from a variety of disruptive events continues to grow across the globe. Recently, a variety of events such as Hurricane Sandy, the Japanese earthquake/tsunami, floods in Thailand, Arab Spring protests, and still more have clearly demonstrated that significant effects to businesses can, and will, result. It is critical that enterprises, in addressing emerging supply chain risks, move from being reactionary to being proactive and resilient, knowing that somehow, perhaps frequently, your business will be affected by a supply chain disruption of one form or another.

A summarized selection of these emerging risks follows, taken from a longer paper published in conjunction with colleagues from the Supply Chain Risk Leadership Council.[4]

Climate Change

How do you respond to these climate changes? There are a number of actions that can be taken both in the short term and the longer term. One of the basic checks that can be made is to understand whether any of your key supplier locations is likely to be affected by floods or other adverse weather events. This should also include consideration of the basic inputs to the production processes, such as the adequacy of the water supply or other aspects of the utilities infrastructure that might be adversely affected by weather conditions. Having established key supplier locations, you can then also look at business continuity planning in terms of its adequacy—both within your own enterprise and in terms of the supplier: Does the supplier have further production sites having adequate capacity? As already observed, companies that were better prepared for issues such as the Thai floods were also been able to use it as an opportunity to improve their performance over competitors who were less prepared.

Global, JIT, Lean Supply Chains

There has been a general trend through the adoption of lean approaches to reduce capacity across industries and in a number of cases to create single points of failure. This has efficiency benefits, but if the right balance is not achieved it can, when combined with JIT, lead to a significant increase in supply chain disruptions.

In May 2012, U.S. total industrial capacity use was 76.3 percent. These overall figures also mask specific capacity constraints in, for example, a low margin sector or one facing new regulations, leading to capacity being withdrawn from the market.

A number of recent disruption events, such as the Icelandic volcanic ash and the massive Japanese earthquake and resultant tsunami in 2011, have quickly stopped sections of automotive and other supply chains at considerable cost. An issue around the destruction of a black pigment plant caused substantial automotive issues, because it was a key point of failure in the supply chain.

How does a supply chain risk management practitioner respond to this increase in capacity constraints and pressure on key commodities? An initial step, as already indicated in this chapter, can be to map the critical supply chains you have and to understand which of the suppliers/supplies potentially represent a single source of failure. Driving transparency is one of the key areas to reduce supply chain risk. There are then a number of other steps that can be taken, such as development of alternative suppliers, technological changes in the product makeup, and so forth. As a means of tracking potential capacity issues, you can also monitor your supplier in terms of delivery times. If there is a slippage in these, it can indicate a capacity or other issue that can be followed up by a supplier audit. In many cases, dual sourcing can be a valid strategy.

Increasing Social Inequity and Potential Supply Chain Risks

Today's news is filled with routine stories of social unease, protest, and violent responses to global and local imbalances in wealth distribution, employment opportunity, and the perceived unfairness of the global economic system. Just a sampling of recent events attributable to social inequity includes the following:

- The Occupy Wall Street movement in the United States—the 99% vs. the 1%
- Violent riots in the UK and France by disaffected populations
- Growing protests and tensions in China on the part of an underclass that feels left out of, and exploited by, China's economic boom

- Millions of unemployed youth across the globe who cannot find meaningful employment in the current economic downturn

How do such conditions, particularly as they worsen, contribute to a potential increase in supply chain risk?

Looking forward, a reasonable person should expect that continuing rise of global social and economic inequity will create increasing frustration and uprisings by a disaffected underclass. These inequities may unpredictably explode into violent protest or revolution at a local, regional, national, or even global scale.

What does this mean for your business and your risk management of existing and future supply chains? A SCRM practitioner must consider how these inequities might affect its supply chain operations, particularly when sourcing from or operating in countries having known social inequities and a history of public backlash that could erupt in an instant.

Evaluate factors such as the following:

- Where do we have supply chains or operations that are exposed to risks from social inequities?
- How would we continue to operate in the event of massive protests, port closures, or even an overthrow of the government?
- Do we have a backup plan or dual sourcing?
- Do we begin to shift or restructure operations to mitigate these risks?

Social inequity, combined with a seemingly growing willingness of local populations to challenge existing systems, is virtually certain to create risks for businesses and their global operations. Think through how this could affect your business, and plan accordingly.

Increased Population and Migration

If we fast-forward to 2050, the environment is likely to have suffered immensely from an economy based on mass consumption on the part of 9 billion people. This will be combined with population migration from rural to urban dwelling. Energy prices may have risen with most easily accessible fossil fuel reserves depleted.

In response to shifts in energy and geopolitical realities, logistics and supply chains will need to react and shift in their turn to meet the burdens of society. In one scenario, it is not too difficult to see Asia as the center of a thriving world trade. Former emerging countries will turn into high-tech locations of global importance and centers of consumption. Low-cost production will shift to other regions previously less economically relevant. The logistics industry is poised to benefit tremendously from the steady increase in movement of parts and goods. Of all modes, maritime is predicted to see the greatest increase.

Population migration will present significant challenges to logistics and supply chain professionals, city planners, politicians, and the like. Some of the challenges that be faced follow:

- Lack of appropriate transportation infrastructure leading to massive traffic congestion. Recent estimates of London traffic movement are in the range of 15 km/h. Even before the advent of the horse-drawn carriage in the nineteenth century, traffic in central London moved more quickly.

- Shortage of (affordable) space leading to urban sprawl. In consequence, freight as well as passenger transport will need to cover additional kilometers.
- Increased pollution.
- Low service levels in central city areas (on-time delivery).
- Higher on-site storage requirements.
- Higher city complexity and customer demand, leading to high logistics costs to service those demands.
- Greater e-commerce use, leading to increased parcel delivery in urban markets, requiring innovative methods to assure on-time delivery.

Dependence on Information Technology

With the world's ever-increasing dependence on information technology, a growing risk that must be confronted is the potential for cyberattacks against governments, business, and leaders by targeting communications, trade, defense, and/or infrastructure. The U.S. administration's study on the current state of information technology has declared that "the cyber corruption threat is one of the most serious economic and national security challenges we face as a nation.... America's economic prosperity in the 21st century will depend on cyber security." The sophistication of cyberattacks reaches beyond computer systems and networks to interdict the sourcing systems of the original information and data. Malware allows electronic intruders to operate unimpeded to disrupt operations or gather sensitive information.

Within supply chain operations, we must improve our resilience to cyber incidents and reduce the cyberthreat. A comprehensive supply chain cybersecurity program includes strategy, policy, and standards for security operations in cyberspace. It addresses threat reduction, vulnerability reduction, deterrence, international engagement, incident response, and resiliency. The program needs to identify recovery policies addressing computer network operations, information assurance, law enforcement, diplomacy, military, and intelligence missions as they relate to the security and stability of the global communication infrastructure. Addressing this problem will require collaboration and goal alignment among security, information technology, and supply chain leaders throughout the whole of each critical supply chain or network. (See Chapter 6, on cybersecurity, for more discussion of cyber risk.)

The Benefits of Improving Supply Chain Risk Management

The benefits of understanding a supply chain better and reducing disruptions manifest themselves in many ways:

- Better agility and responsiveness across the supply chain
- Reduction in the need to incur additional and unexpected costs to deal with disruptions

- Protection of a company's share price
- Ability to focus cost saving and working capital improvement activity on the appropriate suppliers in the supply chain
- Protection against reputation damage
- Avoiding the effects of failure to supply a customer or meet contractual obligations
- Ensuring that appropriate medium- and long-term security is made for key suppliers to protect product profitability and investment
- Closer supplier relationships and trust needed to improve supply chain risk management also often leading to opportunities for improved innovation
- Developing proactive alerts and mitigation strategies that minimize the effects of any single point of failure while reducing both frequency and scale of disruptions

The Supply Chain Risk Leadership Council (SCRLC) has adopted a supply chain risk management (SCRM) maturity model to indicate the levels of maturity that organizations have reached. It sets out how to move from a reactionary approach to supply chain events to a resilient approach in which are put in place many of the risk treatments described in this chapter, including tracking emerging risks as they threaten the supply chain.[5]

Organizations compete and provide their services or products based on their supply chain. Better understanding of the supply chain is not just about risk management; it also the key to driving operational and financial performance gains.

Notes

1. The Business Continuity Institute Annual Survey on Supply Chain Resilience, 2013. www.thebci.org.
2. Taken from Zurich's Supply Chain Risk Assessment Approach. www.zurich.com.
3. Supply Chain Risk Leadership Council Best Practice Guidelines. www.scrlc.com.
4. For the full paper, see "SCRLC Emerging Risks" at www.scrlc.com.
5. For full notes on the supply chain risk management maturity model, see www.scrlc.com.

Intangible Risk

Cybersecurity

Kevvie Fowler

Cybersecurity can be defined as the body of technologies, processes and practices designed to protect networks, computers, programs and data from attack, damage or unauthorized access.[1] The first use of the term occurred in 1994,[2] when few organizations had an Internet presence or were interconnected and data breaches did not capture newspaper headlines. As the years passed, interconnectivity increased, adoption of the Internet soared, and computers became critical components of most businesses.

Today, cybersecurity has captured the attention of employees from the back office to the board room. Furthermore, business boundaries are quickly eroding, and business data is accessed and managed across corporate as well as employee-owned devices such as tablets and smartphones, further complicating data protection.

Despite the increased importance of cybersecurity, many organizations continue to approach the problem as a technological issue, just as they did in the mid-1990s. But cybersecurity is a broader matter that must be embedded into several areas of an organization to protect it against a fundamental shift in the motivation and class of criminals that threaten it.

All organizations share the objective of understanding and managing cyberthreats, and risk management is the critical practice that can be used to accomplish this objective. This chapter will focus on how the practice of risk management applies within the domain of cybersecurity.

Cyber Risk Management Overview

Cyber risk management consists of foundational elements that should be performed by all organizations. An example of a foundational security element is how cyber risk oversight and accountability will be structured within the organization. In addition to these foundational elements there are principles that are used to identify, assess, and prioritize risk and the controls that can be used to reduce or eliminate it. This overview of cyber risk management will focus on the foundational elements of a cyber risk management system and serve as a prerequisite to the risk principles and controls we will look at later in this chapter. The first foundational element we'll explore is leadership and governance.

Leadership and Governance

Years ago, cybersecurity responsibility stopped at the director or vice president level within most organizations. Today, cybersecurity is a top business risk. The board of directors is accountable to ensure that appropriate governance, culture, and systems have been established to protect the organization from cybersecurity risk. The 2013 breach at a leading U.S. retailer shows that cybersecurity accountability resides at the top of an organization. The retailer's CEO resigned[3] amid recommendations to replace several board members for their perceived poor due diligence in protecting the organization from cybersecurity risk.[4] Corporate directors and C-suite executives now place high priority on cybersecurity and are focusing on the following key areas of their organization to ensure that cybersecurity is established and governed appropriately.

Leadership

Responsibility for cybersecurity should reside with senior executives. In most organizations the board of directors or an executive leadership committee is responsible for determining who in the organization will be responsible for information security. This position is often designated chief information security officer (CISO) or an equivalent title and usually reports to a very senior position, such as to another C-Suite role within the organization. The CISO is essential in leading, communicating, and influencing people at various levels across lines of business, often in areas over which the CISO has no direct authority. Having the CISO report into a lower level or a technical area of the organization will reduce his or her influence across the various areas of the business.

Cybersecurity needs to maintain top-level visibility within an organization. The CISO or equivalent security leader should ensure that cybersecurity successes and challenges are communicated to the board of directors. It is ultimately the responsibility of the board to ensure that cybersecurity is effectively managed. This responsibility can only be managed when accurate information flows to board members so that they are aware of the security success, failures and weaknesses within the organization. This area of risk management should be a recurring topic at the board level, not discussed solely in response to individual cyber-related events.

Governance

A proper cybersecurity framework is essential in ensuring clear accountability, communication, and holistic practice within an organization. This framework should be supported by a security policy, standards, and procedures. Figure 7–1 illustrates the hierarchy of cybersecurity framework elements.

Cybersecurity is only as effective as the team devoted to its management. The team should be devoted to managing cybersecurity risks and should contain a range of subject matter experts as well as effective communicators having knowledge of practices and procedures

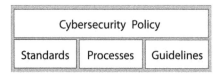

FIGURE 7–1 Cybersecurity framework components.

within other areas of the organization. This mixed skill set is essential in advising, influencing and collaborating with stakeholders across the organization.

Legal and Compliance

The threat of a cyberattack is a significant risk and the potential source of sizeable losses for many organizations. The importance and potential effects of a cyberattack are also well understood by external regulators, legislative bodies, partners, and clients, who impose requirements to ensure that sensitive information is stored, managed, and transferred securely.

Maintaining a compliance requirements register is critical in managing the security and privacy requirements associated with the data you store, process, and transmit. This register should span regulatory, legislative, and corporate requirements set by your organization and should also include commercial requirements, or the requirements to which your organization is held in its business with its partners and clients. Rightly so, your partners and clients will expect your organization to maintain a set level of security.

The complied register should include the different types of protected data within the organization, the specific requirements to protect and manage the information, and notification requirements in the event of data loss or a suspected compromise.

Ensuring that security requirements are embedded within third-party contracts is a necessary but often overlooked method of protecting an organization from cyberattack. Many organizations employ third parties to deliver services and products. In outsourced arrangements, elements of data management or processing are outsourced, but not the governance of the data and systems, which always remains with the outsourcing organization. Any regulatory and legislative requirements that an organization faces will need to be governed by the organization, which remains responsible for ensuring compliance with regulatory and legislative requirements.

Despite the outsourcing of service delivery, the consequences associated with a cyber event experienced at a contracted third party can still directly affect your organization. For example let's consider an organization that maintains a customer database of 1 million data records, backed up by a third party. If the database was accessed by cybercriminals thanks to a lack of basic security practices within the third party provider, the effect, including loss of business, recovery costs, and damage to brand, would lie with the organization. If there was a contract in place between the organization and the contracted third party, the costs associated with the breach would have been covered by the third party and, better yet, the breach might have been avoided all together had there been terms within the contract requiring the third party to implement and maintain good industry security practices to protect the organization's information.

Contract security terms are normally contained in a legal service agreement defining the level of services that the organization will receive and the steps taken by the third-party vendor or service provider to protect the information under its management. When evaluating service providers, it is imperative to ensure that they incorporate and comply with security requirements, including maintaining an adequate level of cybersecurity protection equal to or greater than that of the organization's own industry good practices, including prompt notification in the event of a suspected or confirmed intrusion at the third party provider.

Risk Assessment

As we saw in Chapter 1, risk assessment is the process of identifying, analyzing, and prioritizing risk to ensure that it is appropriately managed within an organization. Risks can be viewed individually as well as collectively; both views should be incorporated into a risk assessment to ensure that the proper level of risk to the organization is identified and managed. Risk assessments can be performed at many levels of an organization, so risks can be identified within a specific technological environment or application or, more broadly, at a project, business unit, or organizational level. A risk assessment can include hundreds of risks, but they cannot all be appropriately covered in this chapter. Our focus in this chapter is on some of the key sources of cybersecurity risk that are applicable to most organizations. These sources of risk should be evaluated for applicability to your organization and augmented with other risks your organization faces as appropriate.

Sources of Risk

Cybercriminals, regulatory and legislative noncompliance, and errors and omissions are key sources of cybersecurity risk affecting most organizations. Each risk may be associated with multiple threats, some of which may have catastrophic consequences. We will begin our look at sources of risk with cybercriminals, the source most frequently discussed among businesses.

Cybercriminals

When one mentions the term cybersecurity, most people are likely to remember a recent news story about a "hacker" who digitally broke into an organization and stole sensitive information, or they may think of the increased need to safeguard their organizations against them. In this chapter, we will demystify the term "hacker" and refer to hackers as "cybercriminals," which better describes who they are and what they do. There are four distinct types of cybercriminals in the world today: petty criminals, hacktivists, organized criminals, and criminals sponsored by a nation-state.

Petty Criminals

Petty criminals are individuals or small groups of criminals who carry out cybercrime. Driven by financial motivations, petty criminals commit computer crimes that can include targeted email campaigns tricking users into divulging sensitive information and exploiting system vulnerabilities to gain unauthorized access to data. Some petty criminals who have special skills also develop computer threats such as malicious software, referred to as malware, that they sell to other cybercriminal groups. A petty criminal may be a trusted internal employee of an organization or may be an outsider.

Most petty criminals lack large resources and thus will typically look for the path of least resistance when committing their crimes. If an organization has superior risk controls, a petty criminal will normally move to another target having a lower level of security. Even when petty criminals possess specialized skills to write and sell malware, they look for a quick return on their product.

The story surrounding a 2013 cybersecurity breach of a leading U.S. retailer includes an example of a petty criminal who sold malware that he authored to a group of cybercriminals. The malware in question was reportedly[5] developed by a 17-year-old petty criminal from Russia, who sold it for $1,800 to a group of cybercriminals who breached the retailer network and installed it across 1,800 store locations. The malware stole a reported 40 million credit card numbers and resulted in one of the largest data security breaches in recent years.

Organized Criminals

Much like petty criminals, organized criminals carry out computer crime for financial gain. Organized criminals consist of large groups of individuals who are well organized and well funded. There are thousands of organized criminal groups in the world. Many such groups are very knowledgeable and highly efficient in execution. Today, malware is a very successful threat used by organized criminals to conduct their crimes. This, however, was not the case in the early 2000's when malware was designed to disrupt operations and spread quickly, commonly resulting in saturated network connections and loss of business service availability. SQL Slammer[6] and Blaster[7] are two examples of this. Malware evolved in the late 2000s and is now stealthy and designed to infect, monitor activity, and steal data without detection. This shift in malware has made it a popular choice among organized criminals.

Despite the growing popularity of covert malware, intrusive malware is undergoing a resurgence. One such example is Cryptolocker, which unobtrusively infects a computer, scanning all local folders in search of documents. It then turns to the network and repeats the search among network files and folders. Using its inventory of the user's documents, Cryptolocker encrypts them, rendering them unusable. It then displays a message informing the user that he or she must pay an online ransom, normally in the form of an cryptocurrency such as Bitcoin or LiteCoin. After being paid, the criminal group will send the individual or organization a decryption key to decrypt the files and return them to their prior state.

Ransomware is usually a threat that is built once and then used multiple times. The organized criminal group either purchases the malware or develops it internally before setting it loose on the Internet, possibly infecting millions of systems around the world.

Petty and organized criminals are financially motivated, but this motivation isn't shared by all cybercriminals. The next group of criminals we will look at carries out crimes in support of political causes, rather than for financial gain.

Hacktivists

Hacktivists are groups of criminals who unite to carry out cyberattacks in support of political causes. Hacktivists typically target entire industries but sometimes attack specific organizations that they believe don't align with their political views or practices. Among the best-known hacktivist groups is "Anonymous," which has carried out hundreds of cyberattacks, including Operation Payback,[8] which included a series of distributed denial of service (DDOS) attacks that disrupted victims' websites, preventing legitimate users from accessing them. A DDOS attack is launched from multiple computers running specialized software that generates a large amount of traffic directed to a website with the intent of overwhelming the system so

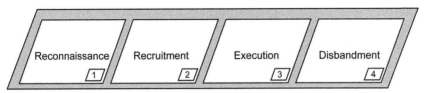

FIGURE 7–2 Stages of a hacktivist's campaign.

that it stops responding to legitimate user requests. Hacktivists typically announce upcoming attacks in advance, hoping to recruit fellow hacktivists and draw media attention to the political cause they support. After recruiting, the operation begins, during which hacktivists perform several types of reconnaissance to identify targets, as well as weaknesses that can be exploited within targeted organizations. The attack is then carried out, typically including the theft of sensitive information or disrupting business operations. At the end of a cyber-operation, the hacktivists disband until they are recruited for the next cybercampaign. In this writer's experience protecting organizations, hacktivists tend to attack in waves, and the attacks continue for a period ranging from a few days to several weeks, sometimes long after a campaign was reported to have ended. Figure 7–2 illustrates the stages of a hacktivist campaign.

The last group of cybercriminals we will look at are nation-state–sponsored criminals, who are not financially motivated and who prefer to operate covertly before, during, and after an attack.

Nation-state–sponsored Criminals

Nation-state–sponsored criminals are highly skilled individuals who are contracted by government departments to launch targeted and complex attacks against unsuspecting organizations in support of a state agenda. Historically Nation-state sponsored attacks have been launched at a number of organizations across industries including telecommunication providers, power and utility organizations and technology manufactures to name a few. In some cases Nation-state sponsored attackers carry out crimes against citizens of their own country. In the past, spies would infiltrate foreign governments and steal sensitive information, such as military plans. With increased reliance on computers, espionage has moved to the cyber realm, where it is commonly executed from secret computer security labs and focuses on the identification and covert extraction of sensitive digital information.

In many cases, governments employ security experts who can plan and execute Nation-state-sponsored attacks. However, some governments also rely on external mercenaries who have specialized skillsets and who are contracted to aid or execute cyberattacks. One such group of mercenaries is known as the Elderwood Group,[9] a group of cybercriminals who have conducted more than 300 cyberattacks over the past four years, including targeted attacks against U.S. military defense contractors as well as against governments and large technology companies.

Considering the substantial investment in cybersecurity protection by governments, military defense and large technology companies, being a good cybercriminal is not enough to ensure a successful cyber-operation. Nation-states also leverage zero-day vulnerabilities, unknown weaknesses within software that provide criminals unauthorized access to any computers running the vulnerable product. In many cases, the vendor of the vulnerable software product is not aware that the vulnerability exists.

These zero-day vulnerabilities are often identified by cybersecurity experts within various government agencies, by independent security researchers, and also by criminals. Nation-state criminals are well funded and often exploit zero-day vulnerabilities in their attacks. These vulnerabilities are bought and sold within hidden online marketplaces that make up the underground economy for prices typically between $5,000 and $250,000 per vulnerability.

The Underground Economy

When financially motivated criminals launch attacks and steal information, the information itself is of no monetary value and must be sold for financial reward. The one exception is ransomware, which holds data hostage until a fee is paid to release it. When data needs to be converted into currency, cybercriminals turn to the underground economy, where large collections of websites sell illegal services and products ranging from drugs and weapons to contract killers and cybermercenaries. Within the underground economy is also a thriving market for data stolen during past cyberattacks. Highly sought after data within the underground economy at the time of this writing are stolen credit card numbers, personal information, healthcare data, and compromised social media and online user accounts and passwords.

All criminal vendors within the underground economy advertise freely and directly compete with each other. Many vendors provide guarantees about the validity of the information they provide, such as credit card information. If you are sold a credit card number that has been canceled by the bank, the vendor will provide a replacement number free of charge. In addition to buying information, you can also lease the services of cybercriminals. One popular service that is frequently leased within the underground economy is the control of a network of compromised computers to carry out activities of your choosing. The most common purpose is to use the network of compromised computers to launch a DDOS attack against a target organization. This service is so popular that vendors within the underground economy frequently offer discounts for a repeat lease. For all cybercriminals' blatant advertising and their commerce of illegal activities, products, and services, it may be asked why law enforcement doesn't just shut down such websites and trace the origins of the individuals involved in the illegal e-commerce. But this is easier said than done. The underground economy thrives on the invisible web, an area of the Internet specifically designed to protect the identity and location of those who use it. The invisible web will be examined in more depth later in this chapter.

Cybercriminals are just one source of risk for an organization. Some sources of cyber risk are not associated with illegal or malicious activity at all.

Noncompliance with Cybersecurity Requirements

Cybersecurity requirements can be found embedded within several sources, including legislative and regulatory standards, corporate standards, and commercial contracts which your partners and clients hold your organization to. Figure 7–3 illustrates some sources of cybersecurity legal requirements.

One example of a cybersecurity requirement comes from a private regulator, the Payment Card Institute (PCI) Security Standards Council. The PCI Security Standards Council is a private regulator formed by executives of major credit card companies, who developed data

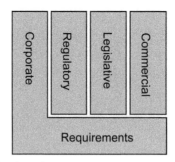

FIGURE 7–3 Sources of cybersecurity legal requirements.

security standards (DSS) and enforce them as regulatory requirements to safeguard payment card information and reduce the losses experienced by merchants and banks at the hands of cybercriminals.

If an organization processes payment card information, it must remain in compliance with PCI DSS requirements or suffer potential fines or the revocation of its ability to process credit card transactions. A recent data breach victim was fined US$13.3 million by the PCI Security Standards Council for noncompliance with PCI-DSS.[10]

Canadian Anti-Spam Legislation (CASL) serves as an example on the legislative side. CASL prohibits the transmission of unsolicited communication, including emails and text messages, to existing and potential customers. Failure to comply with the legislation can carry a fine of up to C$10 million dollars for businesses. Moreover, if an organization has commercial requirements to comply with a base set of security practices and is found not to be in compliance with them, it may be subject to financial penalty, usually in the form of a reimbursement of service fees or termination of the contract with the client.

Considering that in 2014 the reported average global cost of a cyber breach was US$3.5 million,[11] failure to comply with regulatory, legislative, and commercial security requirements can incur a loss in excess of the loss incurred in an actual cyberattack.

Information security and ensuring customer privacy have become a mandatory cost of doing business. Organizations must identify cyber-related regulatory and legislative requirements that apply to them and ensure that business operations are managed accordingly. Aside from cyberattacks and non-compliance with cybersecurity requirements, organizations can still face substantial cyber risks due to mistakes made by employees.

Errors and Omissions

Every digital asset, such as a server, tablet, laptop, or thumb drive, contains data and requires some form of human interaction to benefit from it. This interaction is performed by a human and managed through processes and workflow, with each area serving as a potential area of vulnerability that can be unintentionally or intentionally exploited. Take, for example, an employee who accidentally leaves behind a tablet or a USB thumb drive containing sensitive data in a coffee shop, or an employee who transfers sensitive information to the wrong client by mistake. Errors and omissions caused by such mistakes and system glitches account for a large proportion of data breaches reported each year.[12]

Table 7–1   Common Events and Possible Consequences

Event	Possible Consequences
Loss of service availability	Loss of revenue
	Loss of customer confidence
	Loss of employee productivity
Web application compromise	Loss of revenue
	Loss of data integrity
	Loss of customer confidence
Electronic financial fraud	Loss of revenue
	Loss of data integrity
	Loss of customer confidence
Malware/virus outbreak	Loss of service availability
	Loss of data integrity
	Loss of employee productivity
Physical theft of an electronic asset	Financial loss
	Loss of customer confidence
Unintentional data disclosure	Loss of revenue
	Loss of service availability
	Loss of data integrity
	Loss of employee productivity
Intellectual property theft	Loss of competitive advantage
	Loss of customer confidence

Events

Organizations face many different sources of cybersecurity risk. Each source of risk is associated with one or more events. For example, when considering a hacktivist DDOS attack on an organization, the loss of service availability is the risk, the hacktivist group the source of risk, and the DDOS attack the event. Each risk that an organization faces can be associated with several events. A list of some common events can be found in the table (Table 7-1).

Risk Analysis and Prioritization

Within cybersecurity, the risk analysis process deviates slightly from that discussed in Chapter 1:

- Identifying the value of assets
- Risk criteria definition
- Identifying vulnerabilities and threats
- Determining the likelihood and consequence of identified threats

Identifying Asset Value

During risk analysis, it is important to assign a monetary value to each asset to aid later prioritization. Assigning a value to an asset should be based on both tangible and intangible factors. If an organization purchases a server for $10,000 and spends $20,000 to hire a consultant to install and configure it and $50,000 a year to maintain the server, the approximate value of the server would be $80,000 for one year (assuming the cost of the server is not amortized over several years). Slightly complicating our example, if the organization then copies intellectual property to the server, the value of the server would likely increase to a value far greater than the prior value of a server over a one-year term.

Assigning an asset value based on tangible properties is relatively straightforward, however, intangible properties are a little more complex to identify. It is good practice to consult the asset owner when assigning values and when examining the intangible value properties.

The value of properties will differ depending on the asset under evaluation. The following list describes some of the common properties that can serve as a base when assigning asset values:

- Cost to develop
- Cost to maintain and secure
- Value of the asset to organization owners and users
- Cost of replacement in the event of loss

The properties used to determine the values should be defined and consistently applied to all assets. Some assets may have additional properties, but ensuring consistency will aid in assigning accurate and relative values across all assets. Consistency is important not only when assigning values to assets, but also when defining your risk criteria.

Risk Criteria

As covered in Chapter 1 of this book, defining risk criteria ensures that risk can be compared and aggregated effectively and consistently. Common practice within the industry is to define scales inclusive of multiple rating levels to assess the likelihood and consequence of each risk. Scales can range from two to more than ten, with each level adding a layer of granularity as well as more complexity. Each level within a criteria scale requires a clear definition and should be differentiated from the other levels. Too many levels can result in criteria levels that are too difficult to map, hindering the successful adoption of the risk criteria by others in the organization. Many organizations use five or fewer levels to balance granularity and complexity.

LIKELIHOOD

As already discussed in this chapter, each of the four classes of cybercriminals have different motives for cyberattack, ranging from financial gain to espionage to raising awareness about a political cause. When evaluating the likelihood of experiencing a cyber event at the hands of these criminals, three core factors should be considered that can influence the likelihood of the organization's experiencing a cyberattack.

The data you manage is the strongest influence on your likelihood of suffering a cyberattack. Petty criminals, organized criminals, and nation-states target organizations based on the data they manage. An organization managing financial data will have a higher likelihood of experiencing a cyberattack by a criminal groups motivated by financial gain than that of another organization that does manages neither financial data nor data that can be converted into financial gain.

The industry to which you belong also affects your likelihood of experiencing a cyberattack. If your organization is part of an industry frequently targeted by hacktivists or other criminal groups, you can expect to face more attacks than do organizations belonging to a less frequently targeted industry.

The technology you use is a commonly overlooked influencer in cyberattacks. Technological vulnerabilities are a common way criminals break into organizations. Each vulnerability identified in technology must be either patched or corrected via another risk control to address the exposure. This corrective action is normally dependent on the details of the vulnerability, such as whether it is exposed to a material threats, whether external or internal to an organization. Organizations who use technology commonly associated with a high number of vulnerabilities face increased difficulties in identifying and mitigating these multiple exposures in a timely manner and raises the likelihood of the vulnerabilities' being identified and exploited by a criminal.

CONSEQUENCE

The "consequence" is an event's expected effect on an organization A single cybersecurity event can be associated with several consequences, and such a case, the "high-water mark," or most significant consequence, should be used for the event. For example, if a targeted cyberattack is associated with a loss of brand reputation that carries a consequence rated as "critical" as well as a loss of service availability that has a consequence of "high," the threat's consequence should be rated as "critical." Table 7–2 illustrates a sample consequence matrix including qualitative and quantitative measures.

One of the most significant cybersecurity events is a security breach. It is said by many that thanks to the sophistication of threats and the persistence of criminals, it is no longer a question of whether an organization will be breached, but rather when it will detect the next breach. The covert nature and sophistication of threats make them hard to detect, with some breaches taking months or years to detect. Thousands of organizations each year find themselves grappling with a breach.

The average direct and indirect costs associated with a breach are US$3.5 million.[13] This includes the cost to perform the computer forensic investigation, notification of the people affected, post-breach services such as providing credit monitoring to affected victims, and loss of business.

Table 7–2   Example of a Consequence Scale for Cyber Risks

Consequence	Consequence Consideration		
	Reputational Damage	**Financial Loss (USD)**	**Operational Effect**
Incidental	Limited	<$500	<9% degraded service
Minor	Local/regional Short-term negative exposure	$500–$1,000	10–49% degraded service
Moderate	Local/regional Medium-term negative exposure	$1,000–$19,000	>50% degraded service
Major	National negative publicity	$20,000–$40,000	Complete loss of service
Critical	Global negative publicity Long-term negative exposure	>$50,000	Complete loss of service Loss of employee productivity

A security breach can include several consequences spanning tangible properties such as financial loss, operational effect, and employee safety, as well as nontangible properties such as strategic effect and reputational loss. Take the example of an organization examining the consequence associated with a compromised server. The cost to rebuild the compromised server would be a tangible property, but replacing trade secrets disclosed in the cyberattack, the value of loss caused by degraded brand reputation, and loss of shareholder confidence stemming from the attack are intangible properties. Further complicating the scenario, in several past cyberattacks, the share prices of the breached organizations dropped sharply immediately after the breaches and remained degraded for a period of time, eventually recovering to prebreach value. Within the risk analysis process, do you factor in the loss in share price indefinitely, or just until it's expected to recover? Unfortunately there is no simple answer. It is important to define how a consequence will be rated and consistently applied to all risk events. This consequence should include both tangible and intangible properties, and, much as with the value assigned to assets, the asset owners should be involved to help monetize intangible properties. Another good source that can be used when monetizing intangible properties is a business impact assessment (BIA). BIAs predict the consequences of the disruption of business, which can span tangible and intangible properties applicable within cybersecurity events. BIAs are often completed in conjunction with business continuity planning (BCP). BCP resources may thus also help determine the consequences of cybersecurity events.

An understanding of the consequence of cybersecurity events will allow you to effectively prioritize them.

Risk Treatment

Risk treatment is used to minimize or eliminate identified risk. For example, if an organization owns a server containing a technological vulnerability for which there is no associated patch, the organization could implement additional risk controls, such as by implementing an intrusion prevention system to frustrate attempts to exploit the vulnerability. Alternatively, if the server was not needed in production, the organization might measure the cost of removing it to completely eliminate the risk.

In addition to the foundational cybersecurity practices we looked at earlier in this chapter, which make up the broader cyber risk management system, hundreds of potential risk controls can be used to further reduce or eliminate risk. In this chapter, we'll look at some popular risk controls across three domains: business continuity, human elements, and operations and technology.

Business Continuity

A key objective of every organization or business is to ensure the availability of operations. BCP plays an important role in ensuring that operations can be restored efficiently and effectively in the event of an event such as a power outage, flood, or fire.

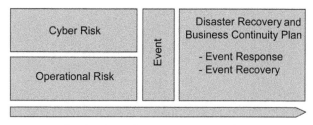

FIGURE 7–4 Linkage between operational and security event response and recovery.

Many security teams are also leveraging effective BCP to prepare, manage, and recover business operations in the event of a cyberattack. The following figure illustrates the linkage between cybersecurity and operational risk, events, and the shared benefit of BCP (Figure 7–4).

When an event is identified, it may involve using additional personnel and transferring operations, partly or fully, to another location or provider to manage. Data from the primary location or from a backup is transferred to ensure that business operations are relocated effectively during the test. The same regulatory and legislative security requirements managed by an organization within their primary location of business apply to temporary data processing facilities. It is also imperative that the effectiveness of cybersecurity in a temporary operating location be the same as in the primary location and that cybersecurity risk continues to be managed at a level approved by the management of the organization.

Most organizations regularly test the response and performance of continuity and recovery plans using tabletop exercises specifically designed to mimic material events likely to be experienced. Organizations using BCP to manage cybersecurity events should also include cybersecurity-related events, such as a targeted cyberattack or a denial-of-service attack, to ensure that cyber events gain the same benefits from testing as other scenarios across the organization.

Securing the Human Element

Successful cyberattacks often include the psychological manipulation of the users of technology so that they perform actions and circumvent processes, knowingly or unknowingly, to aid the criminal. This practice of exploiting people to perform actions desired by a criminal is commonly referred to as social engineering. Cybercriminals often look for the path of least resistance and use social engineering techniques to trick a user into providing physical or logical access to a system or network. For example, a criminal may call up a help desk agent at an organization, pretend to be a member of a project team, and request that the agent verbally provide the password of another team member who is on vacation. To apply pressure, the criminal may add that the agent will get in trouble with his or her manager if he doesn't supply the password and gain access to the files of the other team member to complete a critical project. The organization may have policies that prohibit the help desk agent from providing the

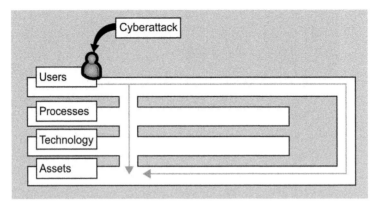

FIGURE 7–5 Human element of security.

password over the phone, but a smooth-talking criminal may be able to persuade the agent to break protocol. Figure 7–5 illustrates how a cyberattack on the human element can circumvent procedural and technological risk controls deployed within an organization.

Social engineering may seem like a trivial or unlikely method of attack, but it remains an effective method used by criminals to gain unauthorized access to systems. Recent breaches, including the breach of a leading retailer in 2013, were believed to be the result of criminals' having used social engineering techniques to entice users at a third party[14] to unknowingly install malware on their computer, granting the criminals remote system access.[15]

Most software and hardware produced today includes a myriad of security features to help protect it from cyberattack. The human element is more problematic and requires users to change deeply rooted behavior. They must be trained to understand the risks they face and how to respond to them.

Security Awareness Training

Security awareness training should include general training on the cyberthreats applicable to all employees and partners as well as targeted sessions for high-risk employee groups, focusing on the specific cyberthreats faced by individuals within key teams.

Security training is an essential component of cybersecurity. It aims to ensure that employees understand the cyber threats that they face, organization security policies and their role in cybersecurity.

Background and Personnel Checks

Employees are an essential line of defense in detecting and preventing cyberattacks. But they also may be the ones conducting the attack, and organizations should ensure that the right employees or subcontractors are hired to interact with systems, data, and other personnel. Background checks are a common method of prescreening to ensure that high-risk individuals are properly evaluated before joining the organization. For additional information on background checks, refer to Chapter 8, on human capital risk.

Operations and Technology

Since the dawn of cybersecurity, technology is the area within most organizations that has received the most attention. But, as we have discussed throughout this chapter, it is just one piece of a balanced and holistic approach to managing cybersecurity.

Technology

When the topic of cybersecurity emerged, there was a belief that the threat could be addressed by means of additional technological risk controls, such as firewalls and antivirus software: The more layers of technology controls, the greater the security. This view has become outdated and is no longer aligned with today's cyberthreats. Previously, IT risk controls were designed solely to detect threats based on signature-based detection strategies. When data was sent to a computer or a file was opened on a computer, the data would be scanned to identify known threats. Now, there are more than 315,000 new threats discovered each day.[16] Product vendors cannot develop signatures fast enough, and system administrators cannot distribute signature files quickly enough to keep up. Some antivirus vendors themselves state that antivirus software alone is not an effective measure against the cyberthreats of today.[17]

Signature-based defense is a necessary form of cybersecurity but is not itself sufficient protection for an organization. Alternative technological risk controls, such as next-generation firewalls and unified threat management devices that combine antivirus, firewall, web content filtering, and data loss prevention provide a reasonable degree of protection. There has also been a surge in the use of anomaly-based detection tools. These tools operate based on behaviors rather than signatures. For example, if a computer is not normally in use between 1 a.m. and 4 a.m., and the software detects an unusually large number of connections with a computer in a foreign country, the software would then highlight the anomaly and alert the user or system administrator. All these controls generate security events that must be acknowledged, analyzed, and acted on. But it remains a challenge to prioritize such anomalies, some of which may be innocuous. Security technology, such as security information event managers, helps organizations analyze large volumes of security data to help ensure that significant threats are focused on.

Operations

Deploying technological risk controls is a start, but effectively configuring controls and actively acting on the events reported by them are equally important steps. In late 2013, a U.S. retailer reported a data security breach and on investigation learned that its risk controls had identified 60,000 events during the attack that were not properly acted on.[18] If they had been acted upon, the retailer may have significantly reduced the scope and effect of the breach it experienced. Organizations looking to assess the effectiveness of their controls should gauge the governance of the control, not just whether the control has been implemented. If there is a control, who is supposed to operate it? Is there a process outlining how events should be qualified and acted on? Do those tasked with following the process have the skills and knowledge to do so? These are just a few examples of questions that should be asked to help ensure that the right people and process accompany a technological risk control.

Transferring Risk

Organizations may choose to transfer cyber risk to a third party, such as an insurer, rather than (or as well as) implementing risk controls on their own. Cyber liability insurance enables organizations to establish coverage to offset the financial cost of a cybersecurity event. In addition to financial support, many cyber liability providers will assist in the actual management of the event for the insured. The goals of cyber liability products are to reduce the effects of a cyber event such as a security breach and minimize the consequences experienced by the insured. Cyber liability insurance can provide support for first-party and third-party costs associated with a cybersecurity event.

First party coverage ensures that financial support is provided for direct costs such as the cost of forensics, notification and recovery of the environment.

Third-party coverage covers lawsuits and other liabilities that the organization may face associated with the event.

A recent example of an organization that used cyber liability insurance to offset breach costs is a leading retailer that received a US$38 million payout from its cyber liability insurer to offset the costs of its 2013 breach.[19]

Risk Monitoring and Review

External Threat Monitoring

Organizations deploy risk controls to reduce risk within an environment. These controls can be administrative, such as a policy or procedures, or technological, such as a firewall or intrusion prevention system. What all these controls have in common is that they are in place to protect against known threats. Known threats are the threats prevalent within the industry that are likely to be experienced by a particular organization. Staying on the forefront of the emerging threats enables an organization to anticipate and protect itself against such threats before they are experienced. This information is known as threat intelligence and requires identifying, extracting, normalizing, and analyzing large volumes of data from the Internet in search of the relevant information.

It is not uncommon for cybercriminals to collaborate and communicate among each other using Internet blogs, chat rooms, and social media sites as they plan attacks against organizations, or to boast about them afterward. Monitoring key Internet locations enables an organization to identify a planned attack scheduled for the future or, in some cases, to identify an attack that, unknown to the organization, occurred but has yet to be detected. This requires the development of robust and sophisticated data analysis systems to store and analyze large and dynamic sets of Internet data. Because the Internet is made up of two segments, the visible and the invisible web, intelligence should be extracted from both segments to ensure that emerging threats are clear.

Visible Web

The visible web is comprised of millions of pages on the Internet. Domains such as .ca, .com, .org, .net, and .biz are merely a few of the popular ones, each containing web pages, social media and chat rooms that may contain data relevant to the organization. The visible web makes up about 4% of networked web pages on the Internet.[20] Access within the visible web is often monitored and mapped back to an IP address of a computer. It is difficult to remain anonymous within the visible web, making it a risky place for cybercriminals to plan or boast about their attacks. The exceptions to this are hacktivists, who seek attention in support of their cause. In addition to keeping track of hacktivists, monitoring the visible web helps identify emerging cybersecurity research and trends that can be used to improve an organization's security program.

Invisible Web

The other 96% of the Internet is made up of several constellations of networks that form the invisible web. The invisible web consists of databases and cannot be enumerated by popular search engines. Many of these database require credentials to access their content. In addition, the invisible web contains several networks of computers specially designed to mask the location and identity of their users and merchants and can only be accessed using specialized software. One popular invisible web network includes sites within the .onion domain. To access this network, users must first download The Onion Router (TOR), software available on the Internet. After installing it, a user can navigate areas such as the invisible wiki and browse the underground market discussed earlier in this chapter. Monitoring the invisible web helps identify past criminal cyberactivity against an organization that may not yet have been discovered. One example of this is associated with a large U.S. bank: One of the bank's fraud analysts was able to monitor underground websites and illegally purchase a collection of compromised credit card numbers that belonging to his institution.[21] Use of the suspect cards was traced back to a retailer and served as an indicator of a breach of which the retailer was unaware. This is a great example of how external threat monitoring can be used to catch exposures missed by a proactive security program.

Whether an organization decides to take on intelligence monitoring itself, or whether it hires a third party, it is important to include data from both the visible and invisible web.

Security Metrics

Security metrics enable an organization to monitor risk controls. The building blocks behind security metrics are good key performance indicators (KPIs) that can be implemented to measure and track the effectiveness and failures of risk controls, as well as positive and negative changes in breaches. An example of a KPI is the number of threats blocked by risk controls within an environment. This can confirm the effectiveness or maturity of a control within that environment. Another example is the tracking of breaches, including the source as well as the amount of elapsed time from cyber event detection to containment and recovery. KPIs allow for the identification of opportunities to learn from past events and manage subsequent events. Security metrics should be reviewed on a recurring basis with managers, who can make changes in response to the metrics and present the information to the company's board of directors so its members understand the state of security within the organization.

Postmortem Cybersecurity Event Reviews

Cybersecurity incidents can harm an organization and can also serve as a way to learn about weaknesses within the security program and gaps in risk controls that require more attention. It is good practice to perform a postmortem review after each material cybersecurity event within an organization. This provides an opportunity to identify a number of things: the risk controls that helped prevent or limit the scope of the event, the response processes that were effective, and the deficiencies of risk controls that, if remedied, could reduce the likelihood of another event in the future. The findings of postmortem cybersecurity event reviews should be formally documented and put through the risk management process to ensure that all cybersecurity risks are assessed and managed accordingly.

Notes

1. http://whatis.techtarget.com/definition/cybersecurity.
2. www.merriam-webster.com/dictionary/cybersecurity.
3. Clare O'Connor, "Target CEO Gregg Steinhafel Resigns in Data Breach Fallout," *Forbes*, May 5.
4. www.huffingtonpost.com/robert-siciliano/data-breaches-may-result-_b_5657961.html.
5. Article: Swati Khandelwal, "BlackPOS Malware used in TARGET Data Breach developed by 17-year old Russian Hacker," *The Hacker News*, January 17, 2014.
6. http://en.wikipedia.org/wiki/SQL_Slammer.
7. http://en.wikipedia.org/wiki/Blaster_(computer_worm).
8. Matthew J. Schwarts, "Operation Payback: Feds Charge 13 on Anonymous Attacks," *Dark Reading*, 10, 4, 2013.
9. http://thenextweb.com/insider/2012/09/07/google-aurora-attackers-still-large-targeting-mainly-us-finance-energy-education-companies/.
10. Kim Zetter, "Retailer Sues Visa over $13 Million 'Fine' for Being Hacked," *Wired*, March 12, 2013.
11. Andrew Ramonas, "Cybersecurity Breach Costs on the Rise, Average $3.5M," *Corporate Counsel*, May 6, 2014.
12. Thor Olavsrud, "Most Data Breaches Caused by Human Error, System Glitches," *CIO*, June 17, 2013.
13. www.ponemon.org/blog/ponemon-institute-releases-2014-cost-of-data-breach-global-analysis.
14. Sabari Selvan, "Target Data Breach Started with a Spear Phishing Attack Targeting HVAC Firm," *eHacking News*, February 13, 2014.
15. Sabari Selvan, "Target Data Breach Started with a Spear Phishing Attack Targeting HVAC Firm," *eHacking News*, February 13, 2014.
16. www.kaspersky.com/about/news/virus/2013/number-of-the-year.
17. Brad Chacos, "Antivirus Is Dead, Says Maker of Norton Antivirus," *PC World*, May 5, 2014.
18. Ben Elgin, Dune Lawrence, and Michael Riley, "Neiman Marcus Hackers Set Off 60,000 Alerts while Bagging Credit Card Data," *Bloomberg Businessweek*, February 21, 2014.
19. Robert Westervelt, "Target Projects Data Breach Costs Total $148 Million," *CRN*, August 2, 2014.
20. Zach Epstein, "How to Find the Invisible Internet," *BGR*, January 20, 2014.
21. http://krebsonsecurity.com/2013/12/cards-stolen-in-target-breach-flood-underground-markets/.

8

Brand Risk

Jonathan Copulsky and Chuck Saia

> *Good name in man and woman, dear my lord,*
> *Is the immediate jewel of their souls.*
> *Who steals my purse steals trash. 'Tis something, nothing:*
> *'Twas mine, 'tis his, and has been slave to thousands.*
> *But he that filches from me my good name*
> *Robs me of that which not enriches him*
> *And makes me poor indeed.*
> **Spoken by Iago in "Othello," Act 3, Scene 3, by William Shakespeare[1]**

Brands matter now more than ever before. It's hard to spend a day without stumbling across endless instances of conventional and digital marketing trumpeting every manner of branded product and service. Brands now adorn a broad range of once unbranded categories—from coffee to chickens to car services. Innovative brands have extended themselves far beyond their tightly focused roots. Just consider how Virgin successfully morphed itself from a recorded music brand to a travel, telecommunications, financial services, and lifestyle brand.[2] Or look at how Amazon has transformed itself from "Earth's largest bookstore" to a purveyor of almost everything under the sun, including business-to-business services, such as cloud computing.[3]

Much like the loss of one's good name, damage to a brand can be devastating. And, unfortunately, not all is safe on the brand front. Risks abound. They range from ill-conceived employee-generated videos that go viral to questionable labor practices of offshore subcontractors to disgruntled customers expressing their frustrations through vituperative reviews on social media sites.

In the past, brand risk management was often synonymous with crisis management—trying to contain the damage from major brand-damaging incidents in an atmosphere of high urgency and a high potential for collateral damage. Leading organizations now recognize that brand risk management is a core component of any robust enterprise risk management program and requires proactive, continuous planning and sensing as well as working closely with key internal and external brand influencers.

The strategies and tactics developed to combat insurgency offer useful lessons for brand stewards. As with counterinsurgency, brand risk management must begin with a compelling narrative. Other steps include training employees, cultivating key influencers, assessing areas of greatest vulnerability, deploying robust sensing capabilities, rehearsing responses to brand-damaging incidents, and executing the actual responses. As with successful counterinsurgency efforts, adopting a "learn and adapt" perspective and measuring results are critical.

Why Brands Matter

The reason for the exponential growth of brands is simple. When done well, branding is an incredibly effective mechanism for taking a rich and complex set of attributes and quickly conveying them through a logo, a tagline, a slogan, a jingle, or an image to inspire passion and loyalty in customers. As brand guru Marty Neumeier writes, "Twenty-first-century companies are learning that, in a marketplace roiled by relentless change and rising clutter, the most effective barrier to competition is not intellectual capital, but branding. A brand—which I define... as a customer's gut feeling about a product, service, or company—is a clever way to keep competitors off your turf... In fact, some of the world's most successful companies have managed their brands so well that their *intangible* assets—i.e., their brands—have achieved a higher market valuation than their *tangible* assets... They would be in serious trouble if they suddenly had to operate without the power boost of their brands."[4]

The Importance of Trust

The nature of the value created by brands, however, is subtly shifting. When British brewer Bass registered its distinctive red triangle as the first ever U.K. trademark in 1876 and emblazoned this mark on the barrels of ales that it shipped all over to the world, a brand signified quality—freedom from defects, deficiencies and significant variations.[5] Today, a brand often stands for much more than product or service quality. We now choose brands because we trust them. We trust that they deliver quality, but we also trust everything that they represent. We trust that they use first-rate ingredients, procured from ethical suppliers and produced by humanely treated workers laboring in a safe environment. We believe that they are based on sustainable and socially responsible practices. When we select a brand, this selection reflects our values and our willingness to associate our values with a brand. We have migrated from mere transactions and consumption to relationships. Because of our willingness to build trusting relationships with brands, brands have become more valuable than ever before.

The byproduct of trust is our willingness to serve as self-designated brand ambassadors by recommending our favorite brands to friends and strangers alike. In a world where the first step in a purchase decision means going to an online recommendation site,[6] this willingness to recommend brands is critical to brands' vitality and success. Pulitzer Prize–winning *New York Times* columnist Thomas L. Friedman attributes the rapid growth of Airbnb, which allows people to rent spare rooms to strangers, to its ability to create "a platform of 'trust'—where everyone could not only see everyone else's identity but also rate them as good, bad or indifferent hosts or guests. This meant everyone using the system would pretty quickly develop a relevant 'reputation' visible to everyone else in the system."[7]

The other consequence of brands' surrogacy for trust means that any breach of trust in our relationship with a brand can be fatal to the relationship. If a brand behaves in what we perceive as an untrustworthy manner, we may terminate our relationship quickly and decisively, unless the brand rapidly takes steps that demonstrate its willingness and ability to restore our trust. For an example, look no further than recent breaches of confidential consumer credit card information.

Who Owns Brand Risk Management?

Brand risk management is the coordinated set of principles, processes, activities, roles and responsibilities, and infrastructure that control the actions of an organization. These are engaged when events threaten customers' trust in a brand.[8] But who owns brand risk management?

Most commercial organizations have an individual and function charged with developing and promoting the organization's brand. This is increasingly true in nonprofit and governmental organizations as well. Typically, these functions are led by a chief marketing officer (CMO) or an equivalently titled senior executive (e.g., chief customer officer), whose duties include understanding the needs of the market, positioning the brand based on market needs, creating the target customer experience, developing platforms for reaching customers, designing offers, and messaging to customers with the goal of driving awareness, consideration, selection, preference, and advocacy. When done well, brand-building activities drive greater loyalty, greater buzz, greater price premiums, and greater growth than those enjoyed by competitors.

CMOs may make decisions that cause customers to lose trust in a brand—a change in product packaging, a revised pricing strategy, the elimination of certain product features, a cheeky advertising campaign, an ill-timed promotion, and so on ad infinitum. It's the job of a CMO to make these decisions and live with their consequences, good and bad. It's a tough job and, not surprisingly, average CMO tenure trails that of other C-suite executives.[9]

Many of the sources of brand risk extend well beyond the direct control, and even the influence, of the typical CMO. Often, brand-damaging events are the consequences of decisions and actions taken by a variety of internal and external players. As our editor notes in Chapter 1, a pipeline spill may create brand risk in addition to health and safety risk, environmental and sustainability risk, supply chain risk, financial risk, political risk, and strategic risk.

Examples of players internal to or closely linked to an organization's ecosystem whose intentional and unintentional decisions and actions are sources of brand risk include:

- Customer service
- Finance
- Front-line employees
- Human resources
- Information technology
- Manufacturing

- Sales
- Spokespeople and brand ambassadors
- Sponsored athletes and celebrities
- Senior executives
- Suppliers and distribution partners
- Supply chain

In fact, it's difficult to identify a single area of an organization that doesn't potentially affect a brand's trustworthiness and, consequently, create brand risk.

The decisions and actions of <u>external</u> players also create significant opportunities—and threats—for brand risk. Although these could be triggered by or a response to specific management reactions (e.g., the decision to use suppliers whose questionable labor practices cause human rights bloggers to spring into action), sometimes these seem to happen without any specific internally generated prompts. Protests by social activists, actions by regulators, and outcries from loyal customers offended by product and policy changes fall into the former category, whereas scathing social media postings from a widely followed celebrity who happens to experience mediocre service during a visit to a restaurant on a particularly busy evening may fall into the latter.

So when it comes to assigning responsibility for brand risk management, one of the key decisions that every organization faces is how to embed a brand risk intelligence mindset across the entire organization. It is unwise to assume that this can be handled solely by the executive who bears primary responsibility for branding and marketing). A brand risk intelligence mindset needs to be supported by principles, processes, activities, roles and responsibilities, and infrastructure that foster alignment and integrated action across the organization.

The High-Speed Landscape of Brand Risk

News of brand-damaging events now travels at dizzying speeds. Today's reality requires compressed timeframes for making critical decisions about how to respond to major reputational challenges. We live in a world in which every individual has a voice and can use social media and the Internet to amplify that voice. Bad news travels quickly and widely.

A movie director who has been kicked off an airplane thanks to overcrowding or a mom who is convinced that a reformulated baby diaper caused her child to develop a rash can quickly garner thousands, if not millions, of supportive fans in a world in which leading social media sites have more than 1 billion users and individual bloggers have millions of followers. Consequently, a strategy based on "wait and see" is rarely viable; organizations need to assume a "zero-latency" world in which there is infinitesimal lag time between when a brand-damaging action occurs and broad public awareness develops.

In the past, managing brand risk was often synonymous with crisis management—responding to (and trying to contain the damage from) major brand-damaging incidents in an atmosphere of high urgency and a high potential for collateral damage. Leading organizations now recognize that managing brand risk is a core component of any robust enterprise risk management program and requires proactive and continuous planning and sensing, in addition to equipping key brand influencers with the information to defuse the damage.

How Counterinsurgency Theory May Help Us Manage Brand Risk

In today's world, there is no single point of accountability for brand risk, and breaches happen with increasing speed. Thus organizations require rapid response capabilities to wildly unpredictable brand-damaging events, which prompted us to search for a model that would help organizations understand how to minimize brand risk by doing the following:

- Assessing brand risk (i.e., the process of risk identification, risk analysis, and risk prioritization)
- Treating brand risk (i.e., selecting options for modifying risks, implementing the options, and improving or modifying risk controls for each risk)
- Monitoring and reviewing brand risk

This search for a model led us to an unusual destination—the world of counterinsurgency. After extensively studying counterinsurgency theory and practice, we have come to believe that the tools and approaches that military and civilian organizations have developed to respond to insurgencies apply to many of the challenges of brand risk management.

An insurgency is an armed rebellion against a constituted authority in which participants in the rebellion are not formally recognized as belligerents. The use of the term is neutral: "When it is used by a state or another authority under threat, 'insurgency' often also carries an implication that the rebels' cause is illegitimate, whereas those rising up will see the authority itself as being illegitimate."[10]

Insurgency is a term frequently associated with the recent conflicts in Iraq and Afghanistan. As U.S. forces struggled with both of these conflicts, military leaders recognized the need to provide their forces with a new playbook, for many "Army officers knew more about the U.S. Civil War than they did about counterinsurgency."[11] Hence the development and publication of the *Counterinsurgency Field Manual* by the Army and Marine Corps in 2006.[12]

The *Counterinsurgency Field Manual* makes it clear that insurgencies are dramatically different than conventional wars. First, in a war of insurgency, it's not always clear whom you're supposed to be fighting, much less why. Attacks come from unexpected sources, at unexpected times, and in unexpected locations, often for hard-to-understand reasons. Second, speed often trumps scale. A nimble organization can often outperform a larger organization, much like the biblical tale of David's felling Goliath. Third, new technologies create new threats (e.g., improvised explosive devices triggered by mobile phones).

Anonymous or unexpected enemies who have hard-to-discern motives, who are operating in a high-speed world, who are using new technologies in unexpected ways—all three are characteristics that seem to apply to brand risks as much as they do to insurgencies. In fact, the more we studied the *Counterinsurgency Field Manual*, the more we came to believe that the approaches developed for combating insurgencies translate directly to brand risk management (Table 8-1).

Table 8–1   Similarities between Counterinsurgency and Brand Risk Management

Counterinsurgency Principles	Similarities with Brand Risk Management
The most effective responses to insurgencies are often not aimed directly at insurgents. "Counterinsurgents often achieve the most meaningful success in garnering public support and legitimacy… with activities that do not involve killing insurgents…"[a]	Appropriately arming employees and other stakeholders with a crisp and compelling brand narrative reduces brand risks and mitigates their effect.
At first you may not recognize that you're under attack. "[T]he government that is being targeted generally takes a while to recognize that an insurgency is occurring. Insurgents take advantage of that time to build strength and gather support. Thus, counterinsurgents often have to 'come from behind' when fighting an insurgency."[b]	Brand risks come from unexpected sources, often without announcement. Understanding potential sources of brand risk, assessing an organization's vulnerabilities, and developing early warning systems or sensing capabilities are critical to effective brand risk management.
The natural tendency to respond to attacks with massive force may be misguided; sometimes the more force you use, the less effective it is. "Another common feature is that forces conducting COIN [counterinsurgency] operations usually begin poorly… They falsely believe that armies trained to win large conventional wars are automatically prepared to win small, unconventional ones. In fact, some capabilities required for conventional success… may be of limited utility… in COIN operations."[c]	Responding to brand risks requires the ability to act quickly. This means careful preparation and frequent rehearsals. A brand risk playbook that spells out roles, responsibilities, types of responses, governance processes, and messaging strategies (informed by the brand narrative) is essential. Response elements include a balance among asking for forgiveness, offering compensation to injured parties, and demonstrating a willingness to take actions to prevent future occurrences.
In wars of insurgency, the winner is the one who learns more quickly. "In COIN, the side that learns faster and adapts more rapidly—the better learning organization—usually wins. Counterinsurgencies have been called learning competitions."[d]	Effective brand risk management must include a significant learning and adaptation component. This is equivalent to military "after action reports" in which an organization focuses on what to do differently as a result of each and every brand risk, with the goal of preventing the event from happening in the future.
If a response works today, it might not work next week. "Competent insurgents are adaptive… Insurgents quickly adjust to effective COIN practices and rapidly disseminate information throughout the insurgency. Indeed, the more effective a COIN tactic is, the faster it may become out of date[,] because insurgents have a greater need to counter it. Effective leaders at all levels avoid complacency and are at least as adaptive as their enemies."[e]	Brand risk management needs to constantly reinvent itself, recognizing that many events that create brand risks today (e.g., cybersecurity, social media) were not threats in the past, and many events that will create brand risks in the future have yet to appear on the horizon.

[a]FM 3-24, 7-2, May 13, 2014, http://fas.org/irp/doddir/army/fm3-24.pdf.
[b]The U.S. Army and Marine Corps, *Counterinsurgency Field Manual* (Chicago, IL: University of Chicago Press, 2007), Introduction, lii.
[c]*Ibid.*
[d]*Ibid.*
[e]*Ibid.*

The remainder of this chapter, consequently, lays out a programmatic approach for brand risk management, consisting of eight steps that brand stewards can take to root out and overcome the myriad brand risks they face daily.

Step 1: Every Effective Brand Risk Management Program Begins with a Clear and Compelling Brand Narrative

According to the *Counterinsurgency Field Manual*, "[t]he most important cultural form for counterinsurgents to understand is the narrative. A cultural narrative is a story recounted in the form of a causally linked set of events that explains an event in a group's history and expresses the values, character, or self-identity of the group. Narratives are the means through which ideologies are expressed and absorbed by members of a society."[13] The manual explains how Americans use the Boston Tea Party to explain why the Revolutionary War began, as well as to remind themselves of why they fought. It also notes that "narratives may not conform to historical facts or they may drastically simplify facts to more clearly express basic cultural values."[14]

In a business context, the narrative is the story around which employees and other stakeholders rally and from which they find inspiration, particularly after a brand attack. A narrative is the ammunition required to restore the trust that previously existed in the brand—without a narrative, it's difficult, if not impossible, to respond to brand risks. The narrative reminds employees, customers, and others of the values, the purpose, and the core identity of the brand. The brand narrative, once deployed, is a type of fail-safe mechanism, implemented by an organization to modify risk.

The most effective brand narratives are developed and socialized with great care and provide a continuous touchstone when events challenge trust in the brand. One of the best known examples of a clear and compelling brand narrative is "Our Credo," authored in 1943 by Robert Wood Johnson, one-time chairman of the health care giant Johnson & Johnson. As the Johnson & Johnson website states, "[t]he values that guide our decision making are spelled out in Our Credo. Put simply, Our Credo challenges us to put the needs and well-being of the people we serve first."[15]

As important as it is to have a brand narrative, it's equally important to embed this narrative in the activities of an organization, including its responses to specific brand risks. The narrative provides the platform for contextualizing a response and allows an organization to go beyond the recitation of facts to remind stakeholders of the purpose and values of the brand that caused them to place their trust in it in the first place.

So, think of the first step within the eight steps of brand management as encompassing six substeps related to brand narrative:

- Developing the brand narrative
- Creating (and regularly updating) the set of proof points and stories that bring the narrative to life
- Deploying the narrative internally
- Deploying the narrative externally
- Training brand stewards in how to incorporate the brand narrative in their responses to specific brand risks
- Updating and adapting the narrative over time

Step 2: When it Comes to Brand Risk Management, Your People Need to be Appropriately Armed

In the brand risk management battle, your people, both employees and senior executives, are your first line of defense. They deliver your brand and are instrumental to creating and maintaining the trust that drives the success of your brand. As public relations firm Edelman reports in its 2014 "Trust Barometer," employees are considered the most trusted source across most clusters of trust attributes outscoring company CEOs, activist consumers, academics, or the media.[16]

When it comes to brand risk management, your people play two roles, both of which represent potential opportunities for controlling risk. The first is to behave in a way consistent with the values and purpose of your brand. Brand-inconsistent behavior can originate from ostensibly innocent activities—more than one fast food chain has been the victim of inappropriate videos created by bored restaurant employees and posted to social media websites. Indiscreet social media postings can also create brand risks by inadvertently disclosing confidential or embarrassing information. But brand-inconsistent behavior can also result from frustrated employees who decide to lash out at employers, including wholesale revelations of proprietary information that could be highly damaging. As an example, think of Edward Snowden, who leaked thousands of classified documents that he acquired while working as a government contractor.

We often assume that if we hire smart people, they will understand exactly what it means to behave in a manner consistent with our brand. Recent episodes suggest that that assumption is unrealistic—not only for rank-and-file employees, but even for senior executives, many of whom have been discovered making statements and behaving in ways creating tremendous brand risk. This expectation seems particularly questionable when it comes to Millennials, many of whom have come of age in the era of social media and oversharing.

This is where codes of conduct and training become critical. Helping your people clearly understand behavioral expectations and training them to behave in a manner consistent with the brand is no longer optional. This is a critical element of the talent management process and needs to be embedded into all aspects of talent management, ranging from selection to evaluation to promotion.

If the first role your people play in managing brand risk is "do no harm," the second role is to play an active role in propagating the brand narrative, responding to events that create brand risk and gathering intelligence about current and emerging brand risks.

In my organization, for example, we have encouraged employees to volunteer to serve as brand ambassadors. In this capacity, they receive social media training and are then provided with a regular stream of messages (customized based on their areas of interest and expertise) they can disseminate on our behalf through social media outlets. No employee is required to participate in the program, and no participant is required to post any particular message. The 1,000+ participants can build their own social media presence (an increasingly valuable asset for almost any employee today) while simultaneously amplifying "trusted" messages created by their organization. We have found that employees who participate in the program have higher employee engagement scores than our employee population as a whole and that the program puts more of a human face on our brand-building activities.

This program also allows employees to assist us with responding to brand-damaging events. We know that employees are invaluable when it comes to creating trust with our clients and the general public. The size of our employee population (more than 60,000 individuals) makes this a particularly potent force. By equipping our brand ambassadors with accurate information year-round, and particularly when we have a brand crisis, we are able to counter some of the external attacks against our brand.

Your people also represent an opportunity to gather intelligence about potential and emerging threats to your brand. Employees encounter conversations about your brand every day in real and virtual spaces. One major consumer packaged goods company tells its employees that they are one of its most vital assets for monitoring the social media landscape and asks that they share positive or negative remarks about the company and its brands online if they believe the remarks to be important.

Organizations that are committed to building and maintaining great brands explicitly invite employees to identify ways that internal and external actions violate the spirit of the brand. We know of one organization in which every employee report of brand-damaging events is posted to an internal social media site, and other employees can comment on these postings, including suggestions of how to change or avoid them, in a 21st-century version of the suggestion box.

Publicly thanking and recognizing contributors is important to their continued engagement—and the success of brand management programs. Experiences with social media have taught us that contributors immensely value recognition, and the opportunity to build their own personal reputations is often more appreciated than any other form of employee recognition.[17]

Step 3: Brand Risk Management Requires Cultivating External Stakeholders before Brand Risks Emerge

When it comes to brand risk management, the cultivation of external stakeholders must closely follow equipping your people.

Every organization has a broad range of stakeholders that influence its success. These stakeholders vary by type of business, but often include the media, legislators, regulators, academics, analysts, think tanks, purchase influencers, alumni, alliance partners, suppliers, and evaluators. In many cases, relationships are handled as a set of discrete activities, where separate parts of the organization own individual relationships and try to influence the stakeholders.

These stakeholders can play many of the same roles your employees can, serving as advocates for your brand, helping you recognize threats to your brand, and helping you tell your story when your brand is under attack. The time to cultivate these stakeholders is before, not after, brand risks develop.

In my organization, we have gone through a detailed process of identifying stakeholders and influencers. For each stakeholder and influencer group, we assessed our current standing with the group, in terms of attitudes and behaviors, as well as the gap between our current standing and our desired standing. We then determined what messaging and interactions would be appropriate to close the gap and developed campaigns to deliver these. As with our people, one of our goals is to cultivate a set of brand ambassadors within these stakeholder groups.

In this process, we have learned that cultivating stakeholders does not happen overnight. Having clear owners for each stakeholder group and key members of each group is important, but it's also important that each owner understand the actions and activities of other stakeholder owners so that our messaging is coordinated.

We have also learned the importance of the brand narrative as the foundation for all of our messaging. Our brand narrative has become the touchstone to which we repeatedly return, and we've started to measure the extent to which we have explicitly incorporated the brand narrative into our stakeholder communications.

The third lesson we have learned is the importance of measuring stakeholder attitudes. Just as we measure client advocacy and employee engagement, we've started to measure stakeholder support, using an influencer perception map that mirrors our customer brand pyramid (awareness, consideration, selection, preference, and advocacy). Over time, we will track our success in moving each stakeholder group up the ladder. As with our people, our goal is to make them our allies in detecting and responding to brand damaging events. Once again, this is a form of risk control.

Step 4: Risk Assessment Begins at Home

The brand risk management program that we have described so far focuses on putting a platform in place to control brand risk. This brand risk platform is anchored in a brand narrative and activated through employees, stakeholders, and influencers. This platform will serve you in good stead as brand-damaging events arise.

But this platform alone is not enough. Brand risk management also needs to include a thorough risk assessment process that parallels the assessment process used for other risks—risk identification, risk analysis, and risk prioritization.

As we discussed previously, brand risks can be the consequences of internal and external events. Often, brand risks fall into the category of "collateral damage," tied to other risks, ranging from financial risks to supply chain risks.

The risk identification process starts with a comprehensive review of what former Defense Secretary Donald Rumsfeld characterized as the "known knowns."[18] We now know, for example, that employees can make brand-damaging videos—even if we have not directly experienced them. We now know, as well, that failing to scrutinize suppliers' labor practices can be brand-damaging. A thorough examination of all internal and external players involved with your brand is a good way to jump-start the risk identification process, coupled with periodic reviews of recent crisis management "fire drills" and scans of the news to discover the brand risk challenges that have confronted other organizations.

After these risks are identified, we can then analyze them to understand effectiveness of existing risk controls, the likelihood of a catastrophic event, and the potential consequences. Because many brand risks are consequences of other risks, it's important to do this as part of an overall enterprise risk management assessment program.

In our work with clients, we recommend the following process:

- Risk identification:
  - Identify and track top brand risks
  - Develop "what if" scenarios
- Risk analysis: Assess overall preparedness and vulnerabilities
- Risk prioritization: Conduct scenario planning as part of brand risk assessment, embedding continuous improvement
- Risk treatment: Adjust mitigation strategies/actions based on outcome of brand risk assessment and scenario planning

We find that scenario planning helps address Rumsfeld's "known unknowns"—the dangers we believe are out there but that may not have yet occurred.

The third part of Rumsfeld's formulation is the "unknown unknowns," or "things that we do not know that we don't know." These words were the source of the ridicule that resulted after a 2002 Defense Department briefing in which he first used this expression. The risk assessment process is unlikely to uncover the "unknown unknowns," so subsequent steps become important to managing brand risk successfully.

Step 5: Risk Sensing Complements Risk Assessment

We often tell clients and colleagues that no organization can effectively escape the possibility of a threat to their brand. It's a question of "when," not "if."

Brand risk sensing allows organizations to track potential risks early in the cycle and detect emerging patterns. Increasingly, there are technology-enabled tools and platforms to facilitate risk sensing.

The key to the successful use of these technology-enabled tools and platforms is identifying the right content sources to monitor, filtering out relevant soundings from the noise, determining trigger points to prompt action, and creating processes that assign responsibility for taking appropriate action.

Evaluating the diverse technologies available for risk sensing is beyond the scope of this chapter. Dell and Gatorade provide examples of how organizations can develop sensing or listening capabilities, specifically tied to social media.[19]

Step 6: Be Prepared to Respond (Quickly)

In the event of a brand threat, all organizations should have a brand risk treatment plan, not unlike an evacuation drill, to ensure order and effectiveness in responding to it.

We can try to prevent brand threats through employee and ecosystem policies and training. We can try to detect them through brand risk sensing. But despite our best efforts, not every brand risk can be successfully prevented or stymied through early detection.

In today's zero-latency world, we find that a brand risk playbook that spells out roles, responsibilities, types of responses, governance processes, and messaging strategies (informed by the brand narrative) is essential.

Although it is extremely difficult to specify responses in advance of specific situations, we find that most responses rely on some combination of the strategies employed by McNeil Consumer Products Company (a Johnson & Johnson subsidiary) in 1982 when the deaths of seven people on the west side of Chicago were linked to Tylenol. As many observers note, the company's response to the ensuing crisis has become the gold standard by which organizations are often judged.

The three major components of the response included asking for forgiveness, offering compensation to injured parties, and, perhaps most important, demonstrating a willingness to take actions to prevent future occurrences.[20]

Just including these three components is not enough, however; every brand risk response strategy needs to be supported by a well-understood execution capability. This means clearly defined processes, roles, and responsibilities and comprehensive employee training. Just as the military uses drills or rehearsals that allow participants to get a sense of executional complexity, timing, and the need for close synchronization of activities, organizations can set up risk response teams that do the same. An untested plan for responding to brand risks is unlikely to generate the success that the planners anticipated.

Step 7: Never Let a Good Crisis Go to Waste

Perhaps in a nod to Rumsfeld's "unknown unknowns," the *Counterinsurgency Field Manual* stresses the importance of learning and adaptation.

Easier said than done. Often, when we're done with responding to a risk, our natural tendency is to move on and not to systematically harvest and insights the hard-fought lessons learned.

A commitment to "learn and adapt" requires organizations to focus on what to do differently as a result of each and every experience, with the goal of preventing the event from happening in the future. As Rahm Emanuel said in November 2008 while serving as chief of staff to president-elect Barack Obama, "You never want a serious crisis to go to waste."[21]

In the military, this process is exemplified by "after-action" reports. The equivalent of after-action reports are also used by the National Transportation Safety Board (NTSB) in investigating every civil aviation, railroad, highway, marine, and pipeline accident and issuing safety recommendations aimed at preventing future accidents.[22]

Whenever an accident occurs, the NTSB deploys a "Go Team" to the accident site. A Go Team is a multidisciplinary group of investigators whose job is to systematically unearth facts related to the accident under investigation. The onsite investigation kicks off the first of a four-step process (investigation, analysis, report, recommendations) allowing the NTSB to determine the cause of the accident and to improve transportation safety for the future.

While the NTSB process is relatively straightforward, several elements stand out and are relevant to brand risk management reviews:[23]

- The investigation is led by individuals who have no direct responsibility for the affected area.
- The investigation focuses on cause and prevention rather than on assigning blame.

- The recommendations include specifics on implementation responsibilities, timeframe, and expected outcomes.
- Results are tracked and reported publicly.

This process can be adopted directly by brand risk management teams.

Step 8: Measure What Matters

W. Edwards Deming, the father of total quality management, was known for his aphorism: "You can expect what you inspect."[24] In another context, Louis Brandeis, who later became a U.S. Supreme Court justice, wrote about the value of disclosure and transparency, "Sunlight is said to be the best of disinfectants."[25] This advice would seem to apply to all types of risks, including brand risks.

In the case of brand risk, the seemingly obvious solution would be to measure brand value and the changes in brand value over time as an organization encounters and deals with various types of risk. The challenge with this solution is that brand valuation approaches vary widely, with no common methodology/framework in place to use as a baseline, much less to assess movement based on specific brand risks.[26]

The alternative (and one that our organization has adopted) is to measure stakeholder perceptions (both internal and external) along a spectrum of awareness to advocacy, recognizing that the metrics represent a point in time to understand how an organization is doing in the eyes of the various stakeholders that matter. Though these measures are far from perfect—they come from surveys and reflected perceptions (versus behavior), they can help illuminate directional trends over a multiyear period. As with brand valuation models, market researchers would argue vehemently about how to approach brand perceptions, and there is no singly right way to evaluate them.

A complementary approach to this type of stakeholder perception capturing is to track specific events tied to brand risks and use media and social monitoring tools to assess sentiments. Sentiment analysis uses natural language processing to determine underlying attitudes, helping organizations understand the extent to which the conversation is favorable or unfavorable. As with sensing, there is no shortage of tools and platforms for analyzing and assessing sentiments that take advantage of the latest developments in technology. Though users of these tools and platforms often discover them to be imperfect (e.g., content sources used, handling of non–English-language sources, analysis of nontextual sources, weighting of different sources), they are a necessary component of any brand risk assessment strategy.

Though the tools used are important, it is equally important that the information gathered from them be shared with important internal parties who can then ensure that solutions are in place to further combat the issues that gave rise to the risk in the first place. We increasingly find that board risk committees are interested in understanding how brand risks are covered in conventional and social media, both in terms of frequency and sentiment.

From a best practice standpoint, we also increasingly find organizations with well-developed enterprise risk management programs use dashboards that include sections focused on key brand-related metrics, ranging from brand valuation to brand perceptions to event tracking and sentiment analysis.

Key Takeaways

In today's high-speed world, brands can be an incredible source of value yet seem to be more vulnerable than ever. With the continued ascent of social media and mobile technologies, brand sabotage incidents seem poised to increase.

Leading organizations now recognize that managing brand risk is a core component of any robust enterprise risk management program and requires proactive, continuous planning and sensing. This is in addition to close alignment with key internal and external brand influencers. The goal is to develop resilient organizations capable of continuously improving their capabilities to manage a constantly evolving set of brand risks.

Building a great and resilient brand now requires playing aggressive defense as well as offense. The strategies and tactics developed to combat insurgency offer a useful model for brand stewards. We have used counterinsurgency theory to suggest eight steps that brand stewards can take to root out and overcome the diverse brand risks they face daily:

1. Develop and deploy a clear and compelling brand narrative.
2. Enlist your employees in the brand risk management efforts.
3. Cultivate external stakeholders before brand risks emerge.
4. Assess brand risks internally and externally.
5. Complement risk assessment efforts with continuous risk-sensing activities.
6. Learn to respond (quickly) to brand risks through the use of playbooks and practice drills.
7. Harvest lessons learned from each brand risk event.
8. Measure what matters.

Notes

1. www.shakespeare-navigators.com/othello/T33.html.
2. www.virgin.com.
3. Brad Stone, "Amazon, the Company That Ate the World," *Bloomberg Businessweek*, September 28, 2011, www.businessweek.com/magazine/the-omnivore-09282011.html.
4. Marty Neumeier, "Foreword," in Jonathan Copulsky, *Brand Resilience: Managing Risk and Recovery in a High-Speed World* (New York: Palgrave Macmillan, 2011), x.
5. www.logoworks.com/blog/bass-pale-ale-brand-and-logo/.
6. Digital interactions influence 36 cents of every dollar spent in the retail store, or approximately $1.1 trillion, according to "The New Digital Divide," Deloitte Digital, www.deloitte.com/view/en_US/us/Industries/Retail-Distribution/5e8b875282d15410VgnVCM3000003456f70aRCRD.htm.
7. Thomas L. Friedman, "And Now for a Bit of Good News," *The New York Times*, July 20, 2014, 11, www.nytimes.com/2014/07/20/opinion/sunday/thomas-l-friedman-and-now-for-a-bit-of-good-news.html?_r=0.
8. A number of organizations rank enterprises based on "trust." See, for example, the Edelman Trust Barometer at www.edelman.com/insights/intellectual-property/2014-edelman-trust-barometer/.
9. Suzanne Vranica, "Average CMO Tenure: 45 Months (but That's an Improvement)," *The Wall Street Journal*, March 23, 2014, http://blogs.wsj.com/cmo/2014/03/23/cmos-work-lifespan-improves-still-half-that-of-ceos-study/?cb=logged0.6447219777919214.
10. "Insurgency," *Wikipedia*, http://en.wikipedia.org/wiki/Insurgency.
11. http://press.uchicago.edu/ucp/books/book/chicago/U/bo5748917.html.
12. "The U.S. Army/Marine Corps Counterinsurgency Field Manual," also known as FM 3-24 and MCWP 3-33.5, was released by the Department of the Army in December 2006. The 2006 version of the manual was previously

available at www.fas.org/irp/doddir/army/fm3-24/pdf. An updated version was released in May 2014 under the title *Insurgencies and Countering Insurgencies* and is available at http://fas.org/irp/doddir/army/fm3-24.pdf. The University of Chicago Press published a version of the manual that includes a foreword by John Nagl and an introduction by Sarah Sewall, director of the Carr Center for Human Rights Policy at Harvard's Kennedy School of Government, in August 2007 (http://press.uchicago.edu/ucp/books/book/chicago/U/bo5748917.html).

13. *Ibid.*, 3–50, p. 93.

14. *Ibid.*

15. www.jnj.com/about-jnj/jnj-credo.

16. 2014 Edelman Trust Barometer Executive Summary, www.scribd.com/fullscreen/200429962?access_key=key-25qv8l25jezgs6th4bfc&allow_share=true&escape=false&show_recommendations=false&view_mode=scroll.

17. Cathy Benko and Molly Anderson, *The Corporate Lattice* (Boston, MA: Harvard Business School Press, 2010), https://latticemcc.com/Site/index.aspx.

18. "In February 2002, Donald Rumsfeld… stated at a… briefing: 'There are known knowns. There are things we know that we know. There are known unknowns. That is to say, there are things that we now know we don't know. But there are also unknown unknowns. There are things we do not know we don't know.' As a result, he was almost universally lampooned since many people initially thought the statement was nonsense. However, careful examination of the statement reveals that it does make sense, indeed the concept of the unknown unknown existed long before Donald Rumsfeld gave it a new audience." Rumsfeld's comments have been cited frequently; this citation is from David C. Logan, "Known Knowns, Known Unknowns, Unknown Unknowns and the Propagation of Scientific Enquiry," *Journal of Experimental Biology* 60, iss. 3: 712, http://jxb.oxfordjournals.org/content/60/3/712.full.

19. Information on Dell's Social Media Command Center can be found at www.dell.com/learn/us/en/uscorp1/videos~en/documents~dell-social-media-command-center.aspx. Information on Gatorade Mission Control can be found at www.youtube.com/watch?v=Y-M2uoNA6Vs.

20. An excellent analysis of the Tylenol case study can be found at www.ou.edu/deptcomm/dodjcc/groups/02C2/Johnson%20&%20Johnson.htm.

21. www.youtube.com/watch?v=1yeA_kHHLow.

22. The NTSB's investigation process is described in Jonathan Copulsky, Alicechandra Fritz, and Mark White, "Brand Resilience: Protecting Your Brand from Saboteurs in a High-Speed World," *Deloitte University Press*, July 1, 2011, http://dupress.com/articles/brand-resilience/.

23. Brand Resilience, *op. cit.*, p. 154.

24. "The Big Apple." www.barrypopik.com/index.php/new_york_city/entry/you_can_expect_what_you_inspect_management_adage.

25. University of Louisville, "Chapter V: What Publicity Can Do." www.law.louisville.edu/library/collections/brandeis/node/196. A perspective on Brandeis and the history of transparency came be found at Sunlight Foundation, "Brandeis and the History of Transparency," May 26, 2009, http://sunlightfoundation.com/blog/2009/05/26/brandeis-and-the-history-of-transparency/.

26. Our colleague Gabriela Salinas evaluates different brand valuation approaches in her comprehensive book, *The International Brand Valuation Manual* (West Sussex, UK: John Wiley & Sons, 2009), www.amazon.com/International-Brand-Valuation-Manual-methodologies/dp/0470740310/ref=sr_1_1?ie=UTF8&qid=1407874588&sr=8-1&keywords=Salinas+brands.

Human Capital Risk: The Threat from Inside

Mitch Albinski

Human capital risk is a broad term covering all aspects of employee and contractor tenure within a corporation. Among direct employees and contracted resources,[1] some "trusted" insiders may be responsible for malicious incidents such as fraud, asset loss, physical harm, and reputational damage.

This chapter will focus on those risks having the potential for malevolent outcomes rather than with the entire spectrum of human capital, such as employee turnover, productivity, or talent management gaps:

- Fraud
- Infiltration
  - Espionage
  - Sabotage
  - Criminal mischief
  - Contracted workforce
- Potentially violent behaviors
  - Harassment
  - Terminations

We will explore these unplanned events and their motivations in the following discussions. It is important to understand that management of these aspects of human capital requires careful assessment, well-defined hiring practices and policies, physical security controls, and corporate awareness programs, thereby forming a holistic approach to the insider threat. These insider threats should also be included in a company's crisis management plan.

The malicious events associated with the insider threat are prevalent throughout the life cycle of the employed or contracted resource and must be managed through **prevention**, **detection**, and **reaction**. The consequences of the absence of appropriate **risk controls** may include incidents of harassment, intimidation, violence, fraud, infiltration, sabotage, injury, intellectual property loss, cyber incidents, higher turnover rates, environmental incidents, and damage to the company's brand or reputation. All these have possible financial loss. There may be indirect costs: lost productivity, vacancy (and the added burden of additional work for existing employees), lag time for the replacement employee, reduced morale, and lost institutional or technical knowledge, for example.[2]

The motivation of an employee or contracted resource to engage in aberrant behavior may be the result of personal conflict, either within or outside the organization, gaps in the perception of the value a resource believes he or she brings to the company, the company's beliefs, philosophical and or ethical differences in how the company is run, the company's products, the company's performance management and personnel advancement systems, and personal financial or family difficulties. It may even stem from allegiance to an outside organization, another competing company, or another country.

Nasty Events Can Happen: Source of Human Capital Risk

Fraud: Deliberate Misuse or Misappropriation of a Company's Resources, Often for Personal Gain

Human capital risks in this area occur across a wide sector of companies as well as at all levels in the organization but usually involve employees, possibly contractors, in a position of trust. These individuals may have access to internal corporate financial resources or have the ability to divert them. The assets may not only be financial but may be physical, with financial returns earned through a third party. It is not uncommon for fraud incidents to occur among individuals who have long service histories and who have thus built a trusting relationship with the company. As a result, evidence of the crime may not be exposed immediately. Under these circumstances, companies may be subject to **overconfidence** in their approach to incidents of fraud and become complacent in their **prevention** and **detection** methods. In such an environment, the classical "motive-means-opportunity" elements are present, but there is also the element of self-justification.

Famed criminologist Donald R. Cressey combined these elements into a hypothesis known as the Fraud Triangle.[3] Cressey's work defines a model that contains three elements, all of which must be present and that together lead to fraudulent behavior:

- **Pressure**: The motivation behind the crime: for example, "I have overwhelming debt and can't see my way clear."
- **Opportunity**: The ability to use a position of trust with little perceived risk of being caught: "I'm a long-term employee"; "My performance is above reproach."
- **Rationalization:** Justification of the crime based on personal ethical values: "I'm borrowing the money"; "I need it for my family"; "The work this company does is harmful to…"

Fraud in the management of human capital is a violation of trust that can lead to financial loss, brand and reputational damage, legal and regulatory issues, and changes in shareholder value. To prevent fraud, the elements of "pressure" and, to some degree, "rationalization" are better addressed through the more traditional human capital processes such as employee assistance plans, development plans, promotion policies, and other retention plans. The element of "opportunity" can be addressed through a review of security policies, internal financial controls, and strict policies on vendor management and procurement practices.

Infiltration: An Insider Threat Having Both Internal and External Consequences

Social beliefs contrary to a company's operations, products, or business philosophy may cause vocal or criminal opposition and efforts to gain access to the company through direct attack or through more common infiltration practices. Some examples of industries where infiltration has been successful include petroleum, chemical refineries, and pharmaceutical research and manufacturing, as well as the U.S. government. Infiltration is one of the most effective public relations and tactical techniques used by groups or individuals. One way of infiltrating an organization is through false employment or through subversion or extortion of an existing employee. With such methods the result is a "wolf in sheep's clothing," an enemy operative undetected within the organization dressed as an employee or contractor. In one example, an infiltrator of a company involved in biomedical sciences released photographs taken out of context of internal projects involving primate research to the media, to animal welfare groups, and over the Internet. The resulting adverse publicity fueled a hostile campaign of protests not only at company facilities, but at homes of employees involved in the research. Probably the most publicized infiltration event in recent history was committed by Edward Snowden, who stated in an interview that he deliberately sought a job with a government contractor with the express purpose of alerting the public about secret NSA surveillance systems. This event, however, was not the typical insider threat. Most insiders who betray their employer's trust do not start out with that intent.[4]

Espionage: A Clandestine Process for Acquiring Secrets

The goal of espionage is to gain firsthand information on projects, technologies, or on research breakthroughs to garner competitive advantage. Espionage may be achieved through infiltration or bribery of insiders. Market competitors, foreign entities, and governments can conduct espionage. Information is a key component to civilian and military advances in both developing and established economies. If countries or companies can reduce their investment and improve results, they can gain an enormous economic benefit from espionage. Some governments actively support their industries to increase competitive advantage and in some cases may use their intelligence and security services to assist in conducting espionage. There has been much public discussion of countries', groups', and individuals' allegedly using cyberattacks to gain information or disrupt operations within other countries and companies. Exploitation of insiders is one of the means by which corporate espionage occurs. (See Chapter 6, on cybersecurity, for more on this; in cybersecurity, exploitation of insiders is sometimes referred to as "social engineering.") The vulnerability to espionage may increase through overconfidence in existing protective measures or complacency in gathering intelligence about the extremes to which other companies or countries might go to gain an advantage through espionage.

Sabotage: A Deliberate Act Causing Destruction, Disruption, or Physical Harm

In today's interconnected and networked economy we hear almost weekly of companies' or governments' having their proprietary data compromised by outside entities, more often than not causing financial havoc for their clients and customers. (For more details, see Chapter 6, on cybersecurity.) With respect to the insider threat, the change from a trusted employee or contractor to one who turns saboteur follows some of the same elements found in Cressey's fraud hypothesis but generally is without the financial drivers found in fraudulent events. Often what motivates saboteurs is dissatisfaction with the work environment, lack of promotion, underappreciation, unkept promises made by management, ethical values or beliefs, downsizing of the labor force, and plant closures. They can sabotage company facilities or systems, cause environmental damage, compromise research projects, and possibly cause personal injuries. Risks posed by these insider threats are significant, and the fallout from the outcomes may extend to adverse corporate publicity, discrediting of a brand, and possibly loss of shareholder value.

Infiltration through the Contracted Workforce

Companies are continually focusing on becoming more efficient and productive, improving shareholder values. They increasingly are relying on outsourced, offshore, contingent, and temporary workforces to perform roles that are not in their core expertise. For example, some work can be performed by other firms less expensively because of their large labor pools and scale. Some work is short-term in nature and does not lend itself to full-time employees. Other work can be performed in other regions where labor costs are less expensive. And some work is so specialized that outside experts are needed to fill a talent void. Though such sources of labor play an important role in controlling top-line expenses, efficiencies, and productivity, they also provides a convenient method for those wishing to do harm through infiltration, resulting in acts of espionage or even sabotage. Companies using contract labor pools often entrust the hiring and engagement process to a third-party agency or firm specializing in the type of skills they are looking for. The contracted employee is usually not provided the benefits or amenities of the full-time corporate employee, and over time, this may cause a pressure situation, driving the contracted employee to contemplate a malicious act. In another scenario, the contracted employee may have sought the temporary position with a particular firm with the express intention of infiltrating the organization for reasons of espionage or acts of sabotage. A couple of theories behind these potential avenues of access is that the hiring process for the contracted resource is not as stringent as that of the corporate employee, or there is no allegiance to the hiring company. In some cases, contracted employees having specialized skills may be given similar access to data, facilities, and projects without higher scrutiny. Additionally, a person whose intent is to infiltrate an organization for espionage or sabotage may simply seek employment through a contracted service provider for a lower-level position—for example, a custodial role (not to single that role out, but access to many areas of a company are granted to custodians, often at night when few others are around, resulting in the classic motive, means, and opportunity).

Employees as Targets

Human capital risk typically is focused on managing the internal risks or the insider threat posed by employee actions or behaviors. There are, however, instances in which an employee's work, position, or function within the organization, places the employee or the employee's family at risk or harm from outside organizations or groups whose beliefs do not align with that of the company, especially if the public becomes aware of the organization's work through publications or presentations. Such groups might include environmental groups, animal welfare groups, anti-abortionists, civil rights organizations, and others. These groups can be segmented into three broad categories of belief and strategy:

- Those who believe the given issue is harmful to society and promote a strategy of public education, information, and vocal but peaceful political action
- Those who believe the issue presents an illegal activity and promote a strategy of public demonstration, media manipulation, and propaganda
- Those who believe not only that the issue is illegal, but also that action up to and including violence is justified in opposition to it

The strategies of this latter group include violent confrontation, infiltration, vandalism, arson, physical attack, identity theft, threats, harassment, and intimidation directed at companies, employees, and sometimes employee families.

Generally, the activities of the majority of these groups fall into the first and, to a lesser degree, second of these categories. Usually groups such as these are vocal but peaceful, and their methods of action are directed through public education, information, peaceful public demonstration, and political action. As in most things human, however, there are fringe elements from such groups whose actions become extreme, usually through direct confrontation, obstruction of employees, vandalism, arson, physical attack, identity theft, harassment, intimidation, and, possibly, unfriendly visits to employees' homes. This, of course, may place a targeted employee and possibly his or her family at some degree of risk. In one incident in the UK, a group of extremists broke into the home of a pharmaceutical research executive and physically beat him. In the United States, some groups have made intimidating threats to targeted employees and their families at their homes.

It is important to be aware of these unlikely but high-consequence risks and to apply consistent and objective criteria to identify employees who are risk from fringe elements and to take preventive measures. Some of these measures may include security briefings on potential threats at locations of future business engagements, as well as security assessment of a residence to identify vulnerabilities and recommend cost-effective measures for mitigation.

The number of employees at risk can be expected to be very small. Nonetheless, a company should include a review of the environment in which it operates to assess the risk of employees' being targeted.

Hostile and Aggressive Workplace Events

Hostilities, harassment, and physical aggression of varying degrees—including the most feared, an active shooter—can be triggered for any number of reasons. These may include domestic issues not related to the workplace, personal bias, belief of unfair treatment, jealousy, drug and alcohol abuse, plant closure, and termination—whether for cause or as part of a reduction in force. This is an important consideration when developing a human capital risk management plan. Though all these examples above can result in malicious acts toward other employees and company facilities, behavioral signs toward coworkers, supervisors, and managers can sometimes preempt an event. We will discuss these points in a subsequent section.

Managing Human Capital Risk

The management of human capital risk is a very important part of an effective risk management and compliance program. However, because of the complex interactions and involvement of many groups in the company, it can end up ill defined.[5] Companies can also fall into the trap of thinking *We've never had an incident before, so why worry about it?* This line of thinking is usually accompanied by poorly written policies on fraud protection, infiltration, and violence prevention and exposes the company to losses and employees or contractors to risk of injury or worse. Within the United States, this line of reasoning may expose a company to legal risks under the Occupational Safety and Health Administration's requirement that employers must maintain a safe working environment. Similar requirements exist in most countries (see Chapter 3 on health and safety risk for more information).

A company may manage some of the risks about which we have spoken through a variety of controls:

- Changing the culture of the organization
- Proper pre-employment screening for employees and contractors
- Effective physical security and information security practices and procedures
- Employee awareness training programs to understand, recognize, and respond to risks in the organization
- Well-designed termination processes
- Management of the employee life cycle

Changing Culture

The **likelihood** and **consequences** of human capital events may vary from company to company, industry to industry, and country to country, but avoiding risk altogether is not possible, for employees and contracted resources are truly what make business run, and they need access to tools, resources, and data to work effectively. The most effective way to reduce risk is to change the culture of the organization. Changing the culture of an organization with respect to the three major elements of human capital risk requires a commitment from the human resources department to focus on the life cycle of employees. This starts with hiring and progresses through career management, employee assistance, and termination. It should include employee and contractor awareness training—not only for security issues, but also threats to the business from malicious cyber activities and the red flags that colleagues may exhibit before physical acts of aggression sabotage or theft.

In this way, employees and contractors become the *neighborhood watch* that assists orga-nizational security. Additionally, it is wise to develop comprehensive physical security poli-cies and practices that match responses to given levels of risk and threats, as well as to develop proactive procurement policies with suppliers and contract labor organizations whose hir-ing practices closely match those of the company. Let's look at these concepts in a little more detail.

Employee and Contractor Screening

Though employee and contractor screening processes do not completely eliminate the poten-tial of the insider threat—after all, many of the malicious events we have described occur after employees and contractors are firmly entrenched within the corporation—good screening programs and process are a key first-line **risk control** for preventing the potential damaging outcomes associated with human capital. Weakness in the initial vetting process, coupled with poor employee life cycle management can result in loss of intellectual property via theft or employee turnover, harm to reputation, loss of capital assets, financial loss, delay of product to market, workplace violence, or damage to the company's reputation.

Basic background screening for all applicants may uncover several red flags that can help in making the best hiring decision. One example of a red flag is inaccuracy in résumés and tran-scripts. A *New York Times* article titled "Fudging the Facts on a Resume is Common, and also a Big Risk"[6] reported that in one study, 43 percent of more than 1,100 résumés examined had one or more significant inaccuracies. These inaccuracies may be deliberate on the part of a prospective employee trying to hide prior associations or activities as part of a quest is to infil-trate a company. Other red flags that can be inferred from the résumé include: frequent or sud-den job changes, particularly those that involved relocation, unexplained gaps in employment, inconsistent educational background, and previous role having a higher salary, complexity, or skill level. The basic background screen will also indicate a criminal record check, which is done under the rules and regulations of the Fair Credit Reporting Act (or similar legislation outside the USA) through a third-party consumer reporting agency. This information allows you to compare what the prospective employee wants you to hear versus what is truly in the record and provides opportunity to probe for an explanation. In any case, though there may be reasonable explanation for such anomalies, companies should have zero tolerance for falsified or information or information that an employee cannot explain.

An *enhanced screening* exercise may be a consideration for reducing human capital risk in specialized areas of a company where the work may be of high intrinsic value and subject to a higher risk of infiltration. Some examples of these include leading-edge technologies for defense or commercial application, rare earth metallurgy, proprietary manufacturing pro-cesses, computer component fabrication, pharmaceutical research, and software design. These decidedly focused fields have a high degree of competitive risk, may involve national defense–related interests, or may be the subject of intense public or special-interest opposi-tion. The enhanced security screening includes a more thorough review of the results of the standard background documentation and may include interviews of relatives and friends, credit checks, and a comprehensive Internet search looking for associations and affiliations.

This additional security measure is designed to identify any individual whose current or past activities, history, or associations may present a risk to company business or existing employees. Results of enhanced screening process may include the following:

- Past or present association with partisan groups having a history of protest, ridicule, or violence against a particular business sector.
- Arrests related to activities conducted with the aforementioned groups, or other criminal activities.
- Record or evidence of harassment or threats made to individuals associated with prior employment. These threats may have been extended to the targeted individuals' families or property.
- Name showing up on a dissenting group's website or on industry-specific watch lists.
- Educational qualifications in excess of the current job requirements and/or frequent job changes within an industry in similar lower-rated jobs.

The enhanced screening process may also be used for existing employees whose job requirements change and who now require access to sensitive, higher-risk areas.

Screening of contingent and contracted workers helps ensure that supplier and vendor hiring practices are in line with that of the company. Though it may be satisfactory for contract agencies to use their own third-party screening services, coordination with supplier human resources departments about expectations of the scope of the background screen is important for building a trusting environment in which employees and contractors work side by side. In the case of the enhanced screening process when the work to be contracted requires access to sensitive areas, it is recommended that the contract agencies use the same screening vendor as the hiring company. This ensures that the background information is researched and analyzed in a similar manner. If any red flags surface, they can be discussed between the company and hiring agency for follow-up discussions with the prospective contract employee.

For key positions, companies may wish to include noncompete clauses in the hiring documentation signed by employees to prevent the loss of key information or technology. Though this latter point is no guarantee of protection of intellectual property, it does provide a reminder to employees tempted to market internal company knowledge after a separation, and may provide some recourse if they do.

The screening practices discussed above may be carried out by the company itself but are generally carried out by third-party employment screening firms, among which there are numerous choices. For the enhanced screening program, the breadth and depth of the work is generally very specific and the parameters should be carefully defined between the company and the service provider. In any event, the results are never simply pass/fail. Usually a report should be made available for inclusion in the hiring decision. When examining the costs/benefits of setting up such programs in-house or through a service provider, the company should look at its own expertise in the process and at the volume of work to be performed. Outsourcing the service to a reputable provider may be preferable to costs of self-performing the work and even more cost-effective if volume contracts are negotiated. In either case, the company must work closely with its legal counsel to ensure that screening parameters are within all local, state or provincial, and federal or national laws governing the searches. Third-party providers typically will have more experience in the process and can put a layer of protection between the prospective employee and the company should any legal issues arise. For screening services in foreign countries, local firms having expertise and knowledge of specific laws governing privacy are recommended.

As an example of laws regarding background investigations, third-party services in the United States are subject to the limits of the Fair Credit Reporting Act (FCRA), in addition to many other local regulations. The FCRA includes a background screen as a consumer report. It establishes very specific parameters for the acquisition and dissemination of pre-employment search results and applies to items such as criminal records, past employment history, and educational verifications. Though adherence to the FCRA is primarily a third-party screening resource matter, the company requesting the work must also certify in writing that the information received is for employment purposes only and that it will not use it in violation of federal or state equal opportunity laws. Within this law, the employer must provide a distinct disclosure to the applicant that the report is for employment purposes only and request his or her written consent authorizing the background screen. This authorization is separate from any other pre-employment documentation and is made available to the third-party screening firm to begin the process.

Should the company decide not to hire the applicant as a result of adverse information in the report, it is required to provide the applicant with a copy of the report and the right to dispute the findings of the report. This is a technical process and, as already seen, can be very complicated; the key points here are to be cognizant of the laws pertaining to the location of the business and to do the search right and do it legally.

Companies may find that cooperative arrangements with respect to screening or mandates with other suppliers may be a point of contention. An example of this may be with unionized labor, or with work councils in some other countries. A specific union or local may provide labor vetted through its own processes. These results may not be subject to review or discussion by the company requesting the labor. When bidding projects or contracting labor under these situations, preliminary due diligence by the hiring company regarding supplier vetting and bonding is recommended. There are exceptions in which a service provider may have control of the background screening in an organized labor situation. For example, in the contracted security industry, many large suppliers of these services must hire unionized labor as a result of country, state, and local labor decrees; however, the security service provider has full control of the background investigation to satisfy state or local licensing requirements for the specific positions.

Over the past twenty years, the personnel testing industry has witnessed a marked increase in psychological test usage for job selection, promotion, and placement.[7] The decision to use these tests to augment typical screening programs is made on a company-by-company basis; much of the testing is done as an aid to determining personal integrity. Integrity testing is highly specialized, and there are three major publishers of tools for these activities—Pinkerton Services Group (formerly the Stanton Corporation) in Charlotte, North Carolina; Reid Psychological Systems in Chicago, Illinois; and London House Incorporated, in Park Ridge, Illinois.[8] If fraud is a risk, and in cases in which trust is critical, companies may wish to include this testing in their screening and overall hiring processes.

Security Policies, Procedures, and Systems

Detection and prevention measures carried out through physical security policies, procedures, and practices can play an integral role in managing human capital risk as well as managing insider threats. The simple practice of visibly wearing an identification badge can go a long way to ensure that the wearer belongs where he or she is. Appropriate visitor management practices also insure that nonemployees and contractors do not have free reign within a facility. Sensitive areas in the corporation, particularly those where disruption from infiltration and deliberate acts of sabotage or espionage can cause financial loss, pose a threat to other employees, or bring reputational discredit, must be viewed as high-risk and be appropriately protected. Recommended strategies for these sensitive areas may include provision of multiple layers of security around the high-risk spaces, with unique identification for authorized employees and contractors required for at least one of the layers. Additionally, systems for accountability for specialized equipment or documentation, review of requests for access, and duration of access to these areas must also be developed in support of the higher security levels.

Security policies, whether they be physical or logical (those pertaining to information systems), should clearly state the consequences to the employee of violation and be reinforced by similar human resource policies.

Awareness and Training

Securing the workforce by implementing awareness and antirisk activities is often an organization's best opportunity to thwart insider threats.[9] Some practical examples of training activities include the following:

- An awareness program for employees describing potential external threats to the organization—for example, the potential for economic espionage.
- A program that develops an understanding of the risks the company faces from both inside and external threats.
- A heightened awareness campaign on the restricted use of cameras and other photo-capable devices in highly sensitive areas.
- Awareness programs designed to protect company assets and employee safety while on travel assignments. This is usually accompanied by intelligence gathering of potential risky locations through the world. (See reference to OSAC at the end of the chapter for more information.)
- Awareness of protection of information policies, including information classification systems, access and destruction protocols, and the proper protective measures for company-provided computers, laptops, tablets, phones, and the like.
- Programs that raise employee awareness of physical anomalies in the workplace as well as behavioral indicators that may foretell a malicious event. In other words, use the workforce as multiple sets of eyes and ears, ensuring that every employee is knowledgeable of the proper course of action should he or she detect something.
- Provision of training to key supervisory personnel in the management of aggressive behavior to recognize, reduce, and manage violent conduct.

The latter point is not meant to turn employees into hostage negotiators, nor law enforcement personnel, but rather to provide effective and compassionate methods for dealing with anxious or aggressive people, better understanding nonverbal signals that a hostile person may exhibit, and potentially delaying the onset of a violent act until appropriate response personnel can be summoned. For more information on such programs, see the references section at the end of the chapter.

Employee and Contractor Life Cycle Management

Though background screening is a key element for managing human capital risk, it is only the beginning. A process known as identity management, which tracks the life cycle of employees and contractors from date of hire through termination of employment, is a key element of minimizing risk over time. Proper employee onboarding (the activities associated with bringing an employee into a company, training the employee, and providing the employee with resources and equipment necessary to perform his or her role) and offboarding (disengagement of an employee from the company and recovery of assigned assets and access) processes link people, job history, assets, physical and virtual access, and training to a unique identifier created during the hiring process, and follows them through their employment history. These systems coordinate new employee integration into the company for the hiring managers, resource administrators, and key service providers. They provide a single interface for initiating and reviewing employee and contractor job-related service requests for assets, IT resources, and physical access to selected areas of the facilities, as well as the level of training required to perform a job. These end-to-end systems track everything concerning an employee's activities during his or her term at the company, which reduces the risk of physical property's and intellectual property's leaving the company upon termination (whether termination for cause or voluntarily) by ensuring that system access and data is properly accounted for and that all access is removed.

Terminations

The process of termination is generally sudden, emotional, and life-changing and may trigger an unplanned response, whether immediately upon notification or after the affected employee has had time to reflect. For these reasons, terminations should be well planned. The timing should be chosen to protect the affected employee from embarrassment and to minimize interactions with other employees—for example, at the beginning of the week, after the workday has started, to minimize interaction with others, or at the end of the day or week, when most employees have already left. In many cases, the end of the week is preferable, for it allows the affected employee time to reflect and, it is to be hoped, cool down while the company is closed for business.[10]

Sometimes a company may choose to have a second person in the room during the discussion, but that should be carefully weighed against the possibility of the affected employee's feeling overwhelmed and becoming belligerent, defensive, or hostile. A representative from the security group should be present and stationed unobtrusively in the area, not directly in the room, in the event of an altercation. It is also good practice for the person leading the discussion to take a position close to the door to avoid being trapped if the discussion turns violent, as well as to have easy access to security personnel if needed.

At the conclusion of the discussion, security should collect the employee's identification access badge and vehicle pass, then escort the terminated employee to his or her vehicle or off the premises. The termination process plan should also make provisions to remove physical and logical access to the company at the same time as the discussion. Physical assets used by the employee should be identified and collected as quickly as possible. Retrieving personal effects from lockers and workspaces can be emotional for the terminated employee and is best done in the presence of a supervisor and observer after the termination. Should the situation be too emotionally charged, arrangements for retrieval can be made at a later time. As a final thought on terminations, if the company had a nondisclosure agreement in place (as discussed in the section on employee screening), this would be the time to remind the affected employee of that pre-employment agreement.

Conclusion: An Integrated Approach to Managing Malicious Human Capital Risks

Within a corporation, "almost everything that can go wrong has a human capital component," according to David Creelman of Creelman Research.[11] We have provided several areas of risk, particularly from the perspective of the insider threat in which the underlying cause is instigated through human capital. We have also discussed several methods to mitigate and manage those risks. However, solutions that are not integrated holistically across the entire workforce will be less effective as a human capital risk management strategy. In their white paper "Building a Secure Workforce,"[12] authors Gelles, Brant, and Geffert propose establishing a workforce culture to manage risk. The cultural awareness is developed through training programs that develop an understanding of red flags for aberrant behaviors, the threats posed by insiders intent on causing turmoil, strong intelligence gathering, and communication of potential risks. This is augmented by sound policies on hiring, physical security, and information security. Last, a strong legal group should provide guidance to ensure that all policies, procedures, and practices comply with local, regional, and national laws. The sum of these initiative forms a balanced and integrated approach to manage risks associated with human capital. It is only through integrated thinking and the willingness of the corporation to make this a key risk management strategy that a more secure organization and workforce can be achieved and the threat from the inside minimized.

Notes

1. The term *contracted resource* will be used in this chapter to denote all human corporate resources not classified as direct employees, such as contingent, temporary, outsourced, and offshore workforces, supplier resources, and those used in the execution of the supply chain.

2. "5 Critical Areas of Human Capital Risk," The Risk Management Blog, Lowers Risk Group. www.lowersriskgroup.com/blog/2013/08/08.
3. Donald R. Cressey, *Other People's Money* (Montclair: Patterson Smith, 1973), p. 30.
4. "Confronting the Insider Threat," Laura Spadanuta, *Security Management Magazine*, October 2013.
5. "Managing Human Capital Risks: Whose Responsibility Is It?" Deloitte Risk and Compliance. http://deloitte.WSJ.com/risandcompliance/2013/04/29.
6. David Koeffel, New York Times, April 23, 2006.
7. *Protection of Assets Manual*, American Society of Industrial Security, Chapter 32, part 1, 2004.
8. *Personnel Screening with Psychological Tests Protection of Assets Manual*, American Society of Industrial Security, Chapter 32, part 1, 2004.
9. Michael Gilles, David Brant, Brian Geffert, "Building a Secure Workforce: Guard against the Insider Threat," Deloitte Consulting, LLP, 2008, p. 7.
10. "Five Tips on Preventing Workplace Violence," Phil Bruce, Employer LINC. http://employerlinc.com/2014/10.
11. "5 Critical Areas of Human Capital Risk," The Risk Management Blog, Lowers Risk Group. www.lowersriskgroup.com/blog/2013/08/08.
12. Michael Gills, David Brant, Brian Geffert, "Building a Secure Workforce: Guard against the Insider Threat," Deloitte Consulting, LLP, 2008, p. 7.

Further Reading

Overseas Advisory Council (OSAC) U.S. Department of State, Bureau of Diplomatic Security, www.osac.gov.

Management of Aggressive Behavior (MOAB). R.E.B. Training International, Inc. PO Box 845, Stoddard NH 03464. www.rebtraining.com.

Financial Risk Management

10

An Aggregated Approach to Risk Analysis: Risk Portfolios

Steven Miller

The Challenges of the Traditional "Siloed" Approach to Risk Analysis

Corporations have traditionally delegated the risk management process to personnel with the appropriate expertise in dealing with a given risk. Examples include cybersecurity and information security risk management delegated to the IT department, financial risk management delegated to the finance department, human capital risks delegated to the human resources department, and so forth. As firms have faced new risks, the new risks have been delegated to and managed by the resources in the firm that have the relevant expertise to manage the risks (those resources are hereafter referred to as the risk owners). Hence a distributed, "siloed" approach[1] to risk management naturally evolved over time. Each department becomes responsible for risk management (as described in Chapter 1) of the risks within its silo.

While this approach has many advantages, it does have its flaws. When risk analysis is performed within a silo (e.g., within the finance department), it can be challenging to optimally prioritize risks for treatment, as individual departments often suffer from an inability to see the big picture—to understand how the risks they manage affect the total risk of the firm[2] (i.e., earnings volatility). Let's look at a real-world example to illustrate this potential problem.

In 1984, the finance department at Lufthansa, a German airline, implemented a hedge to mitigate its foreign exchange rate risk. The company had just purchased a number of aircraft from Boeing valued at $3 billion, to be paid upon delivery of the aircraft. Lufthansa "hedged this exposure by acquiring a forward contract for $ 1.5 billion. Thus, if the dollar strengthened, the firm would lose on its aircraft contracts (which would cost more in D-marks than when the deal was struck) but gain on the forward contract. On the other hand, if the dollar weakened, the firm would lose on its hedge but gain on the aircraft."[3]

Taken in isolation, this approach by Lufthansa's finance department makes a lot of sense; currency fluctuations could dramatically change the ultimate cost (in deutsche marks) of the Boeing planes to Lufthansa. Hence this hedge was designed (net of transaction costs) to reduce by half the effect of exchange-rate risk. This is an excellent example of a department effectively identifying, analyzing, and treating one of the risks within its silo. If all we were concerned about was the effectiveness of risk management within the finance department

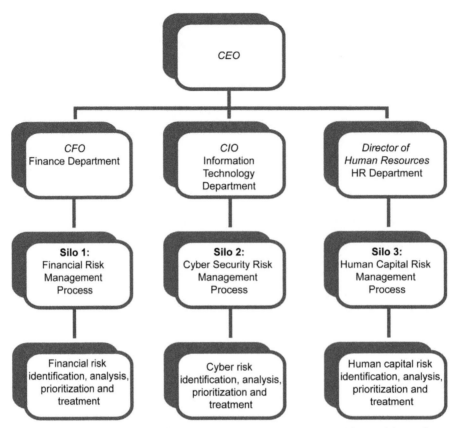

FIGURE 10–1 An illustration of a distributed "siloed" risk management structure. Risks are delegated to a department or operating unit having the appropriate topical expertise to most effectively execute the risk management process. This figure includes only three hypothetical risk silos for illustration purposes, but in practice, numerous departments or operating units are tasked with managing risks.

silo, then the analysis would end here. But if we are concerned about managing the risk to Lufthansa's earnings, then our analysis of this risk management strategy needs to delve a little deeper. Would hedging this foreign exchange-rate risk still make sense if Lufthansa's earnings were highly, positively correlated to the relative strength of the dollar?

Lufthansa's operating expenses (being primarily deutsche mark-denominated) eroded profit margins to a greater extent when the deutsche mark was strong against the U.S. dollar and other European currencies. Conversely, when the deutsche mark was weak, Lufthansa's earnings grew. Thus the contract to purchase Boeing airplanes was, in effect, a "natural hedge" that helped stabilize Lufthansa's earnings irrespective of which direction the exchange rate (i.e., deutsche marks to dollars) moved. So with this new, broader risk management perspective, we are better able to evaluate Lufthansa's hedging decision. The implemented exchange rate hedge counteracted a natural hedge and, by doing so, actually had the unintended effect of increasing Lufthansa's risk.

To draw an analogy, let's imagine that you own a car that has serious mechanical issues. These issues require you to take the car in for service on a regular basis, and the cost of these service visits vary quite a bit. These random increases in expenses resulting from your auto's mechanical failures adversely affect the stability of your monthly disposable income. One day you decide to buy a new automobile that comes with a warranty. Although it is admittedly an imperfect analogy, we can compare your purchase of a new vehicle to Lufthansa's purchase of new Boeing aircraft. In both cases, disposable income (or for Lufthansa, cash flows) will be more stable after the purchase. To extend this analogy to Lufthansa's decision to hedge exchange rate risk, one would have to imagine that you would subsequently pay the automobile dealer a negotiated fee to eliminate the built-in warranty. This extension of the analogy works in that you, along with Lufthansa, have spent both time and money to increase the risk to your earnings over time. Although I acknowledge that the notion of paying a fee to *eliminate* a warranty seems absurd, the idea of implementing a hedge to *increase* a firm's volatility of earnings over time (as Lufthansa did) is similarly irrational and, more important, may reasonably be expected to erode firm value.

To be clear, I am not suggesting that the Lufthansa employee who designed and executed the hedge was behaving irrationally. To an individual operating within a silo, tasked with managing solely the risks assigned to his or her silo, the strategy was appropriate. The suboptimal, value-eroding outcome clearly resulted from the myopia of the individual operating from within the walls of a silo; with the perspective of being enclosed within one silo, one cannot envision what is taking place in other silos. Furthermore, one cannot readily determine how an individual risk is contributing to the total risk of the firm—at least not until the firm starts to develop a broader, more holistic picture of the firm's risks.

The Benefits of an Aggregated (Risk Portfolio) Approach to Risk Analysis

Firms have begun to take a more holistic approach to risk analysis, aggregating individual risks into a portfolio (i.e., the risk portfolio).[4] Although it is true that this evolution in corporate risk analysis is in part a reflection of firms' desire to better recognize natural hedges, as discussed in the Lufthansa case, the value proposition of aggregated risk analysis goes much further. By forming and evaluating a risk portfolio, firms can begin to ask and answer a variety of questions: How much does this particular risk add to the total risk of the firm? Which risks are most important to mitigate? How well does a risk treatment method reduce the total risk of the firm? Are the risk treatment tools that we currently use most effective in addressing our firm's risk? In summary, the formation of a risk portfolio enhances the firm's ability to recognize and exploit natural hedges, understand which risks are driving earnings (and cash flow) volatility, and evaluate the effectiveness and efficiency of potential hedging instruments. Firms with these capabilities gain competitive advantages as they become more expert and efficient at reducing firm risk.

Recent academic research has examined the effects of adopting a holistic approach to risk analysis within a sample of U.S. publicly traded insurers.[5] Researchers find that insurers began

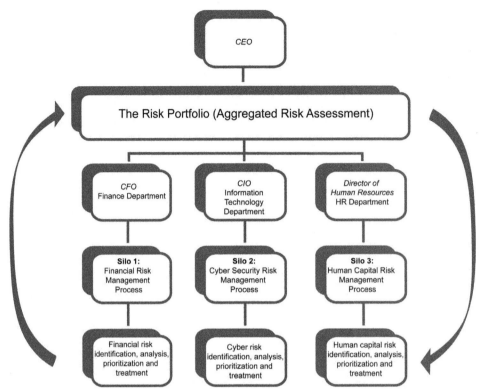

FIGURE 10–2 An aggregated risk portfolio RM structure. Risks continue to be delegated to a department or operating unit having the appropriate topical expertise to most effectively execute the risk management process. Risks that are identified throughout the organization are combined to allow for a more holistic approach to risk assessment. More specifically, the firm's risks are aggregated into a risk portfolio so that correlations and dependencies can be evaluated, diversification (i.e., natural hedging) can be recognized, each risk's contribution to total firm risk can be examined, instruments used to hedge firm risk can be evaluated, the extent of hedging can be evaluated, and so forth. Ultimately, the goal is to enrich the firm's understanding of risks by allowing the firm to ask better questions and make more informed decisions.

to adopt formal aggregated risk analysis programs in the mid-1990s. By 2008, 43 percent of U.S. publicly traded insurance companies had adopted this approach. Regulators and credit rating agencies have strongly encouraged the adoption of holistic risk analysis. For example, A.M. Best started specifically evaluating insurers' holistic approach to risk analysis in 2001.[6] In addition, by 2005, Standard & Poor's began evaluating an insurer's ability to aggregate risks for analysis as a critical factor in assessing the credit rating of the insurer: "Risk models are an integral part of a robust ERM framework. They are used extensively to measure risk exposures, test risk correlation and diversification, validate risk mitigation strategies, and quantify capital requirements for a given risk profile… (and this evaluation criteria) covers… enterprise risk aggregation across risks."[7] Findings from academic research were consistent with the notion that an aggregated risk analysis would make the insurers expert at reducing risk; the enhanced analytical capabilities would make risk reduction efforts more effective and efficient, resulting in a lower marginal cost of risk reduction. Any firm seeking to maximize profits recognizes that a lower marginal cost creates incentives to produce more units of that output (i.e., in this case, produce more units of risk reduction) until the costs of producing the next unit once again equal the marginal benefits. Hence, the additional expertise and efficiency in risk reduction motivates firms to increase (at any given level of firm risk taking) their level of risk reduction while simultaneously realizing increased profits. More specifically, researchers find that firms adopting a risk portfolio to support risk analysis increased the ratio of return on assets over annualized standard deviation of stock returns by two percent, and reduced observable risk by 13.9 percent.[8] Furthermore, research also supports the notion that adopting a more holistic approach would increase firm value (they were found to experience a 20 percent premium in their market-to-book ratio of assets).[9]

Operationalizing a Risk Portfolio

Let's explore an example of a risk-portfolio to gain a better understanding of how an aggregated risk analysis might be operationalized, and of its usefulness to an organization. Figure 10–3 provides us with a sample illustration of a risk portfolio (the figure also references a sample risk portfolio analysis publicly disclosed by Endurance Specialty Holdings, a Bermuda-based reinsurance company). The sample probability distribution aggregates the various risks of the firm and illustrates how a firm can implement a risk portfolio analysis and

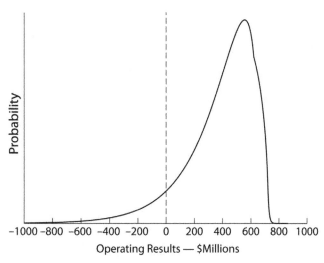

FIGURE 10–3 Illustration of a risk portfolio. An example of a risk portfolio (i.e., an aggregated risk analysis) resulting in a probability distribution of operating profits. That is, the aggregate effect of all firm risks yields the displayed probability distribution of earnings. Hence, a firm performing aggregate risk analysis has the capacity to perform scenario analyses to evaluate different operational and hedging strategies and their resulting effect on expected operating results. This is but one example of how aggregate risk analysis can enhance the firm's ability to evaluate risk managment (as well as operating and strategic) decisions.[10]

seek better understanding as to how a firm's risks impact earnings over time. Such a model can help risk managers ask better questions: Which risks, net of natural hedging, are driving the potential losses in earnings (the left-hand side of the distribution reveals the most severe negative outcomes as well as the negative outcomes with the highest probability)? What hedging instruments would be most effective in mitigating the firm's potential loss in earnings? How would strategic decisions impact firm risk? How would changes in our operating mix (e.g., what products an insurance company sells) affect diversification within the risk portfolio?

The development and implementation of a risk portfolio is typically overseen by a chief risk officer (CRO) and is not designed to supplant the risk analysis being performed by the risk owners housed within the various risk management silos throughout the organization. In fact, to build the risk portfolio, it is essential to receive each risk analysis as an input. That is, Lufthansa still needs the finance department to identify and analyze the foreign exchange rate risk associated with the purchase of Boeing aircraft; after the risk is analyzed, it must then be communicated to the CRO so that it may be incorporated into the firm's risk portfolio. Only after all risks are incorporated can the analysis seek to appropriately recognize the diversification (i.e., natural hedging) taking place within the risk portfolio. Furthermore, after the risk portfolio is constructed, analysis can be performed to optimize the firm's risk retention and hedging strategies (e.g., avoid the Lufthansa blunder), aid the firm in evaluating strategic and operational decisions, and develop allocations that incentivize behavior supporting the firm's risk-adjusted profitability objectives.

The development and implementation of a risk portfolio is meant to enhance a firm's understanding of its risks and, as a result, allow a firm to make better decisions that will increase firm value. It is not intrinsically designed to replace other risk management activities or impair the firm's ability to achieve other risk management goals, such as promoting life safety, meeting safety regulations, or executing disaster recovery plans. And although the goal in constructing the risk portfolio is to encompass the complete set of risks a firm faces, a matter of practicality must be considered. A risk analysis of a pipeline spill, brand attack, cyberattack, and the like can all pose serious financial consequences to the firm; other risks may be less relevant in affecting the firm's earnings volatility. Hence firms may reasonably apply criteria to establish thresholds for risks to be included into the risk portfolio. So if a department's risk analysis finds risks that exceed the established thresholds, those risks are escalated to the CRO for incorporation and analysis in the risk portfolio. As the firm develops its aggregate risk analysis capabilities, such thresholds can be adjusted correspondingly. Aggregate risk analysis can be fairly considered as an additional layer of analysis that may be adopted in such a way that the firm believes benefits are likely to exceed costs.

Constructing the risk portfolio can also highlight risks that reasonably defy modeling. Technological disruptors to the industry or changes in competitive conditions are examples of risks that are challenging to quantify and incorporate into models. Of course, similar challenges may be posed by relatively small risks (e.g., the loss in productivity when a department manager faces personal, family, or medical issues). When faced with such risks, it is important to acknowledge that they exist and to incorporate those risks, when appropriate, in discussions with the relevant risk owners. So to continue with the sample risks above, when reviewing the risk portfolio with the board's risk committee, it is critical to recognize which strategic risks are not integrated into the model and to incorporate those risks into the risk committee's discussion.

Risks Associated with Implementing a Risk Portfolio

To develop such a sophisticated risk portfolio, advanced statistical models are used. It is critical to note the potential pitfalls of relying too heavily upon such modeling tools. As pointed out by statistician George Box, "Essentially, all models are wrong, but some are useful."[11] As firms come to rely upon sophisticated technical tools to help them evaluate risk, there is a tendency to be somewhat overconfident about the precision and the robustness of the capabilities of such modeling tools. Hence it is essential that the potential for modeling error be recognized and explicitly incorporated into the model itself. William Riker, a former president of Renaissance Holdings, warns of what he refers to as "delusional exactitude"—"the tendency to imagine that models provide precise numbers that can be used to diversify or price catastrophic risk; these risks, by their very nature, defy exact measurement."[12]

Building the risk portfolio requires the firm to develop a common framework for evaluating risk and attempt to apply this framework to all of the firm's risks. As described above, a gap in the analysis arises thanks to the risks that seemingly defy objective measurement, and so these risks may necessarily be excluded from the model. In addition, other challenges arise with the risks that can be analyzed within the framework: How do risks correlate with one another, and in what other ways do the firm's risks interact? To take these issues one step further, the relationships between risks may vary over time: "While successful diversification reduces risk by reducing correlation, it is hard to know what areas are correlated when. In times of great stress, new correlations appear."[13] Hence even when a firm feels it has sufficient data and analytical tools to adequately address correlations and other risk dependencies, there are good reasons to challenge whether the model "knows what it doesn't know."

The financial crisis generated a clear opportunity to evaluate the efficacy of an aggregated approach to risk analysis. There clearly were failures. AIG provides us an example of a firm that employed risk portfolio models that failed to adequately assess risk leading into the 2008 financial crisis. "The problem for AIG is that it didn't apply effective models for valuing the swaps and for collateral risk until the second half of 2007, long after the swaps were sold, AIG documents and investor presentations indicate."[14] While discussing the financial crisis with PBS interviewer Charlie Rose, Warren Buffett humorously chimed in to express his skepticism over the capabilities of models to adequately assess risk: "All I can say is, beware of geeks… bearing formulas." That said, there were also successes (that likely went unnoticed and received little attention). The previously cited academic research finds that on average, U.S. insurers that implemented a risk portfolio exhibited less volatility and greater risk-adjusted profitability than those who did not from 1992 through 2008.

Making a Decision to Implement a Risk Portfolio

An important lesson to take away is that models of risk portfolios are not a panacea. Though good theoretical motivations and strong empirical evidence support the hypothesis that aggregated risk analysis enhances firm value, one must maintain a healthy level of skepticism about any specific risk model's predictions. Like many tools, their effect is largely dependent upon who wields them and for what purpose. The quality of the management team and the risk management culture of the organization can play a significant role in how effectively risk models are used.

With all the modeling risks described above, a firm may question whether it should even attempt to implement a risk portfolio (from fear of making an error). This question seems incomplete in its analysis of available options. I think a better way to frame the question is to ask which scenario supports the firm in making better risk management decisions:

> Scenario 1: Struggle to develop a quality risk portfolio that will ultimately help risk professionals gain a deeper understanding of how risks are affecting firm performance. This process helps you learn but requires that you manage the risks associated with what we can anticipate will be an imperfect model.
>
> Scenario 2: Avoid the risks associated with an imperfect model, but, in turn, sacrifice the potential benefits associated with holistic risk analysis. Suffer the same inability to see the big picture that was exemplified by Lufthansa.

Warren Buffett said you should beware of geeks bearing formulas; he did not say that you should kick those same geeks out of the building and refuse to listen to their analyses. There is much to be learned from the formation and analysis of a risk portfolio. When asked for his thoughts on how the implementation of an aggregated risk analysis approach affected their ability to achieve risk management goals, Mike Angelina[15] stated, "[I]t helped us ask (and answer) much better questions… it also allowed us to get a much better grasp on our return on capital." The current state of academic research strongly supports the notion that aggregate risk analysis enhances a firm's ability to manage firm risk and increases firm value.

Notes

1. See Figure 10-1: A Distributed "Siloed" RM Structure.
2. The total risk of the firm is theoretically linked to earnings volatility. Mayers and Smith (1982), Smith and Stulz (1985), and Froot et al. (1993) put forth a theory of how corporate risk management, by lowering a firm's earnings volatility, adds to firm value by lowering expected tax liabilities, financial distress costs, the cost of raising capital, and other contracting costs.
3. Matthew Bishop, "A Survey of Corporate Risk Management," *The Economist*, February 10, 1996, special section.
4. For a visual highlighting the basic differences, see Figure 10-2: An Aggregated Risk Portfolio RM Structure.
5. The discussion of findings from academic research in this section draws heavily from the following papers:
   David L. Eckles, Hoyt, Robert E., Miller, Steven M., 2014. The impact of enterprise risk management on the marginal cost of reducing risk: Evidence from the insurance industry. *Journal of Banking & Finance* 43, 247-261.
   Andre P. Liebenberg, Hoyt, Robert E., 2011. The value of enterprise risk management. *The Journal of Risk and Insurance* 78(4), 795-822.
6. A.M. Best Special Report—A.M. Best's Enterprise Risk Model, A Holistic Approach to Measuring Capital Adequacy (July 2001).
7. Standard & Poor's Rating Services, Enterprise Risk Management, May 7, 2013, 12-13.
8. The research did examine adoption of enterprise risk management, which may incorporate cultural changes as well as a more holistic approach to risk analysis. However, the development of hypotheses in this study was based largely on the economic incentives derived from the formation of a risk portfolio to support risk analysis.

9. The research did examine adoption of enterprise risk management, which may incorporate cultural changes and other potentially value enhancing factors in addition to a more holistic approach to risk analysis.

10. For a publicly disclosed example of a firm's risk portfolio, see slide 19 in the Q4 2010 Investor Presentation from Endurance Specialty Holdings, at http://ir.endurance.bm/phoenix.zhtml?c=137754&p=irol-presentations.

11. G. E. P. Box and N. R. Draper, Empirical Model Building and Response Surfaces (New York: John Wiley & Sons, 1987), 424.

12. William I. Riker, (retired) president, Renaissance Holdings, *Exposure Magazine*, summer 2004, 11.

13. Paul Kneuer, Bubbles, Cycles and Insurers' ERM—What Just Happened? Risk Management: The Current Financial Crisis, Lessons Learned and Future Implications. Copyright © 2008, the Society of Actuaries.

14. Behind AIG's Fall, Risk Models Failed to Pass Real-World Test, *Wall Street Journal*, WSJ.com, October 31, 2008.

15. Mike Angelina, ACAS, MAAA is the former chief risk officer and chief actuary of Endurance Specialty Holdings. He is currently the executive director of the Academy of Risk Management and Insurance at Saint Joseph's University.

11

Managing Common Financial Risks

Sibt-ul-Hasnain Kazmi

Financial risks lurk behind seemingly straightforward everyday business and personal decisions. Businesses face financial risks that originate mainly from credit, liquidity, financial markets, interest rates, exchange rates, stock prices and commodity prices. Financial risks follow a law similar to the law of conservation of energy, which tells us that there is no total change in the amount of energy in the universe, but rather than energy simply changes from one form to another, such as from potential energy to kinetic energy, or vice versa. On a macro level in financial markets, risks are neither destroyed nor created. They exist in every business activity. They correlate, reinforce, or transfer from one form to another. On a firm level, they do not follow this law. They can be hedged, minimized, shared, or simply transferred away.

Knowledge and assessment of financial risk, as for any other risk, is the first step towards risk mitigation.

Types of Financial Risk

Currency Risk

Everyone faces currency risk every day without realizing it. It is quite natural to assume that currency risk only occurs when purchasing a particular foreign currency. In most people's view, the home currency, the currency of their country of residence, is the safest currency bet they can make because wealth is generally described in terms of one's home currency. They consider having currency exposure other than one's home currency as a risk. But we still face currency risk even if we don't own foreign currencies or assets denoted in foreign currencies. Whenever we shop for groceries, cars, or homes, or when we go for vacations, we face it. Products today are imported either partially or wholly from foreign countries. The gasoline we put in our cars is the simplest example of all. Residents of developed countries having stable exchange rates face relatively less currency risk than those living in countries having volatile exchange rates or developing countries where people often expect home currency depreciation. Exchange rate uncertainty affects the cost of living and people's consumption behavior at large.

We live in an interdependent world. The price of one's home currency is relative to a basket of other currencies. What matters more than the absolute stock of wealth in one's home currency is the relative purchasing power to buy other countries' products. Currency risk affects different individuals and businesses differently, depending on their needs and nature. According to economic theory, in the long run, currencies are supposed to revert to their equilibrium value; currency risk, according to the theory, should thus not matter. But in the short run, currency risk does matter, because our daily lives and business decisions are short-term in nature. Devaluation of the home currency may increase costs within, for example, a financial quarter or year. Currency risk thus is part and parcel of life and business. That is especially true for businesses that operate in a multicurrency environment or that have an operational presence in more than one country.

Volatility in the prices of currency and commodity markets can strongly affect the performance of an international portfolio of securities and businesses. Transaction risk is the currency risk associated with the delay between the entrance and settlement of contracts. The greater the delay, the more time there is for two currencies involved in the contract to fluctuate. Translation risk is another type of currency risk that occurs when companies with foreign assets on their balance sheets convert them to the home currency. It is present even if foreign business operations are stable or profitable.

Commodity Risk

Every business faces commodity risk, directly or indirectly. In periods of heightened financial and economic stress, commodity prices rise in contrast to declining values of other assets. Commodities are a natural safe haven when investors run for shelter. For ages, gold has been considered a store of value, something no less true even in today's advanced and thriving global financial system. To own a precious metal such as gold is itself a good risk management technique for risk averse investors. Yet it also introduces additional risks.

A commodity is a tangible asset that is relatively homogeneous in nature. This homogeneity is both a source of boon as well as bane for its users. Homogeneity has led to standardized contracts. This has made buying and selling of commodities in financial market much easier. But it has also added extra volatility and has contributed to quicker spread of sentiments across markets. These commodities are mainly agricultural products, metals, and energy resources. Interestingly, even banks and other financial institutions incur commodity risk. They trade in commodity-based instruments, and they lend to businesses whose core operations are associated with both food and nonfood commodities, such as metal, oil, and agricultural products.

Commodity prices are sensitive to business cycles and correlate positively with inflation (i.e. a general rise in price levels). Commodity prices are also greatly impacted by short-term expectations about the global economy. Oil prices, for example, tend to decline when the world economy is weak owing to weaker global oil demand. Commodity prices also reflect storability. Storability enables commodities to be used as a hedge against unexpected inflation. Unexpected inflation is the component of inflation that is not priced into people's expectations about inflation. There are surveys of expectations about inflation. Actual inflation that is not accurately anticipated in those surveys and the fraction (above or below) market expectations may be considered a proxy for unexpected inflation. The classic case of unexpected inflation in recent history was the great recession of 2007–2008, when commodity prices crashed and then unexpectedly skyrocketed, as did overall inflation. Some frontier markets, such as Pakistan, experienced inflation as high as 30 percent; consequently the Pakistani currency declined in value by about same percentage.

The storable commodities are precious metals, industrial metals and energy. Their prices rise and fall with unexpected inflation. Nonstorable commodities such as agricultural products (wheat, livestock, corn) are negatively correlated with unexpected inflation and the business cycle. Both storable and nonstorable commodities have significant weight in the consumer price index. But it is the storable commodities, such as metal and energy, that are truly a hedge against the surprise of unexpected inflation. There is strong comovement between storable commodities and unexpected inflation. From 1990 to 2004, the correlation coefficient or comovement among various Goldman-Sachs commodity indices such as GSCI, GSCI Agriculture, GSCI Energy and unexpected inflation were 0.44, −0.27, and 0.46, respectively.[1,2] Agricultural commodities cannot be stored, and they tend to have negative correlation with unexpected inflation. Energy commodities can be stored; oil and gas indices are positively correlated with unexpected inflation.

Because of storable commodities' correlations with inflation in general, they can be of use in a risk management strategy, both for individuals and firms. Individuals can invest a fraction of their wealth in gold, silver, or other precious metals. Businesses should consider commodities for diversification with respect to more traditional holdings of bonds and stocks.

Credit Risk

Credit risk is the risk of default by a counter-party, or by a debtor's failure to make a promised payment.

Credit spreads are indicators of default risk. Credit spreads are the difference between the interest rates for a private security such as a corporate bond compared to the interest rate on a relatively default free government bond. Higher oil prices in world markets may lead to a recession that in turn increases credit spreads, as lenders worry that borrowers may have more trouble repaying loans. But this is not uniformly the case. Suppose company A lends to an oil company O. Rising oil price increase the oil company's revenues, which makes it easier for O to repay the loan, despite higher credit spreads in the market. Company O is thus negatively correlated with higher credit risk.

To safeguard against credit risk counterparty limits are the first line of defense. Counterparty limits specify credit limits for each counterparty based on their credit rating.[3] Credit risk can also be monitored by reviewing financial statements, credit scores and market information about borrowers.

Liquidity Risk

Liquidity risk is when a financial instrument or investment can't be sold—i.e., liquidated—at a price agreeable to both buyer and seller. It results in fewer transactions. Illiquidity makes it hard to determine fair market value. The size of the bid–ask spread as a proportion of the ask price is frequently used as an indicator of liquidity risk. For many "over-the-counter" instruments (or "OTC" instruments, which are privately negotiated) a more explicit transaction volume and price (bid-ask spread) is harder to find, so it is hard to get an indicator of liquidity risk. Valuation models rarely incorporate the liquidity risk in their estimates of fair value.

Liquidity risk can be serious, because even after mitigating market or credit risk, liquidity risk remains. Long Term Capital Management, a hedge fund that lost $4.6 billion in 1998, failed primarily due to liquidity risk because it was unable to liquidate its long and short positions at a suitable price. (Ironically, two of the directors of the fund were Myron Scholes and Robert Merton, who had shared the 1997 memorial Prize in Economic Sciences for their research on determining the value of derivatives.) The value in the accounting books may not accurately reflect the value at which the actual transaction takes place—or even whether it will take place. Liquidity risk is particularly important in stressed business conditions.

Market Risk

Market risk is the risk of a loss in asset values resulting from adverse movements in interest rates and stock market prices. Assessing market risk involves assigning the probability of adverse market movements, their duration and volatility, and the magnitude of the potential loss (consequences).

Value at Risk (or VaR) is a commonly used tool for quantifying market risk. The use of VaR itself generates risk, because it treats historical frequencies as probability and erroneously assumes the data generating process to be normally distributed with constant mean and variance. Markets do not have a constant mean and variance except over very short periods. The VaR is a useful tool, but it should be carefully adopted and interpreted owing to its underlying simplistic assumptions.[4]

Another market risk management technique is to stress-test the asset values. This involves stress scenarios that could lead to unexpectedly high losses for the assets thanks to large unexpected movements in a key variable, such as commodity prices, exchange rates, yield curves, or some combination thereof. Although these events are usually hypothetical or have a very small probability of occurring, they have the power to unleash extreme financial destruction. In these scenarios, liquidity risk multiplies and further erodes assets values.

Financial Risk Mitigation Strategies

Financial risk management is not necessarily about eliminating risk altogether. A large part of it is about efficient allocation of risk across different lines of business. Although risk allocation is a valid approach for managing financial risk, it may not be applied as a generalized approach suitable for every form of business risk such as health and safety risk for workers. One does not allocate the risk of being injured or killed: One either reduces or eliminates it. There are hedging strategies for allocating risk, as well as nonhedging strategies for reducing or eliminating it. (Chapter 9 covered one of these, the portfolio approach to enterprise risk management.)

Behavioral Biases that Create Financial Risk

One of the most important strategies for managing financial risk is to be aware of behavioral biases that cause people to make poor decisions that increase their financial risks. Many highly learned and educated people assume away certain risks in their personal or business financial planning. A leading Canadian economist I know was nearing his retirement. He invested most of his retirement assets in banking stocks. He defended his concentrated position by arguing that he knew this industry very well. In his view, heavily regulated Canadian banks—which survived the global financial crisis in better shape than most countries' banks—carried less financial risk than other sectors. The learned economist, like many other ordinary investors, was susceptible to cognitive and emotional biases such as familiarity and overconfidence. There is always a chance that the financial sector might underperform over his horizon of investment. This could entail even greater uncertainty toward the terminal years of his investment horizon, twenty-five to thirty years down the road. Behavioral biases such as these can potentially create substantial financial risks in personal and business planning.

The traditional theory of finance and economics conveniently assumes the perfect rationality of people in complex decision-making. But people are not, of course, perfectly rational. With piles of information and uncertainty about future outcomes, individuals don't synthesize information perfectly rationally, nor do they devise perfect rules for optimal decision-making. Their decisions are based on the limits of their rationality and their inherent biases. They incorporate these behavioral biases while assessing financial risk. Hence perception of risk varies across individuals.

There are two main categories of behavioral biases or errors: cognitive and emotional. Cognitive errors may occur due to either faulty reasoning or lack of understanding in relevant information processing. They can be moderated by education and better advice. Emotional biases originate from the subjective feeling, intuition or impulses. It is said that greed or fear drives markets. The cognitive or emotional errors are at the heart of these overreacting exuberant forces. Perhaps that's why Warren Buffet said: "You want to be greedy when others are fearful. You want to be fearful when others are greedy."[5] It may also help explain why markets remain overvalued or undervalued for the extended periods of time—for example, in an overvalued housing market.

Cognitive Errors

There are two types of cognitive errors, belief perseverance and information processing bias. In belief perseverance bias, people tend to stick to the status quo. They simply don't process new information. It's hard for them to change from their earlier stated position. For example, if a manager has arrived at a particular conclusion about a company she plans to acquire, she does not revise it when she acquires new information, or she chooses only that part of the information that confirms her conclusion and the beliefs that led her to it. Cognitive errors become harder to correct if they comingle with emotional biases and self-esteem. People may defend a stated opinion to preserve their self-esteem.

Information processing biases occur when people process information irrational or illogically. Examples of these biases are anchoring on a previous stated value and then adjusting according to simple heuristics (as described in Chapter 1). Mental accounting[6] is another type of cognitive bias whereby people tend to view different assets in different accounts as watertight compartments having no relation to each other. In contrast, modern portfolio theory thrives on the concept of asset price comovement. (See Chapter 9 for more on the portfolio approach to risk management.) The portfolio approach to enterprise risk management (ERM) is a method to correct such behavior. For example, in some companies, credit and market risks are considered separate risks. There could be separate persons assigned in an organization to monitor these risks. In stressed conditions, both these risks reinforce each other and thus could result in higher financial risks to the enterprise. During economic pessimism, stocks lose their value and credit spreads increase. Not identifying this additional risk of comovement, particularly in a stressed environment, is an example of cognitive bias.

People may become captive to a particular frame of reference, making different decisions in the same situation depending on how a problem or issue is framed. This is known as framing bias.[7] If their frame of reference is too narrow, they can't account for other available and useful information. For example, focusing solely on short-term market price movement without keeping the long-term trend in perspective is called a narrow frame. Someone having a narrow frame overlooks the broader picture and takes risks without taking into account all the relevant factors. Narrow frames lead to mispricing of risk by overemphasizing the short-term market movements without any reference to the long-term trend or the fundamental value of an investment. Commonly used frames of reference, such as a few weeks or years or a 10-year high or low, tend to make us think that data generating processes are stationary over these time periods. Financial markets are nonstationary, and we can avoid this bias by simply looking at fairly long-term trends.

Emotional Biases

Emotional biases include loss aversion, overconfidence, regret aversion, and endowment, which interact with decision making. They are harder to correct than cognitive biases, but having knowledge of them is a first step toward better decision making. We all make decisions based on emotional biases and personal preferences, such as buying a car based more on the shape, style, and color rather than the engine and safety and other mechanical features. The same coffee seems tastier in an expensive and stylish cup then in a cheap cup. But it is the coffee, not the cup, that should matter.

Some emotional biases, such as loss aversion or overconfidence, can lead to more risk taking than someone's risk appetite would otherwise suggest. The gambler who just lost a game may tend to keep gambling to cover his losses, and winning gamblers tend to believe that they will win consistently. Both carry on with more risk taking.

The "endowment effect"[8] is another interesting bias whereby people attach more value to assets they already hold than to equivalent or better ones they could acquire. They undervalue opportunity costs. My friend values his car more than mine although both cars are almost the same in their specification and make. Endowment bias is the difference between the price a person is willing to pay for an asset and the price at which that person is willing to sell the same asset. Familiarity with one's own endowment adds to the perceived value of the asset in the owner's eye. It also happens in the case of inheritance assets. Similarly, a research analyst may value his own quantitative model more than the model of his colleague. Business managers and owners should be cognizant of this bias and objectively analyze the performance of their operations lest they cling to their loss-making businesses longer than they should.

Unhedged Strategies

Risk management is in reality good corporate governance. It is a continuous process subject to evaluation and revision. Financial risk management revolves around following four broad principles:

1. Return versus risk
2. Diversification
3. Discipline
4. Checks and balances

Return should be understood in terms of risk. That's why concepts such as sharp ratio or, more simply, risk-adjusted returns are taken into account to compare different investment results. Sharp ratio is the excess return over risk free rate per unit of risk. The unit of risk is defined in terms of average mean deviation of return, more commonly called the standard deviation. Investment A, having lower 5 percent excess return and 8 percent standard deviation, is better than the one having higher excess return of 7 percent with 15 percent standard deviation. The Sharp ratio of A is 0.63 compared to 0.46 for Investment B.

Diversification is at the heart of contemporary finance and risk management. It is simply putting eggs in different investment baskets that have low comovements among themselves. A disciplined approach incorporating appropriate checks and balances ensures fairness and avoidance of conflict of interests.

The risk management process of the typical treasury of an investment firm embodies these principles. The corporate risk management function determines risk limits. There are usually three offices: front, middle, and back. The front office trades while back office settles trades. The middle office is responsible for overall monitoring of various risks and internal controls emanating from the trades of front office and the settlement operations of the back office. The back and middle offices are fully independent of the front office. They monitor the trading activity of the front office to ensure a smooth and collusion free environment. Breaches of the various risk limits are reported directly to upper management. Defining, devising, and monitoring these risk limits encompasses the assessment and mitigation of risk.

Hedging

Risk management should never be considered an exercise to eliminate financial risk altogether. We cannot eliminate some risks in business, but we can manage and mitigate them through hedging. Hedging means to protect against potential losses by simultaneously holding an asset, or a liability position, or a commitment that cancels the effect of adverse price movement of the initial asset. Perhaps the simplest hedge to understand is insurance (covered in Chapter 11). If you are unfortunate enough as to have your house burn down, your insurance covers the cost of rebuilding it and also pays for your temporary living expenses. An active currency position can be hedged by selling an equal amount of the same currency in the futures market. This can be easily done by buying or selling forwards or future instruments of the same currency. Futures and forwards are the financial instruments that make commitments to buy or sell the underlying commodity, such as currency in our example, at an agreed future date at a contracted price.

I will illustrate this with a simple example of hedging currency risk. Let's say Mary lives in the United States. She has 10,000 euros in cash receipts due at the end of next three months. Presently the exchange rate is 1 EUR = 1.25 USD. If the exchange rate between the euro and the U.S. dollar remains the same, by the end of third month, Mary may convert 10,000 EUR to 12,500 USD. However, Mary expects the euro to depreciate in exactly three months to 1 EUR = 1.10 USD. This means that Mary will only be able to get 11,000 USD at the end of three months and would have to bear the loss of 1,500 USD at that time. To avoid this loss, Mary decides to hedge her currency risk. A hedge could involve selling the future receipts of 10,000 euros now with the help of a three-month euro future or forward contract. The monetary transaction will be settled at the end of three months, but a commitment to sell those is made as of today. Thus Mary sells 10,000 EUR in futures through a currency forward agreement with a local bank at the 3 month forward exchange rate of 1 EUR = 1.20 USD to be settled at the end of three month. Mary thus ensures the amount of 12,000 USD and manages to reduce the probable loss to 500 USD. This is called a fully hedged position, because Mary hedged the full amount of 10,000 EUR. The 500 USD is the cost of that hedged (certain) outcome for Mary. In this fully hedged position, she will get 12,000 USD despite variation up or down in the exchange rate.

Full hedging may not always be the desirable strategy. Its cost is the foregone upside potential in addition to other administrative costs. If, in the above example, the euro appreciates instead to 1 EUR = 1.30 USD, then for Mary the upside potential of getting extra 500 USD is foregone. It is prudent to fully hedge sometimes, yet not prudent at all times. If Mary hedges 5,000 euros instead of the full amount, the hedging cost for her lowers to 250 USD. If now the euro appreciates afterward, she gains 250 USD on the remaining unhedged 5,000 euros. That exactly covers her cost of hedging. This is called the partial hedging.

In another situation, if Mary is very certain that the euro will appreciate in the next three months, then she does not need to either fully or partially hedge. Hedging is like carrying an umbrella in the rain. If the forecast is for sunny weather, she does not need an umbrella at all.

Similarly, firms can hedge depending on their ability and willingness to take risks and their future expectations about exchange rate movement. A risk manager has to trade off between the costs and benefits of hedging. Purchasing power parity suggests that currencies "mean revert" to their fair value in the long run—i.e., they adjust to their true underlying value. Hence fully hedging currency risk does not add value in the long run. This long run, however, could span more than a decade. But the time horizon of business managers is frequently less than a year. And they are highly risk-averse to the volatility in foreign exchange rate movements. They are more likely to fully hedge most of the time.

Hedging may also be done by selling or buying assets of different types that have same or opposite comovement with the original asset price. This is called cross-hedging. For example, suppose Mary can sell 12,000 Swiss francs (CHF) in forwards, and the 3 month forward exchange rate (as of today) is 1 EUR = 1.2 CHF. Until recently, the euro and Swiss franc enjoyed almost perfect positive correlation with each other owing to the Swiss central bank's artificial peg with the euro. For the purposes of this example, I assume that this positive comovement still exists. Mary may decide to sell the Swiss francs against USD (instead of the euro) at the available rate of 1 USD = 1 CHF to cross-hedge her currency risk against euro depreciation. Suppose now that both the euro and the Swiss franc depreciate against the U.S. dollar just after the transaction. If Mary loses because of depreciation of the euro, she avoids loss because of her earlier sale of Swiss francs at the past higher price. In this way, she is fully hedged. Mental accounting may cause managers to ignore this vital comovement between two different currencies.

One can hedge risk in one's daily life as well. Sometimes there are natural cross-hedges available and at other times we can find them with a bit of work. The depreciation of the Canadian dollar when oil prices dropped in 2014–2015 provided Canadians with lower gas prices for their cars and lower consumer prices that offset, to some extent, the higher prices of imported products due to depreciation.

You should bear in mind that hedging may inadvertently introduce additional risks, such as credit risk. For example, Mr. Smith is concerned about the mortgage payments on his house in the event of an increase in interest rates (i.e., the interest rate risk). His mortgage payments are based on a variable interest rate that is reset[9] every six months on the basis of changes in the benchmark rates, such as the prime rate of banks. Because he has a floating rate liability (i.e., the variable mortgage payment), he needs to hedge his liability by owning a floating rate income-generating asset that could match and pay his payments. Assume that Smith can borrow at a fixed rate and invest the proceeds in a floating rate corporate bond that pays a floating rate interest. The interest income from floating rate corporate bond may be matched with variable mortgage payments, and he, by design, manages to convert his initial floating rate liability to a fixed rate loan payment. Another option is that he may rent a basement or a room in his home to generate rental income that could also partially or fully pay his mortgage. This whole scheme of things falls apart for Smith if either the issuer company of the corporate bond defaults or his tenant fails to pay regularly.

This is a simplified example of an interest rate swap, which companies use to hedge interest rate risk. In general, a swap is a private contract between two contracting parties wherein one swaps the return of a position for a return commitment from another party. The swaps, as in the example of Mr. Smith, may also give rise to credit risk if the counterparty defaults. Thus a holistic approach should be adopted while developing the overall hedging strategy. Our risk management strategy is as good as our understanding of the risk and its associated hedging process.

Notes

1. CISDM Research Department, "The Benefits of Commodity Investment 2005 Update," Centre for International Securities and Derivatives Markets. June 2005, 15–17.
2. A positive number indicates positive comovement: When one goes up, so does the other. A negative number indicates negative comovement: When one goes up, the other goes down, and vice versa. Zero means no comovement. The highest possible value is 1 and the lowest possible value − 1.
3. Credit ratings are usually lagged. Forward-looking expectations about emerging risks demand that risk managers be proactive.

4. For more detail on the problems with value at risk, see Green, Philip, and George Gabor, *misLeading Indicators: How to Reliably Measure Your Business* (Santa Barbara, CA: Praeger, 2012), ch. 11: "Misleading Ourselves with Measurements of Risk."

5. Interview with Charlie Rose, PBS (October 1, 2008).

6. Michael Thaler, "Mental Accounting and Consumer Choice," *Marketing Science* 27, no 1 (Jan–Feb 2008): 15–25.

7. A. D. Kahneman Tversky, "The Framing of Decisions and the Psychology of Choice," *Science* 30 (January 1981): 453–458. doi:10.1126/science.7455683.

8. Richard Thaler, "Toward a Positive Theory of Consumer Choice," Journal *of Economic Behavior and Organization* 1 (1980): 39–60.

9. Fixed rates for so called fixed-rate mortgages of longer than a year are reset at their respective maturity. Fixed-rate mortgages may also be viewed as variable mortgages over a longer time horizon with the forgone benefit of a decline in short-term interest rate.

12

The Role of Insurance in Enterprise Risk Management

Greg Niehaus

The purchase of insurance is just one method of treating or modifying risk, but it is a very important method. For example, in 2012, U.S. businesses purchased more than $126 billion of commercial insurance.[1] This chapter will examine the role of insurance in business risk management, primarily from a shareholder value maximization perspective. That is, most of the discussion assumes that the objective of risk management is to increase the value of the company to its owners. Consequently, risk is defined as the effect of uncertainty on value. This approach requires a brief discussion of the determinants of value and how value is affected by uncertainty, which is presented in the next section.

After the section on the determinants of value is a brief discussion of the supply of insurance—i.e., the factors that affect insurers' willingness to provide coverage and the factors that affect the price of coverage. Understanding insurance from the supplier's perspective can help businesses make better insurance coverage decisions.

The chapter then examines factors that influence the demand for insurance coverage by publicly-held companies. Modern finance theory suggests that publicly traded corporations should focus on whether having insurance would positively affect the firm's expected cash flows. This, in turn, largely depends on whether not having insurance would significantly increase the likelihood of financial distress or prevent the firm from having the funds needed for future investment. Other factors that should also be considered are whether the insurer provides valuable claim processing and loss control services, whether insurance is required by regulation, and whether having insurance is demanded by other contractual parties.

All else equal, closely held companies are likely to demand more insurance coverage than publicly held companies, because the owners are less likely to hold diversified portfolios. The lack of diversification is likely to lead to a lower risk tolerance and/or risk appetite. Similarly, managers of companies are less likely to be diversified than the owners of publicly held companies. Consequently, to the extent that managers act in their own interests as opposed to owners' interests, managers could demand more insurance coverage than would be optimal for shareholders.

Table 12–1   Illustration of the Discounted Cash Flow (DCF) Model

Row	Year	0	1	2	3	4	5
1	Expected Cash Flow		$1,000	$1,000	$2,000	$2,000	$2,000
2	Present Value of each Expected Cash Flow*		$909	$826	$1,503	$1,366	$1,242
3	Value of Firm	$5,846					

*Each cash flow is discounted using a 10% discount rate.

Risk and Value

Determinants of Value

A widely used, yet simple model that provides insights about the determinants of value is the discounted cash flow (DCF) model.[2] This model implies that firm value equals the <u>present value</u> of the <u>expected net cash flows</u> generated by the firm over the life of the firm. That is, the value a firm today is equal to the sum of the cash flows expected to be generated by the firm each year, where each future year's expected cash flow is increasingly discounted the farther into the future it occurs. Table 12–1 provides a simple example for a firm that is expected to generate cash flows for five years. The numbers in row 1 are the cash flows that the firm is expected to generate each year. The second row gives the discounted value of each of the individual cash flows using an assumed (somewhat arbitrarily) discount rate of 10 percent. The third row gives the sum of these discounted cash flows, the value of the firm according to the DCF model.

For readers who wish to understand how discounted cash flow is calculated, the following formula will be useful:

In general, the DCF model implies that the value of the firm today, V_0, is equal to

$$V_0 = \frac{E(CF_1)}{(1+r)^1} + \frac{E(CF_2)}{(1+r)^2} + \frac{E(CF_3)}{(1+r)^3} + \cdots$$

where $E(CF_t)$ is the expected value (as of time 0) of the net cash flow generated in year t and r is the discount rate (cost of capital).

The DCF model highlights that firm value is largely determined by the net cash flows that are expected to be generated throughout the firm's life and the appropriate discount rate. If new information is revealed that a firm's cash flows in the future are expected to be higher than originally expected, then firm value would increase. In a well-functioning capital market, new information that the firm is expected to have higher (lower) future cash flows will lead to a higher (lower) stock price today.

It is important to highlight that the cash flows in the future are uncertain. Nobody really knows what the cash flow will be in two years. It is useful to think about each of the cash flows in the future as having a probability distribution that describes the possible outcomes for each

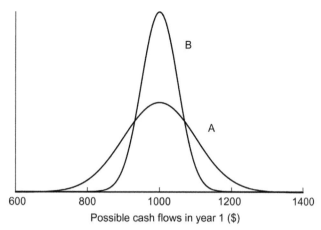

FIGURE 12–1 Examples of probability distributions for future cash flows.

year's cash flow and the likelihood of each of these values occurring. According to the DCF model, the expected value of the cash flow distribution is discounted back to the present. For example, suppose that the cash flows in year 1 have a bell-shaped probability distribution like either one of the two distributions depicted in Figure 12-1. Then, according to DCF model, the number for year 1 that gets discounted would be $1,000, the expected value of the distribution. Of course, the actual cash flows in year 1 could be higher or lower than $1,000.

The two probability distributions in Figure 12-1 have the same expected value ($1,000), but the actual cash flow is more likely to be close to $1,000 with the distribution labeled B than with the distribution labeled A. Using the language of probability theory, the cash flow distribution labeled A has a higher standard deviation than the one labeled B. Using nontechnical language, the cash flows for A are more uncertain than those for B.

It is important to highlight that regardless of whether the firm had probability distribution A or B, the DCF model implies that $1,000 is the expected cash flow and thus, regardless of whether the firm had probability distribution A or B, the value that would be discounted back to the present would be $1,000. The greater uncertainty about cash flows for A would be captured by the discount rate in the denominator of the DCF model (the r), to which we now turn.

The appropriate discount rate (often called the cost of capital) is the rate of return that reflects the time value of money and the uncertainty of the cash flows. The time value of money is the return required by investors to invest in risk-free securities (U.S. government bonds). The additional return to compensate investors for the uncertainty in cash flows is called the risk premium. Thus, appropriate discount rate can be expressed as follows:

$$r = (\text{risk}-\text{free return}) + (\text{risk premium})$$

Intuitively, the greater the uncertainty in the cash flows, the greater the risk premium. The appropriate method for calculating the risk premium is one of the fundamental issues in financial economics and has been the subject of thousands of research papers. A brief summary of one of the most widely used approaches is discussed below.

At this stage, it is useful to illustrate the DCF model using another simple example; this one will be carried through the subsequent discussions. Assume that the firm only exists for one year and that the firm is subject to only one source of uncertainty—whether it has a property loss. The firm's cash flow in year 1 is equal to $1,000 if the firm does not have a property loss, and the cash flow in year 1 is equal to $600 if the firm has a property loss. In other words, the property loss, if it occurs, reduces cash flow by $400. Finally, assume that the probability of a property loss equals 0.1. With these assumptions, the expected cash flow in year 1 is equal to

$$E(CF_1) = 0.9\,(\$1{,}000) + 0.1\,(\$600) = \$960$$

To calculate the value of the firm today (time 0), we need to specify the appropriate discount rate. Assume that one-year government bonds are earning 2 percent and that the risk premium demanded by investors for the uncertainty associated with the cash flows at time 1 (whether cash flows will be $1,000 or $600) is equal to 3 percent. Then the appropriate discount rate is 5 percent, and the value of the firm at time 0 is equal to

$$V_0 = \$960/(1.05) = \$914.29$$

At the end of the year, the firm will be worth either $1,000 or $600, depending on whether the property loss occurs.

Before proceeding, it is useful to consider what would be the value of a firm that generates cash flow in year 1 equal to $960 with certainty. Investors would not require a risk premium in this case, for there is no uncertainty about the cash flows. Consequently, the value of the risk-free firm at time 0 is equal to

$$V_0 = \$960/1.02 = \$941.18$$

At the end of the year, the firm will be worth $960.

How Risk Affects Value

Recall from Chapter 1 that there are a variety of ways that people think about risk. Sometimes people use the term risk to mean the likelihood of a bad outcome or the magnitude of a bad outcome. In the example above, if the probability of a property loss increased from 0.1 to 0.2, then one might say that the firm's property risk has increased. In this case, the expected cash flow of the firm at time 1 would be $920 ($0.8 \times \$1{,}000 + 0.2 \times \$600$), which, holding everything else constant, would decrease the value of the firm. Similarly, if the magnitude of the property loss increased to $500, then one might say that the firm's property risk has increased. In this case, expected cash flow would be $950 ($0.9 \times \$1{,}000 + 0.1 \times \$500$), which, holding everything else constant, would decrease the value of the firm. Thus an increase in risk, where risk means either the likelihood of a bad outcome or the magnitude of a bad outcome, decreases value because the increase in risk decreases the expected cash flows (the numerators in the DCF model).

Another notion of risk discussed in Chapter 1 is the uncertainty, unpredictability, or variability of the outcome. We say that one situation is riskier than another if it is more uncertain— i.e., less predictable. This notion of risk also affects value, but it does so through the discount rate in the DCF model. That is, greater uncertainty in the cash flows (compare curves A and B in Figure 12-1) suggests that investors will demand a higher risk premium, which would increase the discount rate (cost of capital) and lead to a lower value for the firm.[3]

We now have the conceptual framework to consider how the purchase of insurance can affect the value of a firm. The DCF model implies that insurance can increase the value of the firm in one of two ways: (1) by increasing the expected cash flows or (2) by decreasing the risk premium. Perhaps surprisingly, we will end up concluding that for publicly traded companies, the former channel is most important. First, however, we must consider the supply of insurance.

The Supply of Insurance

Insurance Pricing in a Competitive Market[4]

As a benchmark, it makes sense to start by assuming that insurers operate in a perfectly competitive marketplace. Basic economic theory implies that the price of a product or service in a perfectly competitive market equals the cost of providing the product or service. Thus, in a competitive insurance market, the price of insurance should equal the cost of supplying the insurance. There are four factors that determine an insurer's costs:

1. Expected claim costs
2. Time value of money
3. Capital costs
4. Administrative costs

We will consider each one in isolation and then put them together at the end of the discussion.

Expected Claim Costs. Insurers need to charge enough in premiums to cover what they expect to pay in claims. In the example above in which the firm had 0.1 probability of incurring a property loss of $400, the expected loss would be $40 ($0.1 \times \$400$). Thus the premium for a policy that provides full insurance (coverage equals the entire loss) would need to cover the expected claim cost of $40.

The important implication is that any change in the environment that increases the probability of an insured loss or the magnitude of an insured loss would increase expected claim costs and thus increase the insurance premium in a competitive market.

Time Value of Money. In the previous example, let's assume (realistically) that the premiums are paid up front—say, at the beginning of the year—and that claim costs are not paid until the end of the year. Of course, when the insurer receives premiums before the payment of claim costs, the insurer can invest the premium payments and receive interest. Thus in a competitive market, the premium would be reduced relative to the expected claim costs because of the interest that can be earned on the premiums.

The easiest way of incorporating this effect is to find the present value of the expected claim costs. Continuing to assume a risk-free rate of 2 percent, the present value of the expected claim costs would be $40 \div 1.02 = \$39.22$. In other words, the insurer would need to receive a premium of $39.22 at the beginning of the year so that when it is invested for the year at a 2 percent return, it will grow to $40 at the end of the year.

The important implication is that an increase (decrease) in interest rates will lower (raise) insurance premiums in a competitive market.

Capital Costs. To make their promise to pay claims credible, insurers need to hold capital— i.e., insurers need to have assets in excess of what they expect to pay policyholders. These extra assets or capital act as a cushion in case claim costs turn out higher than expected.[5] Certainly, insurers sell a great many policies and diversify geographically and diversify across types of coverage to make their claim costs more predictable. Nevertheless, they cannot eliminate all uncertainty in claim costs because of correlation in claim costs across policyholders and the possibility of extremely large claim costs from some types of business. Thus insurers need to have a cushion (have capital) in case claim costs are high. The problem from the insurer's perspective is that holding capital is costly (the people who contribute the capital want a return on it), so the premium charged to policyholders must include an amount to cover the cost of holding capital.[6]

The important implication is that any factor that makes claim costs to be less predictable for an insurer will require the insurer to hold more capital and will thus increase premiums.

Administrative Costs. Of course, an insurer has marketing, underwriting, claims processing, and management costs. The premium that an insurer charges must cover these administrative costs. For property and liability insurance, the administrative costs can be 30 percent to 50 percent of the premium, depending on the type of insurance.

Putting it all together, insurers must charge premiums that are sufficient to cover the present value of their expected claim costs, capital costs, and administrative costs. A premium that just covers these costs is often called the fair premium. If an insurer has market power, perhaps because of some expertise in a particular market, then the insurer might be able to charge an additional amount above the fair premium.

Factors Limiting the Availability of Insurance

One implication of the previous section is that if an insurer cannot charge a premium that covers the present value of its claim costs, capital costs, and administrative costs, then it will not voluntarily offer such coverage. Thus regulation that restricts the ability of insurers to charge at least the fair premium will cause coverage to be withdrawn from the marketplace. This has occurred, for example, for workers compensation insurance and property insurance in some U.S. states.

Other factors that limit the availability of coverage include moral hazard and adverse selection. Moral hazard refers to the effect that insurance has on the incentives of the insured to reduce expected claim costs—i.e., incentives to mitigate risk. Moral hazard problems tend to be more severe when the insured has a significant influence on the probability of a loss occurring or the size of the loss and when the insured's behavior is costly to observe. The natural solution to moral hazard problems is to reduce the amount of insurance. Consequently, most insurance policies do not offer full coverage; instead, policies have deductibles, coinsurance, limits, and exclusions.

Adverse selection refers to situations in which potential policyholders have different expected losses and the insurer finds it costly to distinguish policyholders who have different expected losses. In this situation, if the insurer charges every potential policyholder the same price, then the customers with high (low) expected losses will tend to purchase more (less) insurance coverage, because the insurance coverage will be perceived to be priced too low (high). In the extreme, the market could "unravel," with only the highest expected loss customers purchasing insurance. Even when the market does not unravel, the low expected loss customers will tend to purchase less coverage—i.e., adverse selection leads to less than full coverage.

Demand for Insurance by Public Companies

Shareholder Diversification of Risk

We now consider the demand for insurance by publicly owned companies and assume that the shareholders of these companies hold well-diversified portfolios. This implies that the owners of the company have diversified away some of the risks that a corporation faces when viewed in isolation. It is important to recognize that the notion of risk we are talking about when we discuss diversification of risk is the unpredictability or variability notion of risk, not the expected loss notion of risk.

The risks that the shareholders can diversify away are the risks arising from factors or events specific to the firm (sometimes called idiosyncratic risks). For example, the risk associated with property damage tends to be firm-specific. That is, one firm's property damage is not typically related to another firm's property damage provided the facilities of the two are not geographically close. Consequently, when holding a portfolio of stocks, the risk associated with property damage across all of the firms in the portfolio will "average out." If one firm has a higher than expected loss, other firms will have lower than expected losses. So, on average, the portfolio has losses that are close to what was expected, and the risk (variability in stock returns) attendant on property damage has been greatly reduced.

However, not all risks can be diversified away. The risk that cannot be diversified away is called the systematic risk of the corporation. Systematic risk is the risk arising from market-wide factors, not firm-specific or idiosyncratic factors. For example, whether the economy is in a recession or an expansion is likely to influence most companies is the same direction at the same time. Consequently, holding a portfolio of stocks does not allow an investor to diversify away the risk (the variability in returns) associated with general economic activity.

Commercial Insurance Reduces Firm-Specific Risk

Commercial insurance typically covers events that are firm-specific. Examples include worker's compensation costs, property damage, liability claims, and earnings lost to business interruption. Thus commercial insurance covers the same type of risk that shareholders can diversify on their own—i.e., firm-specific risk or idiosyncratic risk. Thus the purchase of insurance by public companies with diversified shareholders duplicates what the shareholders accomplish on their own by holding diversified portfolios. We now relate this discussion to the valuation framework presented earlier.

Impact of Systematic and Firm-Specific Risk on Value

Recall that the basic valuation model implies that value equals the discounted expected net cash flows, where the discount rate is a risk-adjusted return. To illustrate, consider a simple model in which a firm is expected to generate cash flow one year in the future and nothing more:

$$\text{value today} = (\text{expected cash flow in year 1}) \div (1 + \text{risk-free rate} + \text{risk premium})$$

Earlier we said that the risk premium depends on the risk of the cash flows. Now we can be more specific: Finance theory implies that the risk premium depends on only the <u>systematic</u> risk of the cash flows. That is, investors demand a risk premium only for the risk that they cannot diversify on their own. Stated differently, investors only require compensation for systematic or marketwide risk. We will not venture down the path of how to measure systematic risk except to state that there are a variety of methods used in practice.

Look at the valuation formula above. What we just argued is that the risk premium in the denominator of the formula does not depend on the firm-specific risk of cash flows (because investors can get rid of that risk on their own). Earlier we made the observation that commercial insurance typically reduces firm-specific risk. Putting these two statements together, we can conclude that commercial insurance typically does not reduce the risk premium demanded by investors. Certainly, commercial insurance does not affect the risk-free rate, the rate of return on U.S. government bonds. Therefore, we must conclude that if commercial insurance is valuable to public corporations having diversified shareholders, then it must somehow increase the expected cash flows of the firm. The remainder of this section paper discuss the main effects of insurance on expected cash flows.

Effect of Insurance on Expected Cash Flows[7]

<u>What is the cost of insurance?</u> A common answer to this question is that the premium is the cost of insurance. Yes, the policyholder pays a premium to the insurer, but the policyholder also receives expected cash flows from the insurer. Assume initially that both the insurer and the policyholder have the same information about the probability distribution of insured losses. Using the example from earlier in the chapter, suppose that both parties believe that there is a 0.1 probability of the firm incurring a $400 property loss. Further assume, for simplicity, that the insurer is willing to offer full insurance. Then the premium for this policy must cover the present value of expected claim costs ($40), plus capital costs, which we will assume is $5, plus administrative costs, which we will assume equals $20. Also assume, for simplicity, that the discount rate is zero. Then the fair premium for this insurance equals $65. Suppose the insurer marks up the price and charges $68.

Now we can discuss the effect of purchasing the insurance on the corporation's expected cash flows. The corporation pays a premium of $68 and in return receives expected claim costs of $40. If this is all the corporation expects from the policy, then the cost of the insurance is $28. That is, the effect of the insurance on the corporation's expected cash flows is − $68 + $40 = −$28. This amount is typically called the <u>loading</u> on the policy—i.e., loading equals the difference between the premium paid and the expected claim costs.

In most situations, however, the corporation obtains claims processing services and often receives loss control services from the insurer when it purchases insurance. Thus, to assess the total effect on the firm's expected cash flow, one must consider the cost of obtaining these services elsewhere, either internally or through a third party. If the cost of obtaining these services elsewhere exceeds the loading on the policy, then the purchase of insurance increases expected cash flows and therefore increases firm value. Note that in this situation, the insurance is valuable because of the services provided by the insurer, not because of the risk reduction provided by insurance.[8]

It is important to highlight that we are not saying that insurance does not decrease risk. We are saying that insurance decreases the risk that can be diversified away by shareholders on their own and thus insurance does not decrease the risk premium demanded by shareholders. To be sure, insurance is decreasing the firm-specific risk. The remainder of this section explains how reducing firm-specific risk can indirectly increase expected cash flows and thereby increase value.

<u>Insurance Can Improve Contractual Terms with Other Parties</u>. Firms can become financially distressed and even go bankrupt as a result of firm-specific risk. Thus by reducing firm-specific risk, insurance can reduce the likelihood of financial distress. If insurance reduces the likelihood of financial distress, then the firm is likely to obtain better contractual terms with customers, suppliers, employees, and/or lenders. For example, most people would pay less for a car from a manufacturer having a high probability of financial distress than for the identical car from a manufacturer having a low probability of financial distress. Similarly, employees and suppliers will demand a premium to provide services to a firm that is close to financial distress. Thus one of the main reasons corporations purchase insurance is to improve the terms at which they contract with other parties by reducing the likelihood of financial distress. Indeed, often other parties will not even contract with a firm unless the firm shows proof of insurance. The important implication is that firms should purchase insurance for extreme losses that keep the firm from financial distress.

<u>Insurance Can Reduce the Cost of Financing New Investment</u>. The methods of financing new investment include issuing new equity, borrowing funds (issuing new debt), and using internally generated funds. Generally, using internally generated funds is a less costly source of financing than issuing new securities.[9] Consequently, a firm can increase its value if it can ensure that it almost always has the internal funds available to finance new investment. This is where insurance comes in. To ensure that internal funds are available for new investment and not used to pay losses from insurable events, a corporation can purchase insurance. This can reduce the cost of financing and reduces the likelihood that the firm would have to forego a good investment because the internal funds were not available. An implication is that firms

having valuable investment opportunities and high costs of external capital are more likely to find insurance to be value-enhancing.

Insurance Can Reduce Expected Tax Payments. When tax rates are progressive, firms have an incentive to reduce the variability in taxable income. This can be seen using a simple example. Suppose a firm has a choice of having very volatile taxable income (either $10 or $100 with equal probability of ½) or having taxable income with low volatility (either $50 or $60 with equal probability of ½). Notice that the expected taxable income is the same ($55) in both situations. Further assume that tax rates are as follow:

- 20% if taxable income is between $0 and $40
- 30% if taxable income is between $40 and $70
- 40% if taxable income is greater than $70

To simplify the calculations (without changing the implication), assume that these tax rates apply to the entire amount of taxable income (in reality, the 20% rate would apply to the first $40 of taxable income, etc.).

With the highly volatile taxable income, the after-tax income would be either $10(1 − 0.2) = $8 or $100(1 − 0.4) = $60, so on average the after-tax income would be $34 (½ × $8 + ½ × $60). With the low volatility option, the after-tax income would be either $50(1 − 0.3) = $35 or $60 (1 − 0.3) = $42, so on average the after-tax income would $38.50 (½ × $35 + ½ × $42). Expected after-tax income is higher with the less volatile income. This effect occurs regardless of the cause of the volatility in before-tax income; the volatility could arise from variability in sales revenue, variability in costs caused by variability in input prices, or variability in property or liability losses. The effect occurs because of the progressivity in tax rates. Thus any action that reduces volatility in before-tax income, such as insurance (or hedging), can increase expected after-tax income when firms are exposed to progressive tax rates.[10]

Demand for Insurance by Closely Held Companies

In addition to all of the reasons for purchasing insurance already discussed, if a firm has owners that are not well diversified, then there are strong reasons to purchase insurance to reduce risk for the undiversified owners. Thus, in addition to the reasons discussed above, some companies purchase insurance because the owners have risk that they have not diversified away, and this risk can be shifted to an insurance company at a reasonable cost.

Other Management Objectives and Risk Management

The discussion to this point has assumed that the managers of a firm are making decisions that are in the interests of the owners. Because of the costs of monitoring and incentivizing managers, situations can arise when managers act in their own interests as opposed to the owners' interests. More specifically, conflicts of interests can arise over risk management decisions. For example, managers who have a large part of their compensation in the form of stock options might have an incentive to take more risk (purchase less insurance) than shareholders would desire, because of the unlimited upside potential and limited downside potential of options. On the other hand, managers who are forced to hold large amounts of stock may be undiversified and therefore attempt to reduce more risk (purchase more insurance) than shareholders would desire.

Interaction between Mitigation and Insurance

Many of the chapters in this book focus on the mitigation (reduction in expected losses) of various types of risk. Thus it is useful to consider the effect that purchasing insurance has on incentives to mitigate risk. For this analysis, we will assume that risk mitigation decisions are made by comparing the cost of mitigation to the benefits of mitigation. Thus the issue to be examined is how insurance affects this cost–benefit tradeoff.

It is important to highlight that the benefits of mitigation are not just the direct financial benefits received by shareholders from reducing the frequency or severity of losses. There can be many indirect benefits of mitigation. For example, a lower loss frequency and/or a lower loss severity can reduce the firm's likelihood of financial distress and thus beneficially affect how the firm contracts with employees, customers, and suppliers. As another example, lower frequency of workplace violence could yield lower turnover and lower costs of attracting new employees. In addition, when a firm calculates the benefits of mitigation, it ideally would include the reduction in expected nonpecuniary losses suffered victims and the effects on people who do have a direct contractual arrangement with the firm, including future generations—who, for example, might enjoy the benefits of lower expected environmental losses.

As described earlier, insurance premiums must cover the expected insured losses. Thus, if mitigation efforts reduce expected losses and insurers adjust premiums to reflect the reduction in expected losses, then one of the direct financial benefits of risk mitigation is the reduction in insurance premiums. On the other hand, if insurers do not adjust premiums to reflect the reduction in expected losses, then the benefits of and thus the incentive to undertake risk mitigation is reduced. This does not imply that risk mitigation efforts should not be undertaken in this situation; it simply points out that one of the financial benefits of risk mitigation is lower than it would be if insurance premiums reflected the mitigation.[11]

In the remainder of the section, we will consider whether there are characteristics of risk exposures that tend to be "treated" with insurance by itself, mitigation by itself, both mitigation and insurance, or neither. In other words, can we identify characteristics of risk exposures that would allow us to place the risk exposure in one of the cells in the following 2×2 matrix?

	Do not mitigate	Mitigate
Do not insure		
Insure		

Earlier in this chapter, we discussed the characteristics of risk exposures that are costly to insure and therefore that tend to not be insured. These are risk exposures for which (1) the insurer needs to hold a substantial amount of costly capital to credibly insure because of correlation in losses across policyholders or because of the magnitude of the potential loss is so great or because there is insufficient information to estimate the loss distribution, (2) the insurer cannot readily distinguish which policyholders have higher expected losses compared to other policyholders (adverse selection), or (3) policyholders have a substantial influence on the outcome and the insurer cannot readily observe policyholders' mitigation efforts (moral hazard). Thus, exposures with these characteristics would tend to be in the first row (do not insure).

We also discussed risk exposures for which businesses would tend to have low demand for insurance. These are exposures threatening relatively small losses that do not threaten the viability of the organization or the ability of the organization to finance future investment. These exposures would also tend to be in the first row (do not insure).

Exposures that would tend to fall in the first column (do not mitigate) are those for which there is insufficient knowledge about the underlying cause of the losses or for which the technology to change the probability of a loss or the size of the loss does not exist or is too costly. An example might be the exposure to a meteorite strike on a firm's property. Of course, knowledge and technology are constantly improving; consequently, the set of exposures being mitigated is constantly expanding.

Many exposures, however, fall in the lower right-hand corner of the matrix (insure and mitigate), because the costs of supplying insurance is not prohibitive and there is demand for coverage, and because knowledge about the cause of losses and the technology to change the likelihood or severity losses exists. In many cases, insurers bundle their insurance coverage with mitigation advice.[12] In other cases, insurers partner with third parties to provide mitigation expertise along with insurance coverage.

Summary Questions to Ask

When deciding whether to purchase insurance, managers should ask themselves the following questions:

- Are your owners' investments diversified?
- Would the financial effect of an uninsured event push the firm close to or into financial distress?
- To what extent would the contractual terms with customers, suppliers, employees, and lenders be affected by an uninsured event?
- Would an uninsured event cause the firm to forego valuable investment opportunities?
- Does the insurer provide valuable claim processing and loss control services?
- Is insurance required by regulation?
- Are there tax reasons for purchasing insurance?

Notes

1. This total consists of $48 billion in workers compensation insurance, $53 billion in other liability, and $25 billion in commercial automobile insurance. Source: National Association of Insurance Commissioners, 2013, www.naic.org/documents/research_top_25_market_share_pc.pdf.
2. The material in this section is found in almost all introductory finance textbooks.

3. As will be discussed later, financial models generally imply that the appropriate risk premium is determined not by the total variability of cash flows. Instead, the discount rate is determined by the systematic risk of the cash flows. Systematic risk is the risk that cannot be diversified away by holding many securities. Intuitively, the risk that cannot be diversified away arises from economywide or macroeconomic factors, not by firm-specific nor idiosyncratic factors.

4. For an expanded version of the material in this section, see Chapter 8 in Harrington and Niehaus, *Risk Management and Insurance*, 2nd ed., Chicago, IL: McGraw-Hill, 2004.

5. This discussion is about economic capital, not capital calculated using statutory nor generally accepted accounting principles.

6. Participants in the commercial insurance market often talk about the underwriting cycle, which refers to periods of high prices and low availability of coverage (a hard market) followed by periods of low prices and readily available coverage (a soft market). One widely accepted explanation for the variation in insurance prices is that the capital of insurers gets depleted after large claim costs occur and that it is costly for insurers to replenish that capital quickly. Consequently, insurers cannot write as much business at a given price (supply shifts back), which causes prices to increase and coverage to decrease—i.e., we see a hard market. Soft markets occur after periods during which insurers have been profitable and have accumulated capital. The supply of coverage increases, so prices fall and quantity increases—i.e., we see a soft market. See S. Harrington, G. Niehaus, and T. Yu. "Insurance Price Volatility and Underwriting Cycles," 2014, in Georges Dionne, ed., *Handbook of Insurance*, 2nd Edition (New York: Springer, 2013).

7. For further discussion of the ideas in this section, see Mayers, D., and C. Smith, "On the Corporate Demand for Insurance, *Journal of Business*, 1982; K. Froot, D. Scharfstein, and J. Stein, "A Framework for Risk Management," *Harvard Business Review*, December 1994; and C. Smith Jr. and R. Stulz, The Determinants of Firms' Hedging Policies, *Journal of Financial and Quantitative Analysis*, 20, 1985: 391–405.

8. Note, however, that the bundling of insurance with services can be efficient, because the incentives to identify fraudulent claims and provide high-quality loss control services increases for the entity paying the costs of claims.

9. There are transaction costs of raising external capital (e.g., investment bankers' fees) as well as potential underpricing costs—i.e., selling new securities at a price below their fundamental value.

10. There are other ways that taxes interact with risk management that can be found in Chapter 21 of Harrington and Niehaus, *Risk Management and Insurance*, 2nd ed., Chicago, IL: McGraw-Hill, 2004. For evidence on the role of taxes in risk management, see Graham, J., and C. Smith, 1999, "Tax Incentives to Hedge," *Journal of Finance*, 54: 2241–2262.

11. Indeed, one of the primary arguments against regulation that forces insurers to charge companies (or individuals) the same premium even though they have different expected losses is that doing so reduces the incentive for the policyholder to mitigate risk. For example, charging all employers of a given size the same workers' compensation premium reduces the incentive to mitigate worker injuries.

12. An example is FM Global, which specializes in providing risk mitigation services along with insurance coverage.

Global and Strategic Risk

Risk Culture

Oliver Davidson, Patricia Mackenzie, Mike Wilkinson, and Ron Burke

The concept of risk culture is relatively new, but recent world events, such as the economic crisis and major industrial accidents such as the Deepwater Horizon oil incident, have brought a sharper focus of attention to the topic in the last decade. Research shows a marked increase in the use of the term risk culture in the past ten years, spiking as the financial crisis hit, as shown in Figure 13–1.

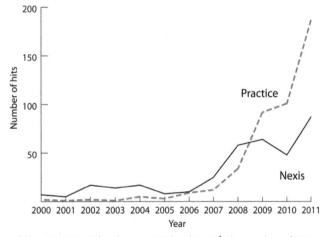

FIGURE 13–1 Summary of "hits" obtained for the term "risk culture."[1] The number of hits were determined from the research news media research tool Nexis and from site-specific searches of websites of firms, professional bodies, and agencies whose work is related to risk ("Practice").

Many commentators have identified issues with risk culture as a fundamental causal factor in such crises.

This chapter is intended as an introduction to the idea of risk culture. We begin by looking at how the concept can be understood in the context of organizational culture more generally, then explore it through several different lenses.

The concept of risk culture is applicable to any organization, but its embodiment will differ widely from one context to another. To provide insight into how the concept of risk culture has developed and can be practically applied, this chapter draws on examples in several different dimensions. First, taking a particular sector, we examine risk culture in the **financial services** *sector*, where the concept has received much attention in recent years. We then look at a particular type of risk culture—**safety culture**, in which the physical impact of cultural shortcomings can be devastating. From there we move on to look at approaches to understanding and **measuring risk culture** in practice, applying lessons learned from other disciplines. In looking at how to shape or manage risk culture, much attention has been given to the role of **reward, incentives, and performance management**, so we also describe some of the considerations, good practice, and limitations in this area.

But first: What is risk culture? There is no universally agreed-upon definition, and some definitions are much wider than others. One is provided by the Institute of Risk Management: "Risk culture is a term describing the values, beliefs, knowledge, attitudes and understanding about risk shared by a group of people with a common purpose, in particular the employees of an organization."[2]

Risk Culture and Organizational Culture

Originating in the 1960s and 1970s, the concept of organizational culture is now commonplace. Although models and concepts of organizational culture are many and varied and can be quite abstract and complex, most managers are familiar with the notion at some level. Of course, the risk culture of any organization is related to that organization's culture overall.

The nature of the relationship between organizational culture and risk culture is a matter of debate and perspective. Some people view risk culture as a subset of organizational culture; for others, it overlaps with, but also extends beyond the traditional boundaries of organizational culture. For yet others, risk culture is simply organizational culture viewed through a risk lens.

Although this chapter is intended as a guide to risk culture rather than to organizational culture more generally, several principles and ideas around organizational culture have an important bearing on risk culture. These are introduced here and are expanded on later in the chapter.

- **Culture Matters:** Culture really makes a difference. Although culture may be regarded as "soft," it plays a powerful role in determining behavior and organizational effectiveness. Many leaders and management commentators now regard organizational culture as the critical factor underpinning the behavior of people at work. This principle is vividly summarized by the statement that "culture eats strategy for breakfast," often attributed to management writer Peter Drucker,[3] as well as by business leader Warren Buffet, who said, "Culture, more than rule books, determines how an organization behaves."[4]
- **Much of Culture Lies beneath the Surface:** Some aspects of culture, such as the management reporting line, are quite visible and are readily apparent. Others, such as unwritten lore, informal relationships, and people's personal attitudes, are more hidden beneath the surface.
- **There Is No "Best" Culture:** Cultures vary between (and within) organizations—and they should. A company competing on the basis of its creativity will need a different culture to succeed from another competing on the basis of operational efficiency. As discussed

in Chapter 1, each organization has its own setting in terms of both its internal context (such as processes, structure and strategy) and its external context (such as its market, competition, regulation, and geography). Although some aspects of culture may generally be preferable to others, each organization thus needs to develop a culture that works well in its own unique situation. Throughout this chapter, we offer a range of frameworks and models of risk culture, indicating this necessary diversity.

- **Culture Can Be Articulated, Measured and Managed:** To some, the very notion of organizational culture seems ethereal and difficult to describe, let alone quantify or manage. However, well developed approaches provide effective ways to do just this.

Risk Culture in Financial Services

Since the global financial crisis of 2008, risk culture has gained importance in the financial sector. There is little doubt that an important contributor to the crisis was the prevalence of a culture that promoted the pursuit of short-term profits at the expense of long-term value generation, which was exacerbated by being entrenched into individuals' rewards. This view was supported by a survey[5] that found that most risk professionals believed the banking crisis was caused not so much by technical failures as by failures in organizational culture and ethics, with 85 percent citing remuneration practices as important or very important.

In recent years, firms have launched reviews of their operational and governance models to address weaknesses considered to have contributed to the increased and often unrecognized risk. These reviews address a wide range of areas, including product complexity, that made risks difficult to assess, as well as incentive schemes and oversight.

Furthermore, companies, advisors and regulators around the world have an increased focus on "risk culture." The Financial Stability Board (an international body monitoring and making recommendations about the global financial system) published a paper offering financial services regulators guidance on risk culture regarding their interaction with financial services institutions.[6] In the wake of the financial crisis, banks and insurers have been working to improve their risk governance structures and, by extension, their risk cultures.

A typical reaction has also been to appoint a chief risk officer (CRO) or to increase the CRO's seniority and status. For instance, in Towers Watson's 2012 Global Insurance ERM survey, 84 percent of respondents had or were planning to appoint a CRO or the equivalent, almost twice the number so reporting in the equivalent 2006 survey. The majority of CROs reported to or had ready access to the board.[7]

Embedding a consistent risk culture beyond the boardroom and into business units remains challenging. Although the board and the CRO have overall responsibility for ensuring that this happens, the direct responsibility for risk management and the risk culture lies with operational management. There may be a tendency to assume that because someone has "risk" in his or her title, he or she must take on all risk responsibility. In reality, although the CRO has overall accountability, risk is "everybody's business," and all employees must take responsibility for it. It is the role of senior management to set the tone and encourage and empower employees to behave in line with the desired risk culture. However, this is in part an issue of maturity, for culture change is a journey that takes time. For example, although risk professionals need to ensure that they use language and concepts appropriate for the wider organization—which is one of the principle aims of this book—there may also be a need to educate people in all roles to bring them up to a common standard of risk management ability, another aim of this book. (For further discussion of the importance and methods of risk training, see Chapter 2, on health and safety risk; Chapter 6, on cybersecurity; Chapter 7, on brand risk; and Chapter 8, on human capital risk). We have observed that in many cases, new governance and processes are put in place in response to recent events and external pressures, rather than taking a longer-term view to engender a culture of risk awareness balancing the downside risk with well-managed opportunities that could result in significant competitive advantages. This requires the board and the CROs as well as other risk specialists to clearly articulate a balanced, business-oriented view of risk as a basis for educating and advising the rest of the business. The communication and education program that results is critical to a successful risk culture and is typically a long-term program involving operational management as much as the risk team. (See Chapter 14 for the role of the board of directors in risk management in setting culture.)

Another consequence of the financial crisis has been that both banks and insurers have been "boxed together" by regulatory authorities. But, as illustrated in the figure below, there are significant and relevant differences between the two, suggesting that they should be regarded and treated differently. This serves to illustrate that a "one size fits all" approach to risk culture is tempting but may be misguided (Figure 13–2).

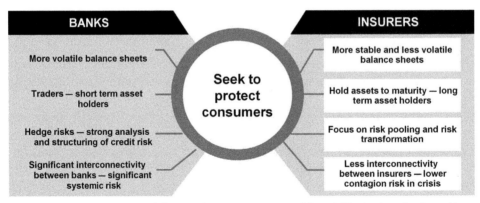

FIGURE 13–2 Illustration of some key differences between two types of financial institutions, banks and insurers. *Source: Towers Watson.*

Indeed, recent years have seen a range of external bodies seeking to describe and influence the risk culture of organizations in the financial sector. National regulators, professional bodies, ratings agencies, academic research groups, consulting firms, and NGOs have all published accounts, recommendations, and frameworks on the topic. Although none of these is definitive, several themes recur throughout and can be seen as central aspects of an effective risk culture. The following table gives a high-level overview of the topics mentioned by three organizations.

	Financial Stability Board	**Standard and Poor's**[a]	**Institute of International Finance**
Dimensions of Risk Culture	Tone from the top	Risk governance and organization structure	Leadership commitment
	Accountability	Risk appetite framework	Communication (vertical and horizontal)
	Effective challenge	Risk reporting and communication	Continuous challenge and active learning
	Incentives	Incentives and compensation	Incentives and performance management
			Governance

[a]Standard & Poor's, "Evaluating the Enterprise Risk Management Practices of Insurance Companies," 2005.

Although the table attempts to align the corresponding concepts across these frameworks, it will be apparent that this is not really possible. Though there are some areas of commonality—the importance of leadership, the effects of reward systems and effective challenge (e.g., both that individuals can challenge one another appropriately and that the risk function can challenge the business effectively)—there are also differences. The content of such frameworks is sensible so far as it goes. However, there does seem to be a clear focus on directly observable systems, processes, policies, and structures. It should not be forgotten that much of risk culture resides in people's attitudes, beliefs, habits, and relationships and is hidden "beneath the surface," which affects how policies, systems, and processes are approached in practice—and thus their success. As an example, after a significant risk event, a colleague was asked to review a company's governance procedures to evaluate whether appropriate decision making processes and levels of authority were in place. The conclusion reached could also apply to many incidents in the sector over the last few years: "There was nothing wrong with their governance procedures—except that they didn't use them." Although the system of internal committees and decision-making processes was well defined, in practice decisions had been influenced by conversations "in the corridors" and by the strength of relationships between individuals. To borrow an oft-used metaphor, the visible aspect of risk culture (such as policies, procedures, limits, and governance) are just the tip of the cultural iceberg. Much more of the iceberg lies beneath the surface, such as people's beliefs, hopes, fears, expectations, assumptions, and relationships. A clear lesson from this is that an organization's formal risk governance processes and its risk culture must be in tune with each other to be effective. To achieve this, it is necessary to gain insight into those aspects of risk culture that are less apparent, lurking beneath the surface of the water (Figure 13-3).

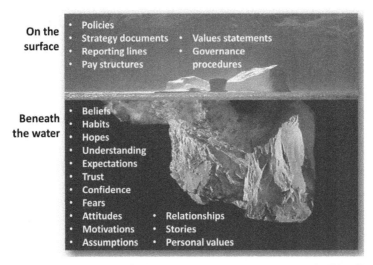

On the surface
- Policies
- Strategy documents
- Reporting lines
- Pay structures
- Values statements
- Governance procedures

Beneath the water
- Beliefs
- Habits
- Hopes
- Understanding
- Expectations
- Trust
- Confidence
- Fears
- Attitudes
- Motivations
- Assumptions
- Relationships
- Stories
- Personal values

FIGURE 13–3 The visible and invisible parts of risk culture. *Source: Towers Watson and Wikimedia Commons (iceberg).*

Safety Culture

Workplace safety is clearly a central issue in many industries (see also Chapter 3, on health and safety risk). Safety breaches can have huge economic, environmental, and, of course, personal consequences. In sectors such as energy, oil and gas, construction, transportation and logistics, mining, and manufacturing, safety is frequently cited as the top business priority. Where safety incidents have occurred, large or small, investigation often identifies organizational culture as an underlying cause. But what aspects of culture are most important in developing a strong safety culture? Towers Watson conducted research into the distinguishing cultural characteristics of businesses recognized for their safety records.[8] Employees were asked about their workplace environment and experience and the results analyzed in the context of actual safety incidents. Some of the findings were fundamental and unsurprising—safe workplaces provide a satisfactory physical environment and good safety training. But the high-performing sites were also distinguished by the cultural environment (Figure 13-4).

Employees reported positive, open relationships with their line managers, who were seen as technically knowledgeable, receptive, and responsive to input and who were forthcoming with recognition for good work. Good line management was found to create a sense of empowerment. Individual employees were able to take responsibility through delegated authority and access to relevant information. They were encouraged to develop innovative solutions to problems. Positive safety environments were also found to have a stronger emphasis on collaboration and teamwork—which was found to be especially important in the context of unusually heavy workloads.

As with all aspects of organizational culture, the tone is set from the top (see Chapter 2, on environmental risk; Chapter 3, on health and safety; Chapter 6, on cybersecurity; and Chapter 7, on brand risk), but front-line management plays an especially vital role in ensuring that a strong safety culture exists on the ground.

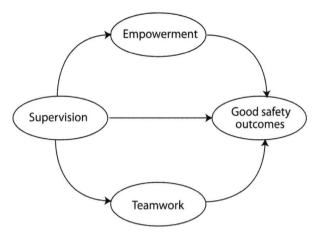

FIGURE 13–4 Good supervision providing empowerment of staff and effective teamwork contributes to good safety outcomes.

Measuring Risk Culture

Some managers, and some risk managers in particular, have shied away from the concept of risk culture, not knowing quite how to approach it. For those from an engineering or actuarial tradition, for example, the notion of trying to measure such an ethereal concept can be troubling. But, in keeping with the mantra that "what gets measured gets managed," if risk culture is to be effectively managed, it surely must be measured. Fortunately, approaches from a social science perspective lend themselves well to this, providing a range of ways to understand, assess, quantify, and analyze risk culture.

Depending on the context and the level of the organization concerned, different approaches to measuring risk culture will be appropriate. Many organizations have progressed from an informal/ad hoc approach through a more structured qualitative approach and now undertake a formalized approach combining both qualitative and quantitative methodologies.

At the less formalized/ad hoc end of the spectrum, organizations have tended to rely on existing data sources, such as by drawing on information from generic staff surveys, policies, and values statements, as well as relying on subjective personal impressions. Such approaches are not thorough enough to provide reliable insights and do not provide an adequate foundation for effective management decision making.

A more structured qualitative approach offers a great deal more insight. This typically takes the form of a series of senior-level interviews combined with focus groups from across the organization. Such an approach can be applied widely across a large organization but also lends itself to smaller business units.

It is important to capture both the senior, strategic perspective and the perspectives of the middle- and front-line roles, for each has access to a different set of information and experiences very relevant to the risk culture.

SIDEBAR: EXAMPLE INTERVIEW/FOCUS GROUP QUESTIONS

Asking open questions of leaders, managers and employees can help bring out the key dimensions of risk culture in a particular organization:

- *In your role, what do you see as the key challenges you have over the coming one to two years? What about over the longer term (say five years)?*
- *In what ways do you think this organization currently does a really good job of managing risk, and how does it need to change?*
- *Are there any aspects of typical behavior or attitudes here that you think need to change to be consistent with your risk management approach? Are there attitudes/behaviors that you think it's important not to lose?*
- *Whose job is it to manage risk in this organization?*
- *When you encounter aspects of risk management that could be improved, what are the underlying causes?*
- *How does this organization learn from mistakes?*
- *What "levers" do you think can be used internally to bring about the kind of changes to risk culture that you'd like to see?*
- *Do people here always know what is expected of them in terms of managing risks?*
- *Which aspects of risk management policies/procedures/controls are the most difficult to stick to in practice? Why?*
- *On what occasions do people try to "get around" risk controls or policies?*

To ensure open, candid participation, the sessions are usually run by an experienced external facilitator who can ask the right questions and also provide an assurance of confidentiality, encouraging people to speak freely in the knowledge that they won't be personally identified. Of course, managers should still feel confident to have such discussions among their team but should remain mindful that people may be unwilling to discuss some topics openly.

The insights from a qualitative approach such as this can be very helpful in identifying issues to be addressed. However, such an approach does not lend itself to quantification and thus makes it difficult to determine the *extent* of an issue, compare within/between organizations, and track progress accurately. A survey approach is able to meet these needs, and many organizations are now using risk culture surveys to monitor this critical business aspect. These range from simple generic questionnaires to those tailor-designed to meet the specific needs of an organization. Again, specialist firms are often called on to provide the right expertise, capabilities, and assurance of confidentiality. Of course, surveys provide a readily scalable approach and thus can be applied across large organizations.

Organizations differ from one another in terms of their strategies, products/services, markets, heritage, structures, and processes—so it is only sensible that their cultures differ, too. Where possible, it is thus preferable to design a measurement approach to fit the specific needs of the organization. If using a survey, this means designing a set of questions that reflect the particular issue most important to the effective operation of that organization. Often a process of qualitative focus groups and interviews (such as that described above) will be used to shape this questionnaire.

A significant advantage of a survey approach is that it can provide precise, quantified measures of each aspect of culture. Results from different groups can be compared to each other. If external benchmark data are available, they can be used to contextualize survey findings in light of what is "typical" or "normal." Though this should not be used to drive diverse organizations to conform to norm or to a single "best" risk culture, it does help in understanding the risk culture profile of an organization in context. Similarly, repeating a survey offers the opportunity to compare results over time, to assess the cultural effect of any changes and monitor progress. Internal comparisons mean that localized "hot-spots" can be identified and addressed, perhaps informed by other parts of the organization identified as exhibiting "best practice" internally.

More sophisticated statistical analysis of survey data can even provide insights into the underlying dynamics of the prevailing risk culture, for example, identifying high-impact topics offering the greatest leverage on people's attitudes, and so informing effective change plans (Figure 13-5).

FIGURE 13–5 Underlying dynamics of the prevailing risk culture. *Source: Towers Watson.*

As well as providing the insights described above, in our experience, a systematic approach to measuring risk culture often also has several less direct but equally beneficial consequences. Firstly, to the extent that it is visible across the organization, it raises the profile of an important, but sometimes overlooked topic. Leader sponsorship of a risk culture initiative demonstrates that it is taken seriously and helps convey a positive "tone from the top." We have found that introducing a risk culture measurement process also makes the topic much more accessible and tangible to both internal and external stakeholders. It provides a common language and set of constructs that managers can use to discuss the topic clearly and constructively, and it helps investors or regulators, for example, understand the value of the existing risk culture. In essence, measuring risk culture begins to give leaders, managers, and employees the concepts and insights they need to begin managing risk culture effectively.

Managing Risk Culture

With the appropriate insights, support, and resources, it is possible to manage organizational culture. However, changing culture cannot be done overnight and is challenging—indeed, many attempts at changing organizational culture come to nothing. Many theorists and practitioners offer guidance on managing and changing organizational culture which are equally applicable to risk culture:

- Culture change is a long process—start the journey prepared for the long haul.
- There should be a clear and compelling vision and strategy that people can understand and which they can "buy into."
- The desired culture should be articulated and modeled from the highest level in the organization.
- Pay attention to the "hidden" side of culture that lies beneath the surface, listening to people's concerns and understanding their personal interests and fears and responding to these. Some aspects of culture (such as systems, procedures, and processes) offer managers the opportunity to address them directly, whereas others (such as people's attitudes and beliefs) can only be affected indirectly.
- Existing systems, processes, policies, and the like tend to support the status quo, so these should be reviewed and modified to reflect required cultural changes. To overcome cultural resistance to change a "one-dimensional" approach rarely works. Rather, it is often necessary to reflect the change through a wide range of levers that are at the disposal of management. These often include changes to
    - education and communication
    - management information
    - leadership
    - governance
    - systems, policies, and processes
    - reward and performance management

Acting through these mechanisms, leaders, and managers can bring about sustained change in the less visible parts of culture, such as beliefs, attitudes, and relationships. For example, formal (or informal) training clearly influences people's level of understanding of and attitudes toward managing risks. Similarly, the availability, accuracy and appropriateness of information has a real effect on judgment and decision making. Although it is clear that leaders and managers are able to shape the risk culture of an organization, there are also limitations on what can be achieved, and experience shows that it is also easy to bring about unintended consequences. We explore these ideas below by focusing on the use of incentives and rewards to influence risk culture.

Rewards and Performance Management

The topic of reward systems and how these affect organizational risk culture has become a focus of particular attention in recent years. Governments and industry regulators have placed a great emphasis on ensuring that how leaders and employees are rewarded is consistent with a sound organizational risk culture. Considering this increased attention, we explore this area in some detail, examining ways that rewards can be used to influence risk culture—but also the limitations of doing so.

Since the onset of the financial crisis in 2008, increased focus has been placed on the relationship between rewards and risk. Though this has been especially pronounced in the financial services industry, it has also featured in a range of other industries. One embodiment of this has been the focus (at times bordering on hysteria) in the press, among politicians, by shareholder activists, and among the general public on the potential use of inappropriate rewards (both the value and methods of reward) at the executive leadership level. In some countries this has led to a range of legislative and regulatory requirements for publicly traded firms—including reporting requirements,[9] "say on pay" shareholder voting,[10] and, in some cases, caps on the amount of pay that can be delivered in incentives.[11] But concerns about the effects of rewards on risk have been equally prevalent at all organizational levels. The increased focus on misselling,[12] particularly in regulated consumer sales environments, is a good example of this. We have seen a large number of accusations, settlements, and fines in industries such as financial services, utilities, telecoms, and pharmaceuticals. In most cases, misselling has been blamed—at least in part—on incentive compensation. Importantly, these cases have involved actions taken by front-line sales and service staff and relatively low- to mid-level managers (albeit generally at the direction of senior management). But misselling has not been the only source of trouble. There are countless other examples in a wide range of industries in which incentives—and the culture that went with them—were felt to have contributed, at least in part, to very negative outcomes. Among the more spectacular examples are the failures of Barings Bank, the "double suicide" of Enron and Arthur Andersen, the failure of Lehman Brothers, and, for BP, both the Texas City oil refinery accident and the more recent Deepwater Horizon spill. The most damaging of these cases often involved not just one or two "bad apples" but rather stemmed from practices that were tolerated—if not encouraged—as part of the cultural fabric of the organization.

There is no question that rewards—and variable incentive compensation in particular—can and do drive behavior. In this way, rewards can be a powerful tool. The problem, however, is that rewards won't necessarily always drive the *desired* behaviors or outcomes. This has led many organizations to focus on the risks, or potential risks, created by rewards. Among the most commonly cited examples of these risks are situations such as the following:

- A CEO or senior leadership team that takes actions to maximize the stock price in the short term, thus risking long-term profitability and growth, because their rewards are linked to earnings per share
- A leadership team that makes overly generous assumptions in recognizing revenue to produce better results that drive higher bonuses
- A sales team that pushes through a large volume of orders, generating high commissions, without considering whether those sales are properly aligned with customer needs, and without caring whether those orders are later canceled or goods returned, because their compensation is linked to gross, rather than net, sales

- Call center staff who are rewarded based on meeting objectives related to the average length of each call and who, in their zeal to meet the objective, push customers along too quickly and fail to listen to their underlying issues, resulting in both unhappy customers and higher costs for the company when customers need to make multiple calls to get their issue resolved

Importantly, the real risk of these situations is faced by the company, not the individuals taking these actions. If we refer back to the definition of risk in Chapter 1 and think about risk in terms of uncertainty and outcomes, the outcome for the employee is earning a bonus, and the uncertainty is whether the employee receives a bonus (or, in many cases, how large a bonus will be received). But for the company, the potential outcomes of the employee's actions (and the related uncertainty) can be much more far-ranging—unsatisfied customers, additional costs to resolve complaints, reputational damage, loss of customers and revenue, and legal action as well as related fines, settlements, and legal costs. In the most extreme situations, as noted above, it has led to the failure of the company.

Much of the blame (and, by implication, possible solutions) has been placed on the role of rewards and incentives in particular. This focus on incentives, we argue, is prudent but also dangerous. It is prudent because we know that poorly designed incentives can create bad outcomes. But it is also dangerous for two reasons:

1. It leads to a false notion that incentives can be used to "control" risk.
2. It places an unreasonable burden on incentives and rewards in general to serve as the primary (or exclusive) tool to manage behavior—ignoring the role played more broadly by the organization's risk culture.

Incentives Create Rather than Control Risk

Many organizations have launched initiatives that seek to determine how they can "control" risk through their rewards. But no incentive or reward program design can be used to control risk. Rather, incentives—any incentive—create risk. Changing the design of the incentive plan can reduce or eliminate certain risks, but in doing so it creates other, new risks. In extreme cases, this has led some companies to question whether they should have an incentive plan at all. But this too creates risks—in this case, the risk that the company's compensation costs are not aligned with its financial results (see Chapter 2, on environmental risk, and Chapter 3, on health and safety risk, for comments on the effect of incentives in managing risk in those fields).

This is not to suggest, however, that firms should not worry about their reward design and just get on with things. Conducting a comprehensive risk assessment of incentive programs is a process that companies should periodically undertake, as outlined below.

Risk Identification

Risk identification involves identifying the sources of incentive risk, which requires creating an inventory of all the incentive plans that are currently being used in the organization. Though this may sound like a simple task, in large multinational organizations there can be tens or even hundreds of different "local" plans (local to a geography, a business unit, or a function). Few organizations have historically had a formal process for gathering this information. In creating the inventory, it is useful to understand such things as the following:

- What incentive plans are in place?
- How many plans exist?
- How much is spent on these plans?
- What do they reward for?
- What outcomes are they driving?

The best way to conduct the inventory is to collect actual plan documents for each plan, but it can sometimes be more efficient to prepare a survey-based instrument that is provided to the plan owners to populate with the required information.

Risk Analysis

Risk analysis is focused on understanding the causes and sources of incentive risk. Organizations use a variety of methods and tools to analyze the risk of their incentive plans—some involve very quantitative, formulaic scoring algorithms, while others take a more qualitative approach. However, the most important factors tend to revolve around two categories:

1. Technical plan design details (e.g., the use of thresholds and caps, the degree of upside opportunity and acceleration in payouts, the existence of clawbacks and deferrals, the types of measures that are paid for)
2. The materiality of the plans in question (e.g., the relative amount of earnings any one person can earn, as well as the size of the population affected and the total costs involved)

Risk Prioritization

Having completed the risk analysis, it is then possible to identify the incentive plans that require further attention. The matrix in Figure 13-6 provides a simple means of prioritizing incentive plan risk for many organizations. It looks at two dimensions.

Incentive plan risk relates to the likelihood that the incentive plan design could lead to undesirable outcomes. Though specific criteria will vary from one organization and one industry to another, these would generally align with the two categories identified under risk assessment (technical incentive design and materiality).

Business impact risk relates to the potential consequences that may be caused by the incentive plan. This is a function of the degree of risk that the business itself faces in the course of its operations. For example, in a financial services firm, the consequences of a "higher-risk" incentive plan could be very different for a firm that is committing capital and underwriting risks (where the potential returns could be quite volatile and unknown) compared to a firm that is operating in a more fee-based mode (where it is quite clear at the time of the sale exactly

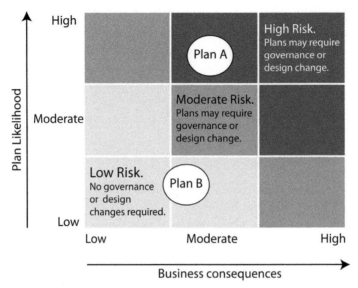

FIGURE 13–6 Incentive plan risk assessment matrix. *Source: Towers Watson.*

how much money the firm will make). In an industrial environment, the consequences could vary, in part, in relation to the degree of danger involved in the firm's production facilities and operations. In both cases, it is important to understand the extent to which the jobs in question can affect potential risk outcomes based on decisions they are making, where such decisions are likely to be influenced at least in part by the behaviors driven by their incentive plans. The business itself may have high risks (e.g., a potentially dangerous manufacturing environment), but the plant employees' effect on this risk is substantially different from the salespeople's effect on it (Figure 13-6).

An example of how to apply this would take the following steps:

1. Identify the risk event. This could be a group of sales incentive plans that could lead to misselling.
2. For each plan in question, evaluate the likelihood that the incentive plan will lead employees on that plan to cause the event (e.g., misselling).
3. Evaluate the potential business consequences (loss of > $X million in revenue, loss of > Y% of customers, regulatory fines and/or legal costs of > $X, etc.).
4. Based on this process, place the plan on the matrix above.

Actions to Treat Incentive Risk

Changing the design of the incentive plan is one action that can be taken. For instance, you may decide that using an uncapped incentive plan for certain jobs creates too great a risk of windfalls that are not reflective of the effort required to drive the result. Or you may find that a plan contains a "cliff" mechanism, whereby earnings increase dramatically upon reaching a key milestone—which, in the case of a sales plan, may increase the risk of misselling to get over the hurdle. But in other cases, it may be felt that such features are important and that the risks can be managed through other means. This is where two other important elements come into play—incentive governance and performance management.

Incentive Governance

Incentive governance refers to the oversight and control processes that are in place to monitor and manage the incentive plan. We think of it as all of the things that need to happen throughout the lifecycle of an incentive plan—starting with the establishment of principles and objectives that should underpin the plan design, moving through the plan design process, goal setting, budgeting, and then administering and managing the plan throughout the year.

In the above examples, a company that decides that the value of not having caps outweighs the risk that putting them in place could establish an incentive governance process requiring formal review and approval of all incentive earnings before they are paid. They could establish a process whereby any individual payments above $X value, or above X% of the target payout, are automatically reviewed. In the case of an extraordinarily large payout, this gives the company the opportunity to confirm the validity of the situation. And language in the incentive plan terms and conditions may also be included to stipulate that although the intent of the plan is to operate in an uncapped fashion, payments above X level will be reviewed and must be approved by management before they are made.

Performance Management

There is a fundamental law of incentives that all too many organizations are quick to overlook—you can't pay for everything that you need someone to do. If you try to do so, you end up with an incentive plan that is overcomplicated and that fails to drive the desired behavior. Incentives can be a powerful motivator and driver of certain results and outcomes—but not all results and outcomes. And part of how incentive plan risk can and must be controlled is through the role that managers play—the goals and objectives they set, how they provide feedback to their team, and how they coach and direct the team's performance (as well as when and how they provide recognition). Clear guidelines, criteria, and tools need to be developed to support managers in this regard. Individuals who are behaving in ways merely maximizing their earnings while creating inappropriate risk for the company or its customers need to be addressed promptly, first via feedback and coaching, and eventually, if required (and certainly in more egregious cases), through the threat of employment termination. Tolerating certain behavior just because the incentive plan "pays" for it must be viewed as inexcusable—and a sure sign that there is not a healthy risk culture in the organization.

SIDEBAR: THE EFFECTS OF RISK CULTURE ON INCENTIVES

The retail industry provides a particularly good example of this link. Many retail organizations are placing greater emphasis on their customer service orientation as a means of differentiating themselves in an increasingly commoditized world. In so doing, they also question whether using a highly variable commission plan for their store staff creates a potential conflict between how their employees are paid and the focus they want them to place on serving customers and creating a positive customer "experience." Some retailers have felt very strongly that they need to place more emphasis on base salary and have a relatively small incentive linked entirely to team (store) results, with particularly strong emphasis on customer satisfaction scores. It is felt that this will reduce the temptation of store staff to look after their own interests first (i.e., commission earnings) over the interests and desires of their customers.

However, one leading retailer has taken a very different approach. It has traditionally paid a large portion of compensation in the form of an individual sales commission. Top sellers can earn very handsome rewards—resulting in significant differentiation in earnings between lower and higher performers. At the same time, this organization is also routinely seen as leading the industry in its customer orientation and responsiveness. It sets a standard to which many others aspire. And yet it pays its staff in a way that would seemingly create a high likelihood of misalignment of interests between employees and customers. If one were to conduct a risk analysis of its incentive plans, they would be rated as having relatively high risk for the organization.

And yet somehow it all works. Why? Because of the overriding effect of the organization's culture. The culture of customer service is so deeply embedded in this company that store staff would not even think of taking an action that would drive their commission if they felt that it was not also helping to serve the customer and meet the customer's needs. This means, at times, spending time with a customer to take back a good being returned, or to manage a very small-value transaction, when instead the salesperson could potentially be selling a very high-value designer bag. The culture is such that if someone were seen to be taking a "pushy" approach to customers, failing to listen and serve, not only would their manager address the behavior in the performance management process, but the employee would be ostracized and disrespected by his or her coworkers.

This is not, of course, to say that no one who has ever worked for this firm has ever "pushed" a sale based on the commission that could be earned while failing to serve a customer appropriately. But those who have a pattern of doing so are dealt with quickly and efficiently—and they either shape up or ship out very quickly. This culture effectively serves as a control mechanism over the risks created by the reward structure—a risk that might not be as easily controlled in a different organization having a different culture.

Conclusions

Although the term "risk culture" is used by people in a variety of ways, we consider that the broad concept is fundamental to an organization's ability to manage its risks and so to achieve its strategic objectives. This is best demonstrated by briefly considering the contrary—there are too many cases of organizations (and their stakeholders) suffering from the consequences of a poor risk culture.

Just as no two organizations are exactly alike, so there is no single "ideal" risk culture. Rather, each organization should develop its own understanding of the risk culture that works best in its own circumstances.

Much of an organization's risk culture lies beneath the surface, so important cultural characteristics may not be immediately apparent—but they can be identified, measured and understood using a range of qualitative and quantitative approaches.

Leaders and managers have access to a range of "levers" that they can use to shape the culture (including the risk culture) of their organization. These include things such as training, communication, management information reporting, and governance. However, managing culture is not easy, and attempts to shape culture are prone to unintended consequences. In particular, attempts to use incentive/reward systems as a silver bullet to control risk culture are ill founded. Though financial reward can play an important role in shaping risk culture, it is important to realize that a more holistic approach is needed to bring about a more robust and appropriate risk culture in most organizations.

Notes

1. Power, M. K., Ashby, S., & Palermo, T. Risk culture in financial organisations - A research report, pp. 1-103. London: Centre for Analysis of Risk and Regulation (CARR), 2013. Retrieved from http://www.lse.ac.uk/researchAndExpertise/units/CARR/pdf/Final-Risk-Culture-Report.pdf.
2. IRM, "Risk Culture: Guidance from the Institute of Risk Management," London: Institute of Risk Management, 2012.
3. European Business Review, 2014, www.europeanbusinessreview.com/?p=2817.
4. Warren Buffet, "Memorandum to Berkshire Hathaway Managers," in *Financial Times*, October 6, 2006.
5. "The RiskMinds 2009 Risk Managers' Survey: The Causes and Implications of the 2008 Banking Crisis," www.moorecarter.co.uk/RiskMinds%202009%20Risk%20Managers'%20Survey%20Report.19March2010.pdf.
6. FSB, "Increasing the Intensity and Effectiveness of SIFI Supervision: Consultative Document Guidance on Supervisory Interaction with Financial Institutions on Risk Culture," Basel, Switzerland: Financial Stability Board, Bank for International Settlements, 2012.
7. Towers Watson, "Global Insurance ERM Survey," 2012.
8. Towers Watson, "Building a Safer Workplace," 2010, towerswatson.com.
9. For instance, U.S. Securities & Exchange Commission (SEC) requirements.
10. For example, UK regulations related to nonbinding "say on pay" shareholder votes, as set forth in section 439 of the Companies Act 2006, and later revised in the Enterprise and Regulatory Reform Act 2013 section 79.
11. Most notably in CRD IV—the Capital Requirements Directive IV, which applies to credit institutions and investment firms in the European Union and has capped bonuses at 1X base salary, with the potential to increase the cap to 2X base salary with shareholder approval.
12. There is no legal definition of misselling, but it generally refers to situations that include one or more of the following outcomes: A salesperson has sold a product that is not suitable for the consumer; a sale has been made based on the provision of advice or information that is misleading or outright false; a sale has been made with the omission of a key piece of information. It is most often thought of in the sale of financial products that involve some degree of advice, but it can apply equally in other situations as well (e.g., someone buying a piece of clothing in a store but who is misinformed about the returns policy). Such acts may be unintentional (products sold by someone who is not qualified to sell them, but who is not purposely trying to mislead the customer) or intentional (stretching or glossing over relevant facts to get a sale, or knowingly selling something to a customer that is not a suitable product).

14

The Role of the Board of Directors in Risk Management

Peter Whyntie

A chairman of a major bank was quoted in a national newspaper as saying that he was "no longer losing any sleep over the financial planning scandal that has tarnished the bank's name."[1] The timing could not have been worse. In the same week, that bank had been forced to admit to a parliamentary senate inquiry that it had misled both the inquiry and the securities regulator concerned. Already operating under an enforceable undertaking relating to significant customer losses incurred thanks to seriously flawed advice, the bank had just had new conditions to its financial services license imposed by the regulator. Should those conditions be breached, the bank would face license suspension, cancellation, or even prosecution. In monetary terms, the bank faced potential consumer recompense in excess of $250 million.

The same chairman had only a week earlier "warned [that] boards could face serious 'unintended consequences' if more regulation forces directors to become too involved in management issues."[2]

This illustrates the challenge facing boards of directors in a world in which the expectations of a wide range of stakeholders on what role directors should play is constantly evolving.

Directors Govern, Managers Manage

Though broad consensus holds that directors should govern and managers manage, there is less consensus on what that actually means. Neither is there much guidance in legislation. At the level of legislation, various jurisdictions across the globe codify directors' liabilities for corporate failure but generally do not specify duties to the level at which it is possible to discern where a directors' role ends and a manager's role starts. Where there is more specific guidance, it tends to be directed to financial responsibilities and to health and safety (which in some jurisdictions also incorporates environment), often making directors and officers liable for noncompliance, but not enterprise risk management in its broad sense. A prominent New Zealand professional director, Rob Campbell, has challenged what he calls the "popular governance mantra [that] 'directors govern, managers manage'" as overly simplistic. He points to a number of factors, including increasing legislative provisions bearing directly and personally on directors; the responsibility of directors for the content, accuracy, and compliance status of financial statements; and many directors' also being managers—i.e. executive directors. In the face of this complex mix, he poses an alternate: "[M]anagers manage and directors manage the managers, change the managers, or take the consequences if the managers don't manage well."[3]

Curiously though, perhaps the most prominent legislation introduced in recent times purporting to deal with financial failures on a large scale, the U.S. Sarbanes–Oxley Act of 2002, is essentially silent on the specific topic of risk management other than financial risk management. It has driven a very heavy regime of detailed compliance and audit, including of financial risk controls, but it is in stark contrast to other jurisdictions, such as the UK, Australia, Malaysia, Singapore, to name but a few, that have all introduced regulatory governance codes or stock exchange governance guidelines explicitly setting out duties of boards in relation to risk management on a broad scale. The London Stock Exchange, for instance, has said that "[w]hatever risk framework is adopted by a company, clear risk oversight from the board, as distinct from management, is essential."[4]

Although the United States tends toward rules-based prescriptive law, the majority of English-speaking jurisdictions have tended toward principles-based law whereby legislation sets high-level objectives and the market and/or regulators set more detailed guidelines. An examination of the NYSE Listed Company Manual also failed to find a single mention of risk management, even in the section on corporate responsibility.

Largely as a result of the global financial crisis of 2007–2008, financial services prudential regulators have not only increased their focus on financial risk management, but have also extended to enterprise risk management and specific requirements for board governance of risk. For instance, the Australian Prudential Regulatory Authority (APRA), which has been recognized as one of the strongest prudential regulators, has issued a number of prudential regulatory standards setting out its requirements for governance of regulated entities and for specific categories of risk for each financial sector:

> *This Prudential Standard requires an APRA-regulated institution to have systems for identifying, measuring, evaluating, monitoring, reporting, and controlling or mitigating material risks that may affect its ability, or the ability of the group it heads, to meet its obligations to depositors and/or policyholders. These systems, together with the structures, policies, processes and people supporting them, comprise an institution's risk management framework. The board of an APRA-regulated institution is ultimately responsible for having a risk management framework that is appropriate to the size, business mix and complexity of the institution or group it heads. The risk management framework must also be consistent with the institution's strategy and business plan. For instance, if a company sets an aggressive strategy with aggressive business goals and also adopts a conservative risk appetite[,] there will likely be irreconcilable tensions.*

The key requirements of this prudential standard are that an APRA-regulated institution must do the following:

- Have a risk management framework that is appropriate to its size, business mix and complexity.
- Maintain a board-approved risk appetite.

- Maintain a board-approved risk management strategy describing the key elements of the risk management framework that give effect to its approach to managing risk.
- Have a board-approved business plan that sets out its approach for the implementation of its strategic objectives.
- Maintain adequate resources to ensure compliance with this prudential standard.
- Notify APRA when it becomes aware of a significant breach of, or material deviation from, the risk management framework or aware that the risk management framework does not adequately address a material risk.[5]

As can be seen, that sets general responsibilities for a company with some explicit responsibilities for the board. Though the standard was developed for financial services entities, the responsibilities outlined are applicable across virtually any organization. Perhaps these could be restated as board responsibilities:

- Ensure that management establishes and maintains a risk management framework that is appropriate to its size, business mix and complexity.
- Approve the risk appetite.
- Approve a risk management strategy that describes the key elements of the risk management framework that give effect to the entity's approach to managing risk.
- Approve a business plan that sets out the entity's approach for the implementation of its strategic objectives.
- Ensure the entity maintains adequate resources to ensure that it effectively manages its risk within the risk appetite.
- Ensure that management reports when it becomes aware of a significant breach of, or material deviation from, the risk management framework or aware that the risk management framework does not adequately address a material risk.

Providing Leadership and Affecting Risk Culture

The board has a critically important role in setting the culture necessary to support and maintain effective risk management. The Institute of International Finance[6] identified risk culture "as a crucial element in strengthening risk governance." It went on to state that "the 'tone at the top' is crucial to building and embedding a strong risk culture." These and other findings arose from a series of global studies and reports of the IIF conducted since the global financial crisis.

Essential elements to developing and sustaining an effective risk culture include the following:

- Committed leadership
- Horizontal information sharing
- Vertical escalation of threats or fears
- Continuous and constructive challenging of the organization's actions and preconceptions
- Active learning from mistakes
- Incentives that reward thinking about the whole organization

- An effective governance structure:
  - Access of CRO to authority including ability to escalate to Board,
  - A Chief Risk Officer (CRO) with extensive influence,
  - Communication of risk tolerance to the organization and external parties, and
  - Evidence of management objectives linked to risk management objectives.

Three key factors then required to be in place to demonstrate commitment, support the culture and ensure that the framework has the resources and infrastructure to operate effectively follow:

- Tone at the top
- Strategy and budget
- Transparency and accountability[7]

Consideration also needs to be given to whom do we mean when we say the "top." Is this the chairman? The whole board? The CEO? Some factors to consider in determining that include influence, longevity, and consistency.

A study of the demographic effects on the role relating to board chairmen found that "the influence of 'the leader,' namely the individual, irrespective of the role held, was recognized as the ultimate driving force of the firm. Whoever that leader is, still the leader was reported as the critical factor in determining firm success. Irrespective of governance practice and role separation or duality, one person was seen to determine the success or failure of the enterprise."[8] What is particularly telling in these findings is that the influence is equally relevant to positive or negative performance. So a takeaway from this is that the influence of the leader, whether chairman or CEO, is likely to be a critical factor in the effect of the "tone at the top" when it comes to how effective the risk management culture is.

Cultures are a long-term matter, so the longevity of the leader is likely to significantly influence the consistency of culture over the long term. If the board allows ownership of culture to be left to management, and particularly the CEO, consistency is likely to be affected by the trend to shorter CEO tenure. In 2008, *Forbes* reported average North American CEOs' tenure as 6.8 years, down from 8.6 years two years previously.[9] By 2013, the average Fortune 500 CEO tenure was 4.6 years.[10]

The tenure trend for directors appears to be heading in the opposite direction. In 2013, 64 percent of directors of S&P 500 companies were reported as having served 10–15 years.[11] So that might seem as a counterbalance, allowing for boards to set and own culture over the long term and drive consistent implementation by the shorter-tenured CEOs. However, that must be tempered by studies that have found that long-term tenure can hurt performance. In scanning articles and studies on the effects of board tenure on performance, there seems to be a diversity of views. However, a recent empirical study across a sample of S&P 1500 firms from 1998 to 2010 has identified nine years as the optimal tenure. The study partly attributed that to the learning effects in the early years of tenure's becoming outweighed by the entrenchment costs as tenure extends beyond optimal length.[12]

Perhaps a practical observation to make from these various findings is that an organization needs to be very cognizant of the interplay between the need for a strong and influential leader to drive a positive risk culture while also recognizing that applying the culture consistently over the long term requires ownership to reside where there is greater longevity—i.e., at the board. The organization must also recognize that this is likely to be less effective when a board is dominated by, rather than driving the behavior of, its CEO. When some of the more spectacular corporate failures are examined, such as that of Enron, very dominant CEOs appear to be a factor. (For more on culture and risk management, see Chapter 13.)

Structuring Boards to Govern Risk Management

This section has been derived from an article written by the author and published in the **Journal of Chartered Secretaries Australia Ltd.**[13]

Considering risk management's newly perceived importance to the effective governance of organizations, there is a growing trend ensuring that it is the focus of appropriate board committees.

The most common approach is to assign the oversight of risk management to the audit committee. When risk is assigned to other committees, the governance structure will often be influenced by the organization's industry. Across the financial services sector, particularly since the global financial crisis, there has been a move toward adoption of dedicated risk committees that look at risk on an enterprise basis. In the resource and energy industries, some companies have created risk committees focusing on combinations of corporate responsibility, environment, and health and safety.

There is considerable debate over whether governance of risk management is better left to a generalist audit committee or to a dedicated risk committee. What, then, are the pros and cons of generalist audit versus dedicated risk committees?

A useful starting point is a very recent APRA prudential standard that addresses this exact topic: CPS 220 Risk Management. It sets out the different roles of both a board audit committee and a board risk committee. It stated in its announcement of the standard on May 9, 2013, that one of the two most important enhancements is "the establishment of a board risk committee that provides objective non-executive oversight of the implementation and on-going operation of the institution's risk management framework. The committee must be chaired by an independent director who is not the chair of the board."[14]

The reference to the role of the audit committee within the standard is limited to ensuring that the institution's "compliance with, and the effectiveness of, the risk management framework is subject to review by internal and/or external audit at least annually. The results of this review must be reported to the board audit committee."[15]

Clearly APRA has formed a view that the audit function is about assurance, whereas the risk function is about the implementation and ongoing oversight of risk management. Is this supported on a wider basis?

In his highly influential review of corporate governance in the UK financial industry, Sir David Walker made a very clear distinction between the "essentially, though not exclusively, back-looking" responsibility of the audit committee "relating to the effective implementation by the executive of policies decided by the board as part of the strategy of the entity." In then addressing the risk responsibilities, the review states, "[T]hus in parallel with, but separately from, compliance and audit the board has responsibilities for the determination of risk tolerance and risk appetite through the cycle and in the context of future strategy and, of critical importance, the oversight of risk in real-time in the sense of approving and monitoring appropriate limits on exposures and concentrations. This is a forward-looking focus." It concludes that section saying, "[B]ut a clear differentiation is needed in ensuring that appropriate and separate attention is given in [sic] to backward and forward-looking risk functions."[16]

The review recommends dedicated board risk committees by saying, "[B]ut the potential or actual overload of the audit committee and the need for a closely-related but separate capability to focus on risk in future strategy leads this Review to the conclusion that best practice in a listed bank or life insurance company is for the establishment of a board risk committee separate from the audit committee."[17]

In December 2010, SpencerStuart, a global executive search firm, published its findings from interviews of audit and risk committee chairs of leading international corporations in industrial, life sciences, banking, and financial sectors across Europe and the United States.[18] It specifically addressed the pros and cons of creating a separate risk committee.

It found mixed support for the concept of a dedicated risk committee, with a finding, not surprisingly, that "the nature of the organization and the kinds of risks the business faces can significantly influence which approach makes the most sense for a specific company."[19]

One view was that "the more a business is dependent upon the proactive taking of risk in a dynamic way, the more likely it is to be better served by a risk committee separate from audit".[20]

The findings also echoed concerns raised by Walker about the overloading of audit committees if they also had oversight of risk. The danger is that risk can then become a lower priority. In this writer's experience, that is frequently the case, with risk often relegated to last on the agenda. It then tends to be either starved of appropriate discussion time or, in the worst case, dismissed with a "can we take the risk report as having been read?" attitude.

The topic was also addressed by Protiviti.[21] In stating that it is not a one-size-fits-all matter, it went on to say that it can be a good idea under some circumstances. It identified companies that have "complex market, credit, liquidity and commodity pricing risks"[22] as examples. It also stated that it "fosters an integrated, enterprise wide approach to identifying and managing risk and provides an impetus toward improving the quality of risk reporting and monitoring, both for management and the board."[23]

Protiviti also points out that establishing a separate risk committee is no "panacea." "It may be more important to evaluate whether a sufficient number of independent directors possess deep knowledge and experience in dealing with the industry and its critical risks." He later adds that "the board needs to be careful that the creation of a risk committee does not result in a subconscious attitude of delegation by the rest of the board on risk matters, such that the non-committee members begin to view risk as a matter for the Committee and not the full board."[24]

The risk of disaggregating specific risk categories to separate committees is that the holistic view of the organization's enterprise risk is obscured or even altogether missed. Hence the board, when employing separate risk committees, needs to ensure that it brings all the intelligence from those committees together for review on an enterprise basis.

Having explored what others are saying, it might now be illustrative to look at some practical examples based on some client engagements the author has undertaken.

Those clients having dedicated board risk committees did demonstrate a singular focus on risk management governance across the enterprise and all risk categories, undistracted by an agenda often weighted to financial oversight and assurance matters that were typically the province of the audit committee. Relevant to both models, the focus of the full board and leadership (or lack thereof) in respect to risk management from both the chair and the CEO appeared to be critical.

When the board led culture and the CEO was tasked with its implementation, risk management not only was supported, but was clearly adding value. This was demonstrated by fewer customer and supplier complaints, lower staff turnover, lower error rates, and better project completion rates.

Unfortunately, ASX Governance Principle 7, Risk Management, relies entirely on self-proclamation of compliance by companies. There is no requirement for a company to demonstrate that it actually has anything in place, and there is no external independent review process required. Hence examples are seen of statements about risk frameworks made in annual reports that are then shown to be essentially absent or deeply flawed when the company announces a significant failure.

Early in 2013, an ASX-listed company had to issue a correction to its annual report: It had entirely neglected to address Principle 7. Even in its correction, the wording showed that the board's understanding of risk management seemed to be limited to financial risk management. Within days of issuing the correction, it announced a serious incident that, among other things, had resulted in the death of a worker. It suffered a 60 percent drop in share price from which it has yet to recover, and its operations had to be suspended for several months. It had to demonstrate to the country regulator that it had put in place an effective risk management framework before it could resume its operations.

In conclusion, it appears that there is far from being a consensus on the pros and cons of a dedicated risk committee. There is stronger support when organizations are more complex and when there is a need to take a dynamic approach to risk. There is also strong recognition that it may be an appropriate solution when the sheer volume of work already undertaken by an audit committee is already a burden and adding oversight of risk might overwhelm it.

There is also a concern that regardless of whether risk oversight is assigned to an audit committee or a risk committee, the board must never take its collective eye off the ball. Indeed, in all papers reviewed, the board is cited as having the responsibility of setting the risk appetite, driving risk culture, and always retaining overall responsibility for the oversight of risk.

Finally, a common view is that the capacity of the individuals on the board or relevant committee, including their understanding of the organization's business and industry, their ability to challenge, and their competency to exercise independent judgment, is paramount to the effective management of an organization's risk.

The Information on Which Boards Rely

Fundamental to directors' being able to effectively discharge their risk governance responsibilities is their receiving accurate, relevant, and timely information and data.

Over the course of many years of consulting to boards on risk management, the most frequent complaint heard by the author has been that the sheer volume of risk reporting overwhelms directors and obscures important information. However, when confronted with these complaints, management invariably argues that directors fail to spell out what information they wish to receive. All too often this becomes a very circular argument, with no "winners."

It behooves both boards and their risk management teams to work together to devise the optimum solution. The starting point should be to ask the following question: "What information about risk management is needed to properly inform the board's decision making?" If that is always applied as the test of what information should be provided to the board, it is more likely that management will avoid the temptation to just deliver everything that seems to be relevant—or, worse, deliver whatever it can collect!

Other chapters in this book discuss risk reporting in specific areas of risk. For example, Chapter 2 looks at the information that boards need if they are to manage environmental risk. Accordingly, this section will look at the subject from a very high level.

The diagram below was developed for use with boards and senior management to explain the difference between the strategic management of risk versus the operational management of risk. (Note that the concept of operational management of risk is not the same as the risk category of operational risk management, the subject of Chapter 5; likewise, the concept of strategic management of risk is not the same as strategic risk, the subject of Chapter 16.) Though this concept is not generally used, the author has found that it resonates with boards and senior management. It simply illustrates broadly where the focus of each should be (Figure 14–1).

The board's primary focus should be on the top crescent. Hence it should receive management reporting that provides information on the current status of the enterprise risk profile (e.g., the aggregated assessment, analysis, and prioritization of risks discussed in Chapters 1, 5, and 9) in respect of the organization's risk appetite with specific reference to the vision, corporate code of conduct, and strategy. Because the board retains responsibility for the oversight of these, it should have a strong say in how it wants this reported, as well as with what frequency, and should be very engaged in discussing it with management. Many boards will want this to be discussed at the full board meeting, not delegated to a single risk committee or multiple category-specific risk committees. The risk committee might receive it initially and review the detail, but it will often then be tabled for discussion at the full board.

The bottom crescent is what is managed day to day. Depending on the industry and the sophistication of the organization, there will be very detailed risk monitoring, analysis, and reporting of all categories of risk across the organization. The challenge for management is to work with the board and relevant risk committees to then determine what of that is relevant to the board. The risk appetite will be of assistance as a means of prioritizing information and data. If management is focused on establishing what information will enable the board to see what material affects or relates to the organization's meeting its vision, staying true to its

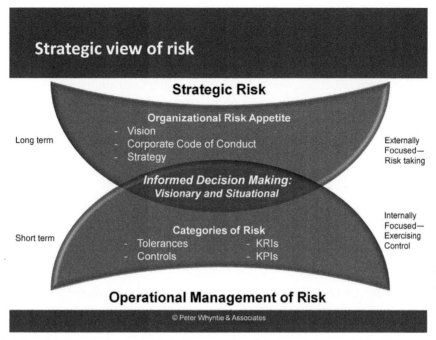

FIGURE 14–1 Focus of strategic management of risk versus operational management of risk. *Source: Peter Whynties & Associates.*

corporate code of conduct, and achieving its strategy, there is a good chance that it will get the balance right.

A practical suggestion to boards and management is to view the development of the appropriate balance of risk reporting as a journey. If boards and their risk or audit committees set aside some time in the risk segment of the agenda to review with the CRO or Risk Manager the effectiveness of the reporting, over time, they will see a marked improvement in the value derived from it.

One word of warning. Risk reporting often follows a strict pyramid approach based on severity tables. That is useful to filter out "noise." However, sometimes seemingly small or minor events can have catastrophic consequences. Thus it is important to build in the ability for a risk manager to be able to quickly escalate matters when a judgment is formed that senior management, and perhaps board, attention warrants it (this is discussed further in Chapter 5, on operational risk, and Chapter 9, on risk portfolio).

Demands on Directors from Stakeholders and Litigation

We live in an increasingly litigious world. And the fines being meted out for compliance breaches have reached astronomical heights. The most recent example is that of French bank BNP Paribas, fined US$9 billion in June 2014 for violations of U.S. sanctions laws and enabling the activities of terrorists and human rights abusers in Sudan and other countries. It would be difficult to find a better example of the cost of cure vastly overshadowing that of prevention.

Though financial services appear to have attracted the biggest fines, examples of other hugely costly fines and civil damages are replete across industries and jurisdictions. Some of the biggest have involved anticompetitive behavior arising from antitrust breaches and cartel behavior. Civil damages and fines from major disasters such as that of the Deepwater Horizon, or BP Gulf of Mexico, oil spill of 2010 have been in the billions of dollars.

Curiously, to date, actions have not generally been taken against directors. However, the cost to shareholders has been extremely damaging, and it would seem only a matter of time before we see class-action civil suits launched against directors and executives.

Many companies are now taking actions to minimize their exposures to the potential effects of global warming. The insurance industry is leading because of its exposure to claims resulting from climate-related disasters. Investment funds are increasingly reducing their exposures to climate-damaging industries, such as carbon energy production and coal mining. Companies are starting to explicitly state their environment or sustainability risks in their reporting.

Boards and their risk or audit committees are likely to be increasingly focused on their governance duties as regards minimizing their organization's risks. The author was asked by two large listed companies to conduct reviews of their conflicts of interest governance frameworks immediately after the global financial crisis. The boards had directly commissioned these reviews, concerned that transactions involving related parties could come under shareholder scrutiny. The directors of both organizations were motivated by both their potential personal liabilities and the potential costs to their shareholders and reputation damage.

Of significant concern to directors facing the challenge of these exposures is the challenge to maintain a governing role and not to end up micromanaging. Part of enabling that outcome is to ensure the following:

- The board's risk management charter is clearly defined. A board and committee risk charter is a basic and essential governance document that sets out what the role and responsibilities of the board and committees are with respect to risk.
- The appropriate risk governance structure is in place.
- The right mix of experience, knowledge, and capabilities is represented among the directors, particularly on risk and audit committees.
- The board reporting of risk provides information "that allows it to understand and appreciate risk issues, challenge management on risk decisions, and have a plain language conversation about risk at the board level."[25]

Conclusion

Risk management is increasingly becoming a significant part of the focus of boards. In light of the relative recency of risk management as a formal discipline, especially outside financial services, it is not surprising that there are as yet few decided cases to which to look for guidance.

Since the global financial crisis of 2007, there has been a gradual introduction of formal codes and standards by some regulators and stock exchanges.

The literature on the topic is also gradually expanding, providing useful insights into how different organizations are dealing with developing effective risk governance structures, addressing the appropriate director versus management balance of responsibilities, exploring the board's role in risk culture, and looking at effective value adding risk reporting.

The best practical advice to managers and directors with which to close this chapter is that it is a journey. Boards and management that work together to find the balance that works for them will do the best. If directors continually investigate whether reporting is informing the board and its decision making, then management will better appreciate what is required.

Notes

1. C. Kruger, *Sydney Morning Herald*, May 29, 2014.
2. D. Kitney, *The Australian*, May 19, 2014.
3. R. Campbell, *The National Business Review*, June 2, 2014.
4. LSE Corporate Governance for Main Market and AIM Companies, September 2012.
5. APRA Prudential Standard CPS 220-1 Risk Management, January 2015.
6. Institute of International Finance, *Governance for Strengthened Risk Management*, October 2012, p. 1.
7. "Risk Culture—Reform in the Financial Services Industry: Strengthening Practices for a More Stable System," The Report of the IIF Steering Committee on Implementation (SCI), Institute of International Finance, December 2009.
8. N. K. Kakabadse and A. P. Kakabadse, "Chairman of the Board: Demographics Effects on the Role Pursuit," *Journal of Management Development* 26, no. 2 (2007): 188.
9. M. Kirdahy, "Executive CEO Tenure," Forbes.com, March 7, 2008.
10. G. Burnison, "The CEO Pay Circus of 2013," The Exchange—Yahoo! Finance, March 21, 2013.
11. C. Hymowitz and J. Green, "Corporate Directors Get Older, Hold Their Seats Longer," *Bloomberg BusinessWeek*, May 23, 2013.
12. S. Huang, "Board Tenure and Firm Performance," INSEAD Business School, May 2013.
13. P. Whyntie, "Pros and Cons of a Dedicated Risk Committee: Keeping Good Companies," *Journal of Chartered Secretaries Australia Ltd* (now *Governance Institute of Australia Ltd*), 65, no 7 (August 2013): 400–402.
14. APRA announcement to all ADIs, general insurers, and life companies, dated May 9, 2013.
15. APRA Prudential Standard CPS 220 Risk Management, May 2013, para. 43.
16. "A Review of Corporate Governance in UK Banks and Other Financial Industry Entities: Final Recommendations," November 26, 2009, p. 93.
17. Ibid., p. 94.
18. Kevin M. Connelly, Carolyn C. Eadie, and Valerie R. Harper, "The Growing Role of the Board in Risk Oversight," December 2010, www.spencerstuart.com/research/articles/1471.
19. Ibid., p. 2.
20. Ibid., p. 2.
21. "Board Perspectives: Risk Oversight—Should the Board Have a Separate Risk Committee?" *Protiviti*, iss. 24, October 2011.
22. Ibid.
23. Ibid.
24. Ibid.
25. Institute of International Finance, "Governance for Strengthened Risk Management," October 2012, p. 30.

15

Political Risk

Elizabeth Stephens

Mention the words "political risk," and most business people will have an idea what you mean. But probe more deeply and ask for examples of how political risk events have affected business returns or about their implications for future growth, and your audience may become vague.

One of the reasons for this is the absence of a universally agreed upon definition of political risk and its consequences. For the purposes of this chapter, political risk is understood to mean

The risk of a strategic, financial, or personnel loss for a firm because of nonmarket factors, including action or inaction by a government authority, macroeconomic and social policies (fiscal, monetary, trade, investment, industrial, income, labor, and developmental), or events related to political instability (war, civil war, coups, insurrection, riots, and terrorism).

Political risk events can be triggered by a disparate and wide-ranging array of factors. The "butterfly effect"—the sensitive dependency on initial conditions according to which a small change at one place in a deterministic nonlinear system can result in large differences in a later state—is an apt description of the superficially unrelated chain reaction unleashed by seemingly disparate political trends.

Political risk events—that is, action or inaction by a host government that can deprive a foreign investor of assets or impair return on an asset—include the following:

- Russia imposed a ban on grain exports in August 2010 after drought and wildfires devastated crops. The measures were designed to keep domestic food prices low. Russians consume large amounts of bread, and rising prices have the power to provoke popular unrest. The government was particularly keen to avert price rises in the run-up to parliamentary elections the following year. International commodity traders with contracts to export grain were unable to meet their contractual obligations.
- Argentina introduced a bill in April 2012 for the partial renationalization of YPF, the country's largest energy company, with the government seizing Spanish Repsol's stake in the company. The government cited underinvestment in future production as justification for the nationalization, which Repsol denied. Repsol countered with claims that the

government drove down the YPF share price ahead of the announcement to minimize compensation payments. Analysts viewed the move as politically motivated by the government's desire to own a larger stake in the country's energy sector.

Globalization has created greater interconnectedness and, by implication, greater vulnerability to events beyond the boundaries of sovereign territory and far beyond our control. Though the search for greater economic rewards and economies of scale presented by globalization is clearly understood, the concomitant impact of heightened exposure to political risk is often ignored.

This is a significant risk management failing when one considers the tremendous influence that politics exerts on market movements and how the most unexpected economic events are often triggered by political action or inaction.

Today several clearly discernible trends dominate the investment environment: interconnectedness of financial markets; reliance on global supply chains and offshoring; the rising power of nonstate actors, including terrorist groups; national energy insecurity; commodity price fluctuations; and high youth unemployment.

Anticipating the risks associated with each of these trends requires understanding the political and economic environment in each territory, the separation of powers and the independence of the various branches of state, institutional independence, the prevalence of the rule of law, and the preferences of leaders who determine policy choices and thereby political and economic outcomes. Often a lack of political capacity or willingness to maintain a stable society and predictable economic environment leads to financial loss.

Political developments can make a mockery of even the best considered investment decisions. This is particularly true in territories where populist governments come to power or autocratic leaders dominate the political environment. Yet developed nations are not immune from manipulating legislation and investment laws[1] in response to the dictates of the electoral cycle or as a device to plug ever-increasing budget deficits.

Though businesses go to great lengths to model risk scenarios that may affect their business return, political risk events are generally not calculated with the same degree of rigor. This is often because political risk can seem so amorphous that business leaders lack a framework for assessing their risks. In reality, political risk, like other elements of risk management, comprises components that can be identified, analyzed, and prioritized by those who have an understanding of variations across political systems and an understanding of the effects that political risk events will have on different political systems. Events surrounding the Arab Spring provide a pertinent example.

The Arab Spring

Right up until protests swept across the streets of Sidi Bouzid on December 18, 2010, in response to the self-immolation of Mohamed Bouazizi in protest of police corruption and ill treatment, many investors believed that autocratic leaders and hereditary monarchies had made the Middle East and North Africa a quiescent investment environment.

In retrospect, the immediate underlying causes of the Arab Spring were economic.[2] Rising food and fuel prices, combined with high unemployment, particularly among the young male population, created unsustainable pressure on rigid political structures. Undemocratic, weak political institutions, controlled almost exclusively by one individual or one family, were unable to meet protestor's demands for meaningful political reform that would prevent the escalation of violence and the rapid deterioration of law and order.[3] Similarly these governments were unable to convince their western backers that they had the ability to rein in protests and restore stability without resort to violent suppression, thereby forfeiting international political and economic support.

As a result, the crisis has endured for almost five years at the time of writing, spreading from Tunisia across Arabia. By December 2012, rulers had been forced from power in Tunisia, Egypt, Libya, and Yemen. Civil uprisings had erupted in Bahrain and Syria. Major protests had broken out in Algeria, Iraq, Jordan, Kuwait, Morocco, and Sudan, and minor protests had occurred in Mauritania, Oman, Saudi Arabia, Djibouti, Western Sahara, and the Palestinian territories. Weapons and Tuareg fighters returning from the Libyan civil war stoked a simmering conflict in Mali that resulted in French intervention to prevent the seizure of the country by Islamic insurgents.

As investors tried to ascertain how governments would respond to the uprisings and the long-term implications, political risk analysis would have posed a series of questions to determine the different responses in each territory:

- Which governments were most stable?
- Where was economic pressure the highest, with consequent potential for political unrest?
- Which governments would be able to respond by implementing political reform and/or raising subsidies?
- What would be the response of the international community, and with what consequences?

Analysis of these answers would have helped investors foresee the following:

- The monarchies would survive because of their subjects' belief in their legitimacy. Saudi Arabia would lend support to pressurized monarchies in Bahrain, Jordan, and Morocco as a device to shore up the institution of monarchy across the region.
- Hydrocarbon-rich territories would use their reserves to increase social subsidies to buy the quiescence of the population, as occurred in Algeria and the Gulf states.
- Foreign intervention in Libya would lead to the overthrow of Muammar Gaddafi and create a security vacuum in Libya and surrounding territories.
- Territories where leaders were overthrown would be unable to undergo a smooth transition to democracy as had occurred in eastern Europe after 1989.[4]
- Terrorist networks would spread across the region, taking advantage of the security vacuum created by the demise of the autocrats.

Identifying Sources of Political Risk

Crisis Contagion

The Arab Spring provides a pertinent example of how investors can incorrectly perceive risk when diversifying investments across regions and using the past as a guide to future behavior.

Many investors ignored global trends, such as high food and fuel prices and youth unemployment, that made the status quo in many Middle Eastern and North African states unsustainable. Combine inflationary pressure with the concentration of wealth in the hands of autocrats in power for decades, insufficient transparency of its redistribution, corruption, social media, and the WikiLeaks scandal that revealed the willingness of the U.S. government to allow Tunisian President Ben Ali to fall in the event of a sustained uprising, and the combustible mix that gave rise to revolution was apparent.

How Likely Are the Risks You Face?

Hugo Chavez's election in Venezuela and Vladimir Putin's election in Russia illustrate how changes in the individuals who control governing institutions affect the "stability" of a territory for investors. In contrast, unexpected shifts in power do not have a substantive effect on markets in "stable" territories that have well-established institutions, vibrant civil societies, and representative political systems. Risks to investment are far lower in territories where political and economic decisions are institutional rather than led by personalities.

Responding to the Unexpected

The capacity of political leaders to implement policies of their choosing during times of turmoil and their ability to do so without triggering further negative repercussions is one of the hallmarks of a "stable" country. Countries with neither capacity are the most vulnerable to political risk. The challenge of acting decisively while maintaining political stability is one that governments grapple with at times of extremis.

The economic orientation of an economy and its integration into global financial markets and trading systems is a determining factor in assessing how a country will respond to shocks. The United Kingdom provides a pertinent example. With a high concentration of political power vested in parliament, it is theoretically possible for the government to enact rapid policy changes, which could be perceived as an indication of low policy stability. In practice, the capitalist and market-oriented nature of the UK economy means that policy changes are usually economically rational and accompanied by a period of transparent evaluation and debate. In contrast, the concentration of political power in the opaque Chinese Communist Party Politburo[5] creates a high level of political stability but heightens the risk for investors that decisions are motivated by nonmarket factors and implemented without consultation.

Political Risk May Be Counterintuitive

Systems of government and political ideologies play a significant role in determining the risk profile of a territory. Democracies are often associated with stable operating environments and autocracies and other nondemocracies with instability. In reality, the risk environment on the ground is more complex. For example, the governments of many newly democratizing countries in promising mining locations, including Liberia, Sierra Leone, and Guinea, recently beset by turmoil, have sought to rescind and renegotiate mining and oil and gas contracts signed by previous military or authoritarian governments for a larger share of the profits.

Such action contradicts the standard business position, which relies upon the sanctity of contracts irrespective of the circumstances in which they were signed, so long as those signing the contracts have the authority to do so at the date when they were signed. It raises the highly subjective concept of "legitimacy" in contractual agreements and the circumstances under which a contract should be considered secure. If a contract were entered into when the host country was experiencing a period of heightened political tension, does the foreign investor have the right to expect the contract to be honored when the country moves into a period of political stability, even if the process of wining the contract was transparent? This is a challenge confronting many investors in developing territories, and as a consequence, few of the mining majors are jumping to conclusions about the security of their investments or future contracts.

Although resource nationalism is more prevalent in South America, central Asia, and Africa, it has become a notable trend in some of the world's richest territories. Despite the United Kingdom, Canada, and Australia offering some of the world's most hospitable environments, with highly developed infrastructure, a low risk of political violence and robust legal systems, acquisitions perceived to be contrary to the national interest have been prevented and retrospective taxes imposed on the extractives sector.[6] In this regard, the developed world is equally capable of creating an unstable risk environment for foreign investors. Australia provides a case in point. Once considered a safe haven for mining investors, the risk profile of the country has rapidly deteriorated.

The greatest source of political risk affecting companies operating in Australia's mining sector are legal and regulatory reforms, including the impositions of a range of additional taxes and royalties that discriminate against the mining sector.[7] (See Chapter 2, on environmental risk, for more discussion of these risks in mining and other sectors.)

A left-leaning political agenda, combined with a decision to adhere to a tight fiscal policy, means that the natural resources sector will remain vulnerable to government attempts to extract greater revenue for the duration of this political cycle.

The willingness of western governments to intervene in the operating of the markets in this way has given greater legitimacy to the governments of developing nations' doing the same.

Reputational Risk

Political risk can become inextricably linked with reputational risk, particularly in the liberal west. It is no coincidence that China and Russia have been particularly successful in operating in territories considered to be "high risk." This isn't because Chinese and Russian companies have more effective political risk management strategies in place than their western counterparts; it is because the nature of their governments and societies mean that they are less accountable for the ways that their enterprises operate in overseas territories. They have proven particularly effective in thriving in Africa, the Sahel, and central Asia, where they have fewer constraints than their western counterparts in paying officials or turning a blind eye when it comes to issues of transparency and accountability. The Chinese presence in Sudan, Libya (now accounting for 10 percent of Libya's oil output), and, more recently, Niger, demonstrates the importance of these players within the hydrocarbon market[8] in territories where western governments have serious concerns about corruption and human rights abuses. (See Chapter 7, on brand risk, for more discussion of this topic.)

POLITICAL RISK INSIGHTS

- Political risk is a real and present issue even in relatively stable markets.
- Political risk should be analyzed—it is rarely a consistent or coherent threat even within the same country.
- Despite the risk, there are significant rewards associated with trade and investment into the emerging markets, and many elements of political risk can actually be managed.
- Political risk insurance is a very effective mitigation tool, especially when risks are well understood and cover is tailored.

Political Risk Assessment

As companies expand across borders to tap into new markets or to exploit new resources, a key determinant of their success is the ability to manage political risk. Long-term sustainability is dependent on integrating political risk management into enterprise and business risk management in a methodological way. This enables companies to make more informed decisions about global expansion, government relations, community engagement, operational structures, supply chain management, and other issues relating to sustainability.

Management teams often feel that they lack the requisite tools to adequately assess political risk. Its nebulous nature can create the impression that it is impossible to rate and prioritize risks based on seemingly amorphous concepts such as "political stability," "regulatory risk," and "terrorism risk." In reality, much can be done to quantify and systematize political risk assessments, which is reassuring, for it is often political risk factors that make or break an investment.

Political risks should be assessed at the time of an investment and a risk management structure put in place. These risks should then be monitored on an ongoing basis to enable the risk management framework to be regularly updated to reflect fluidity in the risk profile of a host territory.

Though the most effective political risk ratings tools are based on a combination of quantitative and qualitative sources, deciding between these different types of sources is not as important as developing a systematic framework for the modeling of the data. The use of multiple sources of data enhances political risk models and allows for cross-referencing and sense checking of economic and survey data. Each source of data will have its merits and demerits and should be weighted accordingly.

Internationally respected and independently verifiable data sources may offer a level of reliability that local sources of information do not. Expatriates and local employees have a tendency to "go native" and underestimate the risks inherent in the host political environment. Alternatively, they may be too closely tied to the host government to feel safe providing an objective assessment of reality on the ground. Governments themselves also have an incentive to falsify data when economic performance is poor. Inflation data published by the Argentinian government is often inaccurate and, when compared with International Monetary Fund or World Bank data, indicates that the government underreports inflation rates by 10–15 percent.

Many banks, export credit agencies, multinational corporations, and insurance underwriters develop political risk matrixes to assign a quantitative weighting to their risk exposure in overseas territories. Country risk ratings often focus on the credit risk posed by a territory and different forms of political risk that have the potential to destabilize the operating environment. In addition to the currency, sovereign debt, and banking sector risks posed by a country, political risk assessment also looks at political stability, institutional resilience, legal risk, regulatory risk, and investment risk, such as government propensity to forcibly renegotiate contracts or seize foreign-owned assets. Because many investments are of a medium- to long-term nature, it is useful to develop short-term forecasts (six months) and medium-term forecasts (twenty-four months) for each territory. Developing meaningful ratings over a long-term time horizon is challenging, particularly in developing markets, where governments are vulnerable to sudden violent change. Scenario modeling, a process of analyzing future events by considering alternative possible outcomes, may provide a more viable alternative.

Risk ratings provide a benchmark for investment risk in different territories and the risk that investments will be affected by a range of perils. They are an effective tool for benchmarking risk between countries and regions and for highlighting exposure to concentrations of perils. For example, mining companies are likely to find themselves disproportionately exposed to the risk of expropriation than companies operating in the non-extractives sector, and they are vulnerable to the same risks even if their portfolio of assets is diversified across a number of continents.

It is important to note that political risk ratings are an art and not a science. A level of subjectivity is inherent in each rating, which often acts as a strength rather than a weakness. Economic data alone was unable to indicate the effects that the election of either Jakarta Governor Joko Widodo or former General Prabowo Subianto in Indonesia would have on the investment environment, but a qualitative view, provided by an expert on the Indonesian political environment, could provide valuable strategic insights to the potential changes to the investment landscape.

The International Monetary Fund or World Bank provides information on the past performance of the world's economies, but this isn't necessarily an indicator of future performance. On the contrary, GDP data for the Eurozone growth in the years preceding the financial crisis created the impression of linear growth and gave no indication that sovereign states in the developed world were on the precipice of the largest debt crisis in history. However, discerning investors who analyzed data relating to consumer and government debt were more likely to consider the unsustainable trajectory of many western economies.

Political risk ratings reflect the risks facing a country; they are not meant to predict a crisis. Many investors I worked with before the Arab Spring had assigned relatively low risk ratings to their investments in Libya. Their justification for so doing was that the investment environment under the leadership of Colonel Muammar Gaddafi was stable. He had ruled Libya for more than forty years, and there was no evident challenge to his authority. I found this bemusing, as I generally do when investors assure me that their contracts or assets are safe in territories where power is vested almost solely in one individual. In such territories, the risk of an abrupt correction cannot be discounted, and from an actuarial perspective at least, the dictator in whom you have placed your trust will, at some point, die, potentially taking political stability with him.

Similarly in 2009–2010, I had discussions with investors over political risk ratings I produced for Egypt. Working on a ratings scale of 1 (low) to 10 (high), ratings I produced were in the medium-risk range of 5–6. Investors with experience in Egypt often considered these too high, whereas my perception of Egypt was that of a simmering cauldron waiting for the lid to blow off. Ratings can't predict the timing of a crisis, but elevated ratings provide investors with important insights into the nature of the risk environment.

There are reasons why credit rating agencies often assign a 4-point deduction to the sovereign ratings of oil-rich Gulf states like Saudi Arabia. Though their debt:GDP ratios are positive and their foreign exchange reserves are the envy of the Western world, the undemocratic nature of the regimes and the absence of the rule of law heighten the risk of a sovereign default. In contrast, the strong track record of the United Kingdom in honoring debt obligations and international confidence in its institutions and the rule of law enabled the country to maintain its triple A credit rating for much longer than underlying economic data indicated that it should have.

Political risk ratings should be granular. They are less valuable as a risk management tool if they posit a single numerical rating for a territory. A ratings system that provides a rating of 4 for Portugal and 7 for Nigeria tells a risk manager very little about the underlying challenges to be confronted when operating in those territories. A granular breakdown of the risk environment that highlights economic and credit weakness in Portugal as compared with terrorism risk and corruption in Nigeria is of far greater value in directing the risk management process.

Political risk ratings are fluid and will change to reflect alterations and evolutions in the political landscape. Generally, these alterations should be small and incremental, for significant shifts in ratings indicate that the underlying assumptions about a territory were incorrect. More dramatic ratings changes do occur as black swan events, but these are, by definition, infrequent.

Although ratings are fluid, they must also be relative. In 2002, Moody's Investors Service infuriated Tokyo by downgrading Japan's sovereign credit rating to one notch below Botswana.[9] Though the southern African nation was performing relatively well, it seemed illogical to attribute greater risk to the sovereign debt of the world's second largest economy.

This aptly demonstrates that although political risk ratings provide a valuable guide to assessments of the risk environment of divergent territories, the output is only as logical, robust, and meaningful as the thought process and data that comprise the inputs. Even leading rating agencies can misjudge the creditworthiness of sovereign states and corporations.

Mitigating Political Risk

The global risk environment remains very challenging, and this will require effective management by companies seeking to invest, particularly in the rich natural resources sector. Historically management of political risk by corporations was considered an oxymoron, whereas credit risk management tended to be either a question of trust or the elimination of risk through structure/collateral or transferring to local banks.

Today we recognize that companies change the political risk environment within which they operate. There are a number of steps companies can take to manage political risks and maximize investment returns.

An effective political risk strategy must be about identifying challenges and understanding how risk may be anticipated and effectively managed to safeguard the opportunity presented by a trade or investment. The political risk management process can be broken down into a number of stages.

The first is to acknowledge that the belief in "good" versus "bad" countries when contemplating political risk is something of an illusion. Trade flows to high-risk countries like Sudan remain significant, and oil companies are prospecting in Somalia despite perceptions that it is a dangerous place to do business. In reality, political risk is not generic across a region or even within a country, and foreign investors must analyze the specific environment in the specific region of the country for their specific project. Several steps can be taken in structuring a trade or investment to minimize the likelihood that a political risk event will disrupt activities.

The second step is to acknowledge that the origin of an investment plays as significant a role in determining the risk profile of a venture as the destination of the investment. The meaning of this may not be immediately apparent, and the key point to note is that investors play a crucial role in the creation of the risk environment in which they operate and their investment profile is a key determinant of this. A Russian, Brazilian, Chinese, or American company making an investment in the same oil project in Angola will be perceived in entirely different ways by the host government and local population even before the project commences and its effects felt. Acknowledging this and actively engaging with host governments and local communities to alter negative cultural stereotypes that may adversely affect a project are important parts of the risk management process.

The third step is to do effective due diligence. This will include a review of security on the ground, legacy issues, reputational risk, social effects, environmental effects, and relations with the current and potentially future political decision makers in the host country. The adoption of a coherent political or country risk strategy can neutralize potential sources of risk and reduce, or at least identify more clearly, those risks that cannot be satisfactorily managed.

Similar due diligence may be needed for transit route countries to ensure the integrity of the supply chain and export routes.

The fourth step is to ensure equitable reward sharing among sovereign states, private companies, and other participants. A major driver for expropriation and contract agreement repudiation, particularly in the natural resources sector, has been perceived inequality in returns when commodity prices rise or tariffs and tolls are increased. One way to address this is to link the royalties of all parties to project profitability. Direct government equity participation in projects can also be a risk management tool and may be an alternative to the royalty structure.

The fifth step is to consider engagement with nongovernmental stakeholders that can enhance the stability of a trade or investment. Many operational nongovernmental organizations (NGOs) are becoming increasingly cognizant of the developmental benefits of investing in infrastructure projects and are willing to work with foreign investors to enhance project management. An NGO's local expertise may prevent a project company from inadvertently creating new risks by advising on such matters as balancing the interests of competing tribal groups, employing from across ethnic groups, and sensitivities to such potential tension-infliction points as the sacred status of religious and historical sites.

As a sixth step, the benefits of working with multilateral organizations should be considered. As a preferred sovereign creditor, the World Bank wields considerable influence in the event of contractual disputes and defaults with emerging governments. This influence is reinforced by the World Bank's likely involvement in other projects within a host territory and its status as a key source of liquidity when a country is in turmoil.

The seventh step is to ensure that dispute resolution mechanisms are in place at the time of contract signing. Clarity on law and jurisdiction, dispute resolution, and arbitration provisions if dispute resolution fails are important considerations. Recourse under bilateral investment treaties (BITs) may provide a further source of redress if the treaties have been signed and ratified by the respective governments.[10]

In the event of a dispute with a host government or local investment partner, a foreign investor is more likely to receive a favorable hearing outside the project's host state. The most favored jurisdictions for legal contracts are England, Wales, France, and New York. These territories are considered to have robust and impartial legal systems, staffed by highly competent legal practitioners that will consider a dispute without favor.

Step eight is to consider threats beyond merely payment or political risk, such as property or personnel threats in the form of political violence or employee risks such as kidnap for ransom or extortion. Implement appropriate security planning measures. For very unstable territories, consider emergency evacuation procedures. Seek the advice of security companies as applicable.

Depending on the nature of your investment and the profile of your company, the final step may be to consider the utility of political risk insurance (PRI) as a risk transfer mechanism. PRI works well where risk is well managed and defined. It does not compensate for deficient contracts, poor development processes, or lack of political risk planning. To the contrary, PRI is most effective when risk is well managed; under these circumstances, it provides an effective safety net, effectively neutralizing political risk and allowing you to maximize the returns on your investment.

POLITICAL RISK ASSESSMENT AND MITIGATION

- Identify, analyze, and prioritize the potential risks in each country where you trade or have investments.
- Define the perils on a micro-level, for political risk is rarely consistent or coherent, even within the same country.
- Quantify the consequences on your investment if these risks occur.
- Structure the project in a way that minimizes these threats.
- Decide how to distribute these risks among all the parties involved—e.g., risks you bear, joint venture risks, and lender and investor risks.

Notes

1. Ian Bremmer and Preston Keat, *The Fat Tail: The Power of Political Knowledge for Strategic Investing.* Oxford, UK: Oxford University Press, 2009, p. 4.
2. Jack A. Goldstone and John T. Hazel Jr., "Understanding the Revolutions of 2011: Weakness and Resilience in Middle Eastern Autocracies," *Foreign Affairs*, April 14, 2011.
3. Jason Brownlee, Tarek Masoud, and Andrew Reynolds. *The Arab Spring: The Politics of Transformation in North Africa and the Middle East.* Oxford, UK: Oxford University Press, 2013.
4. Steven A. Cook, "How Do You Say 1989 in Arabic?" From the Potomac to the Euphrates: Council on Foreign Relations, March 28, 2011.
5. Bremmer and Keat, p. 2.
6. Elizabeth Stephens, "Exploring Coal's New Frontiers," *World Coal*, June 2013.
7. Elizabeth Stephens, "Political Risk in the Australian Mining Sector," *Industrial Minerals*, July 2013.
8. Elizabeth Stephens, "Operating in the Sahel and North Africa," *Petroleum Review*, April 2014.
9. Mure Dickie, "Japan Still Stronger Than Botswana," *Financial Times*, January 28, 2011. www.ft.com/cms/s/0/15aba75e-2a37-11e0-b906-00144feab49a.html#axzz37iSNeB3y.
10. It should be noted that there is an increasing trend among developing nations to allow bilateral investment treaties (BITs) to lapse. Indonesia announced its intention, in March 2014, to terminate sixty-seven BITs, a policy South Africa initiated last year. These announcements are a product of the perception among developing countries, most notably those having sizable extractive sectors, that the treaty-based system favors foreign investors. The renunciation of these treaties removes an important form of protection that investors consider when assessing political risk.

16

Strategic Risk: The Risks "of" and "to" a Strategy: The Case of Blockbuster and the Need for Strategic Flexibility

Michael E. Raynor

In the realms of physical, intangible and financial risk management, the topics of the previous chapters, the primary goal is to optimize a company's ability to achieve its objectives despite the uncertainty surrounding future events. Bad luck, incompetence, or malfeasance—each of which can be dimensions of an organization's internal context—can derail even the best-laid plans. Quite reasonably, much of risk management assumes that the plans themselves, if implemented as intended, will achieve specified objectives, and that achieving those objectives will deliver the desired outcomes.

Other risks lie entirely in a company's external context, risks that threaten an organization's very existence because they undermine not merely the execution of a plan, but the value of the objectives themselves. The risk that a company is pursuing the wrong objectives can be thought of as "strategic risk."

There are further two types of strategic risk: the risks *of* a strategy and the risks *to* a strategy. The risks *of* a strategy are created by the choices that define the strategy itself. That is, in choosing to compete in one way—e.g., with a low-cost position or a highly differentiated one—a company necessarily becomes *unable* to compete in another way. If the path you have chosen turns out to be economically unviable because consumer tastes change or because new competitors make different choices that consumers prefer, then you have been undone by the risks *of* your strategy.

Risks *to* a strategy are risks arising from new competitors that find ways to invalidate the choices you made. Whereas your strategy might have been based on providing low-cost solutions that were lower-performance, a competitor that finds a way to provide high performance at low cost creates a risk *to* your strategy. In both cases, you might find yourself implementing your strategy very effectively yet fail to achieve the results you seek because the strategies themselves have been undermined.

To illustrate, consider the case of Blockbuster, the once-ubiquitous video rental chain.[1] Its first store opened in 1985 in Dallas, Texas. The details of the company's growth are unique, but the essence of its story is universal. Beneath the inevitable drama of acquisitions, competitive struggles, and personality clashes, Blockbuster's success was built around holding on tight to two rules that drive long-term success. First, don't compete on price; that's a race that has only one winner. Second, don't rely on cost leadership as a source of superior profits; that's self-immolation to a false god.

The general case for these rules is made in prior research.[2] In the case of the video rental industry, consider that during the 1980s, tens of thousands of mom-and-pop stores tried to stay afloat by cutting prices and just about every convenience store in the United States tried to create "free revenue" by cramming a few dozen tapes into their magazine racks. Blockbuster, on the other hand, competed on selection, stocking not only the latest blockbusters, but also building a carefully chosen catalogue based on an analysis of neighborhood demographics. That selection came at a price, however: Building out lots of large stores and keeping them stocked was an expensive proposition. To pay for it all, Blockbuster did not focus on the "obvious" price—the rental fee—but instead on the far less obvious price that few customers think they will need to pay: the late fees.

This was pure strategic brilliance. The video rental business had been characterized by cutthroat price-based competition and commodity products. In response, Blockbuster created strong differentiation and barriers to entry by providing asset-efficient availability and selection and generating superior profitability through a price premium that was largely invisible to customers. At its peak, in 2004, the company had more than 9,000 stores and more than 60,000 employees.

Blockbuster's relatively rapid and total collapse is perhaps the only thing more dramatic than its impressive rise. Filing for Chapter 11 bankruptcy protection in September 2010, the dwindling asset base was picked up by Dish Network in April of 2011. As operations around the world were divested or closed down, Dish explored a variety of new (for Blockbuster) approaches, including by-mail and online options, but to no avail. On November 6, 2013, the last video rented out by a Blockbuster store was, in what had to be a deliberate irony, *This Is the End*, a movie about the apocalypse.

The mere fact of Blockbuster's demise is not a reason to think that anything went particularly wrong. Nothing lasts forever, and a curious fact of the study of decision-making is that simply because a decision made under uncertainty yielded a bad result doesn't mean that it was a bad decision. Even so, these inescapable facts of the human condition did not dictate the nature or timing of Blockbuster's demise. Neither was it bad luck, incompetence, or malfeasance that proved the company's undoing. Rather, it was largely Netflix's fault. More remarkable still, Netflix's success was not a function of finding a way to do better what Blockbuster had been doing. Rather, Netflix found a way to change the game—to invalidate the assumptions that had made Blockbuster's strategy so successful.

In other words, Blockbuster didn't go "blockbusted" because it was unable to implement its chosen strategy. It came undone because its strategy was simply no longer viable thanks to the actions of, in this case, a specific competitor. Blockbuster is no more not because it failed to grapple with the risks associated with its internal context, but because it failed to assess correctly a specific risk in its external context—specifically, the risks *of* and *to* its strategy.

Tradeoffs and the Risks *of* a Strategy

Strategic is a term that in general usage has indistinct contours. As a colloquialism, it is often little more than a synonym for "important." This meaning-in-use will not suffice when addressing the concept of risk, for a strategic risk is something much more precise than simply an "important" risk.

Every company has an "activity set"—those activities it performs that allow it to provide products or services that customers value. An automobile manufacturer, for example, must design, manufacture, sell, and service its cars—either on its own or via a more extended ecosystem.

Every company's activity set is subject to certain constraints, limits on what it can do and at what cost. These constraints are determined by engineering tradeoffs. For example, a company that has chosen to focus on high-end performance automobiles will typically be unable to provide leading-edge low-end, highly fuel-efficient automobiles—and vice-versa for a company focused on the low end. Think of the range of what each company can produce as its own possibility frontier. The possibility frontier for the industry is therefore that segment of each company's individual frontier that is farther from the origin that any other company's frontier (Figure 16–1).

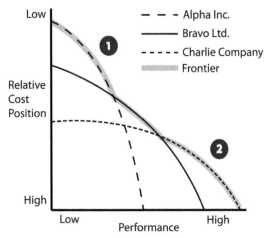

FIGURE 16–1 Imagine for a moment an automobile industry with only three competitors: Alpha, Bravo, and Charlie. Each company is able to provide cars with different performance attributes at different costs, and the range of cars each company can provide defines each company's possibility frontier. The frontier for the industry is the concatenation of all the maxima for the three companies—that is, the combination of the highlighted segments of each company's frontier. Where a company's frontier is the above all the others (the highlighted segments), it enjoys a particularly powerful competitive position: It can provide the highest level of performance at a given cost. The value of that position will be a function of how many customers want cars with those performance attributes and how much more than the company's cost they are willing to pay. Where a company's frontier lies relatively close to another company's, in the vicinity of points ❶ and ❷, competition can be fierce, especially if large numbers of customers desire cars having those performance attributes. *Source: Adapted from Porter (1996) and Raynor (2011).*

A company's strategy can be usefully thought of as the tradeoffs the company embraces with the intent of creating an activity set with some segment of that activity set's possibility frontier defining the industry's possibility frontier.[3] That is a somewhat cumbersome, but precise, way of saying that a company's strategy consists of the choices it makes to serve some segment of the market better than the competition does.

The risks *of* a strategy are the risks arising from the tradeoffs embedded in a particular activity set. If you are good at serving the low end of the market, you are unlikely to be good at serving the high end of the market. Your strategic bet, the strategic risk you accept, is that there will be enough customers to make your strategy economically viable. You still have to deal with physical, intangible, and financial risks in the execution of your strategy, but these risks are quite different from the risks that arise from the tradeoffs that define the strategy—risks that, though manageable, are inescapable.

Blockbuster's nearly twenty-year run of success can be attributed to a terrific strategy: Its activity set consisted of a relatively asset-intensive, but asset-efficient, approach enabled by savvy data management. (It would have been called "big data" if we had had that term in the late 1990s.) Other providers—the mom-and-pop shops and the opportunistic grocery stores—had much lower investment levels and lower absolute costs, but that meant they couldn't match Blockbuster's availability of hit titles or provide an appropriate back catalogue. At best, they pipped Blockbuster in the "convenience" or "impulse purchase" category when they happened to have just the right movie at just the right time in just the right place. In more technical terms, the tradeoffs that Blockbuster embraced meant that its productivity frontier defined a segment of the industry's frontier that more closely matched the requirements of a great many more customers (Figure 16–2).

When Netflix first entered the fray, in 1997, there were two new elements of its activity set, or "business model," to use a more conventional term. First, the company had an exclusively online interface, and videos were delivered via the U.S. Postal service. Like Blockbuster, videos

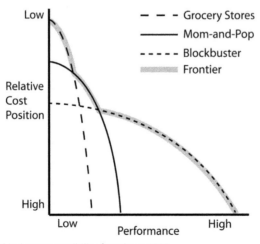

FIGURE 16–2 The video rental industry's possibility frontier *c.* 1995.

were rented one at a time, and late fees applied—even though it was (perhaps apocryphally) a $40 late fee that Reed Hastings, one of Netflix's founders, had been assessed by Blockbuster on his rental of *Apollo 13* that had motivated him to launch the company.

In terms of its possibility frontier, Netflix had embraced a different set of tradeoffs. It was offering one sort of convenience (you didn't have to leave your home to select or receive a DVD) at the expense of another (you had to wait for the video to be delivered). These tradeoffs had one additional advantage: They allowed Netflix to launch at much lower cost than a brick-and-mortar rental outlet; Hastings invested only $2.5 million of a $700 million payday on the sale of his software startup, Pure Software, whereas Blockbuster had to deploy thousands of stores and construct multi-million-dollar warehouses to achieve the sort of nationwide coverage Netflix achieved from its inception.

The dimensions of convenience embodied in the two companies' respective activity sets were very different. Consequently, Netflix—like the grocery stores and single-location players before it—served to define more sharply the risks *of* Blockbuster's strategy. That is, Blockbuster had bet that enough customers would value what it could offer sufficiently highly that the company would have a viable business. Alternative providers were making different bets. As new providers make different bets, the risks *of* a strategy increase. Netflix defined a new risk *of* Blockbuster's strategy, insofar as it might turn out that many customers would actually prefer to wait several days for a single DVD rented from a company with less selection that was marginally less expensive than what was available at Blockbuster.

Whatever Netflix's early success, however, the risks *of* Blockbuster's strategy did not materialize in any significant way. Blockbuster's possibility frontier still defined most of the industry's frontier.

Innovation and the Risks *to* a Strategy

As is often the case with new ventures, however, Netflix's initial model evolved dramatically and rapidly. By 2000, the company had migrated to a monthly all-you-can-watch subscription (subject to a limit on the number of DVDs being rented at any one time), dropping both late fees and explicit charges for postal service. In addition, the online interaction with customers allowed Netflix to gather detailed customer-specific information on what people were watching and, consequently, to make customer-specific suggestions about what they might like to watch. This led to the development of powerful "suggestion engines" that directed customers to movies they might not have otherwise considered but were likely to enjoy. Consequently, Netflix could now guide customers to movies it had in stock, mitigating customer frustrations at not finding what they were originally looking for.

Where strategy is embracing different constraints in order to serve specific customer segments with more targeted offerings, *innovation* can be seen as breaking the constraints that define the limits of a given strategy. When a competitor pursues a different strategy than you, they manifest a risk *of* your strategy: They might have guessed better about which sets of tradeoffs customers will value more. Netflix in 1997 served to define some of the risks *of* Blockbuster's strategy: Providing convenience and selection meant asset intensity and higher costs. Lower prices meant waiting.

When a competitor begins breaking the constraints that define your strategy, it is *innovating* in ways that pose a threat *to* your strategy: The tradeoffs that separated the two of you begin to erode, and your competitor is able to provide similar or better products and services at lower or similar cost.

Netflix's changes between 1997 and 2000 served to break some of the tradeoffs that had defined Netflix's and Blockbuster's initial strategies. Netflix had dramatically lowered the per-video cost by shifting to a subscription model; it had dramatically changed its relationship with customers by creating "watch lists"; it had blunted the "out-of-stock" problem with its accurate suggestion algorithms. In other words, Netflix was no longer merely embracing different tradeoffs in the pursuit of strategic differentiation. It had innovated and so expanded the possibility frontier of its activity set, allowing Netflix to occupy a greater expanse of the industry's possibility frontier. Netflix no longer served merely to define the risks *of* Blockbuster's strategy by highlighting the tradeoffs inherent in Blockbuster's model. Instead, Netflix was on the cusp of becoming a threat *to* Blockbuster's strategy by invaliding the assumption that such tradeoffs were binding on all industry players.

The video rental market continued to fragment with the introduction of Redbox in 2003, a kiosk-based rental service that focused on new releases provided at very low cost. Although Redbox could be immediate and convenient in a way that Netflix couldn't, and thanks to its low capital and operating costs could offer its services at much lower prices than Blockbuster, its kiosks could initially stock only 100 disks, which made it difficult to maintain Blockbuster's levels of availability and selection.

Because it embraced a different set of tradeoffs, Redbox served largely to define new risks *of* Blockbuster's strategy. But then, as with Netflix, innovation kicked in: Improvements in kiosk design increased inventory to over 700 discs, dramatically lowering the "stock-out" rate while increasing selection. Connecting the kiosks with an online interface allowed Redbox customers to determine availability in advance and reserve titles for pickup. All this without compromising its structurally lower costs, which kept Redbox's prices lower than Blockbuster's, even as Redbox enjoyed strong profitability (Figure 16–3).

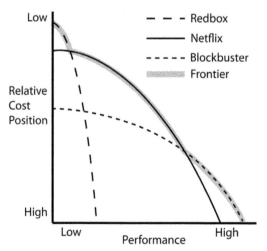

FIGURE 16–3 The video rental industry's possibility frontier c. 2004.

By 2004—the peak of Blockbuster's growth—the strategic landscape had changed in ways that had greatly increased both the risks *of* Blockbuster's strategy and the risks *to* that strategy. Those portions of the industry's possibility frontier that had been captured by Netflix and Redbox had dramatically reduced that portion of Blockbuster's frontier that defined an industry maximum.

The risks *of* Blockbuster's strategy were captured primarily in the possibility that there was simply no longer enough business along that portion of the industry's frontier that Blockbuster defined to sustain the company's current operations, never mind continued growth. The risks *to* Blockbuster lay predominantly in the possibility that either or both of Redbox or Netflix would continue to innovate—to break the tradeoffs that defined their own frontiers in ways that allowed them to subsume that remaining portion of Blockbuster's frontier that still defined the industry's maximum.

Assessing Strategic Risks

The disaster that eventually befell Blockbuster was by no means assured, but neither was it entirely unforeseeable. The tradeoffs at the heart of Blockbuster's strategy had not changed since the company's inception: Convenience, selection and availability defined the company's value proposition to customers. Providing that value demanded a capital- and labor-intensive model. Embracing these tradeoffs in ways that mom-and-pop stores couldn't (for lack of capital) and grocery stores wouldn't (because it would have corrupted their ability to compete as grocery stores) allowed Blockbuster to outcompete its rivals. Thanks to its scale, Blockbuster very likely also had lower unit costs than its would-be competitors. Leveraging its position and assets, the company was able to branch out into game rentals and all manner of ancillary retail: once you have the locations and the labor, it's easy to plug in a different kind of disc (the games) and to sell soda pop and candy to go with the movie. The result was more than fifteen years of remarkable, and remarkably profitable, growth.

New models defined by Redbox and Netflix created new risks *of* Blockbuster's strategy. They had not broken the fundamental tradeoffs among capital, labor, convenience, and selection that defined Blockbuster's position. Rather, these entrants embraced fundamentally different tradeoffs. The only way Blockbuster could have responded was by emulating them, creating new divisions that embraced the same tradeoffs these entrants were exploiting in order to hive off some of Blockbuster's market share.

Why didn't Blockbuster start its own mail-order operations in the late 1990s or at least the early 2000s? In fact, why didn't Blockbuster simply acquire Netflix in 2000, when it could have been had for $50 million and had fewer than 500,000 subscribers? But Blockbuster waited until 2004 to launch Blockbuster Online, by which point Netflix was closing in on 5 million subscribers.

In hindsight, it is easy to fault Blockbuster for not having pursued a different course. Such finger-pointing might be entertaining, but it is not instructive. Through the mid-2000s, it was entirely defensible to interpret both Netflix and Redbox as manifestations of the risks *of* Blockbuster's strategy and little more. Creating new divisions or acquiring these entrants would have almost certainly have been material drains on management time and attention, creating new and potentially dysfunctional levels of complexity within the organization. After all, the dangers of unfettered diversification are well documented and well understood, and the bankruptcy courts are replete with the stories of those who succumbed to what turned out to be corporate bloat. Similarly, the virtues of focus are amply heralded in the popular and scholarly management literature. There was good reason for Blockbuster to stick to its knitting.

The framework used in this book prescribes that the first step in effective risk *assessment* is *identifying* the risk. The definitions of "strategy" and "innovation" offered here provide a rigorous analytical framework for identifying your strategic risks, specifically, the risks *of* and *to* your strategy.

Identifying strategic risks requires that you understand the relative shape of your competitors' possibility frontiers compared to your own, as well as how each maps to the critical elements of customer value.

At first blush, this might sound a little bit like "figure out whether competitors can give customers what they want better than you can," but this extended discussion of Blockbuster's travails has given us a powerful language that reveals important subtleties.

Every strategy necessarily embraces tradeoffs among different dimensions of performance. A successful strategy embraces tradeoffs that maximize what the greatest number of customers is willing to pay the most for. This can be difficult to determine in advance, so a great deal of competitive activity takes the form of jockeying for position, testing different approaches to a market, and finding out via trial and error what really works.

Once a successful strategy has been found—either through careful analysis and bold commitment, or through experimentation and incremental evolution—existing and new competitors will define the risks *of* your strategy as they create their strategies. That is, the risk implicit in the choices you have made will become explicit in light of the choices they make.

Blockbuster bet on the primacy of convenience, availability, and selection and invested heavily to deliver on those dimensions of performance. That meant big investments in assets and people, which, in turn, required high prices in the form of rental and late fees. This particular combination of performance attributes was better than the available alternatives for almost fifteen years and was possible only by embracing the very same tradeoffs among those attributes.

Netflix and then Redbox made very different choices, giving up specific dimensions of convenience (Netflix) or availability and selection (Redbox) in exchange for dramatically lower prices. In both cases, these companies enjoyed some material success, and Blockbuster would have done well to keep an eye on just how much of the market for rentals was migrating to these alternative offerings.

It is at this point that we can move from *identifying* strategic risks to *analyzing* them. To understand the risks posed by competitors' strategies, it is worth looking to the nature of the competitive offerings that a successful incumbent has vanquished in the past. Blockbuster, having put paid to literally tens of thousands of smaller focused rental operators and the deeper-pocketed but less committed convenience and grocery stores, might well have taken the view that Netflix and Redbox were simply sequels to a movie it had seen before. But whereas earlier competitors were playing essentially the same game as Blockbuster, but less well, Netflix and Redbox had fundamentally different strategies: They were playing a different game.

Beyond understanding simply the shape of the frontiers defined by these alternative strategies, it would likely have been possible to generate meaningful insight into the nature and rate of the expansion of these frontiers. Whereas customer reaction (demand-side response) would help limn the threats *of* the strategy, looking to potential technological and process changes relevant to your competitors (supply-side evolution) provides insight into the risks *to* the strategy.

Once again, it is only in hindsight that online video streaming and high-density kiosks were the "inevitable" innovations that would invalidate the tradeoffs that defined Blockbuster's strategy. Deciding precisely what to do, when viewing Blockbuster's choices from Blockbuster's perspective at that point in time, requires not post hoc mockery but a fair-minded attempt to *prioritize* (the next step in risk *assessment*) the risks *of* and *to* the strategy that these competitors had created.

First, the question is whether the risks *to* the strategy are sufficiently grave to warrant a significant and immediate response. That is, were first Netflix and then Redbox actually bleeding away enough business that Blockbuster could simply no longer compete with its assets-and-selection model? Given Blockbuster's growth through the early 2000s, and the relatively small size of Netflix and Redbox, it would be difficult to claim that these entrants, in their initial forms, posed the sort of challenges that required a dramatic and drastic shift in Blockbuster's strategic position. Competition is rarely good for your business, but it is often manageable risk. Emulating a competitor's successful model is often an option even after a competitor has captured a viable and durable market niche. Competitive, if not peaceful, coexistence is often possible even after a late entry.

In contrast, despite the uncertainties, the gravity of the threats *to* Blockbuster's strategy posed by the effects of innovation by Netflix and Redbox were, even at the time, relatively predictable. Netflix's online customer interface was Internet-based. Internet-based music services were bubbling up in the late 1990s and became especially credible with the rapid success of Apple's iTunes, launched in 2004. Early 2005 saw the launch of YouTube, which made video streaming over the Internet increasingly credible. This made the commercially viable streaming of movies over the Internet at least thinkable. The full scope of the risk *to* Blockbuster's strategy could have been seen quite clearly by combining these technical and business model advances with the observation that all content migrates to every possible medium: After all, Hollywood studios fought the rise of videotape rentals!

This discussion has implications for the *treatment* that Blockbuster might have applied to these risks. The risks *of* Blockbuster's strategy very likely demanded a "watchful waiting" response. Mail-order and kiosk distribution channels were not characterized by significant barrier to entry or material customer switching costs, so being a relatively late entrant would not have been debilitating. Moving too soon or, worse, unnecessarily would have meant making significant investments in businesses that would have very likely cannibalized its existing business. It was therefore entirely defensible to *mitigate* this risk *of* the strategy by simply paying very close attention to the evolution of the market and developing contingency plans.

The risks *to* Blockbuster's strategy, defined largely by Netflix, were quite different. The nature of the deals Netflix struck with customer premises equipment (e.g., game console makers and consumer electronics companies) and with Hollywood studios for distribution are far more difficult to replicate than simply alternative distribution channels for DVDs. Customers tend be much less likely to subscribe to multiple services than to shop at different stores, creating switching costs. Consequently, the downside of being late to the video streaming business was far greater. Innovation within Blockbuster's bricks-and-mortar based activity was fundamentally limited: Its core assets simply weren't sufficiently fungible to respond to Netflix's expanding frontier. That was not a consequence of bad management, but of the ineluctable differences between atoms and bits. An effective response very likely demanded emulating that new strategy. But when? Committing or waiting were both very risky bets given the uncertainty.

A more effective treatment here is one that actively *reduced* the risk, and that would have meant setting up an independent division that had the explicit mandate of exploring the potential of video streaming as an alternative distribution channel for video entertainment. Doing this effectively can be tremendously difficult, but research in this area has some practical advice to offer.[4]

Perhaps the most critical dimension is understanding that in these circumstances, launching a new division creates value by reducing strategic risk, not by generating cash flows. In Blockbuster's case, that would have meant that a video streaming division would have been best valued as an *option* on future possibilities rather than a *commitment* to a specific commercial opportunity. This, in turn, would mean that the division would operate under a clear and often constraining strategic mandate: Do *not* attempt to build a successful video rental business; seek *only* to build a successful video streaming business. Commitment to this success would lie entirely at the level of this new operating division, while the division's value to the larger corporation would have to be assessed at the corporate level based on the combination of the operation's cash flows, the effect on the effectiveness of the larger organization (thanks to the burdens of incremental complexity), and the reduced strategic risk Blockbuster faced thanks to the division's existence. The resulting option is correctly seen as a *strategic* option because it creates the possibility of changing Blockbuster's activity set in a way that alters its frontier—that is, in a way that fundamentally changes its strategy (Table 16–1).

Table 16–1   The Elements of Strategic Risk Assessment

Stage of Risk Assessment	Activities
Identification	Specify the shape of the frontiers of competing activity sets
Analysis	Estimate the rate and nature of customer adoption the expansion of competitors' frontiers
Prioritization	Estimate the timing and magnitude of the resulting risks *of* the strategy due to customer adoption *to* the strategy due to frontier expansion
Treatment	Decide whether the nature of the risks permits mitigation: watchful waiting and contingency planning treatment: the development of strategic options through targeted investment

Strategy, Innovation, and Flexibility

Every company operating in dynamic and competitive markets is playing at least three games at once. The first is the current, cross-sectional, or point-in-time game, defined by the strategic choices made by the company and its competitors. The rules of this game are defined by the tradeoffs that define each company's activity set and, hence, competitive position. The second is the future-oriented, longitudinal, or across-time game, defined by innovations that change the rules by breaking those same tradeoffs. And the third is defined by the uncertainties that surround each of the first two.

Successful strategies are often characterized by deep commitments to building capabilities optimized to meet the particular needs of specific customer segment.[5] Yet committing in the face of uncertainty necessarily creates the risk that the wrong—and perhaps very wrong—commitment has been made.

The identification and analysis of strategic risks has tended to focus on the need for more creative and less hide-bound thinking. Individual and collective cognitive biases can make it very difficult for people and organizations to see what they should. Proposed remedies can be very helpful in expanding the horizons of corporate leaders, allowing them to take seriously credible threats that might otherwise have been dismissed.

Being too expansive in risk identification can be just as damaging as, if not more damaging than, being too limited, however: Once unleashed, our imaginations can concoct all manner of horrors lurking in the shadows. The hope here is that thinking of strategy in terms of tradeoffs among activities within an activity set provides a rigorous and systematic way to identify the magnitude and nature of strategic risks—namely, in terms of risks *of* and *to* a company's chosen strategy.

When it comes to treating strategic risks, there has been a tendency among many researchers to favor adaptability—the ability to change strategies rapidly. This, however, begs the question of how to create a changeable strategy without undermining the defining characteristic of a good strategy—namely, that it is built on commitments made over time and hence intrinsically difficult to change quickly. And so a central challenge that has long defined attempts to manage strategic risk is what might be called a "meta tradeoff" between commitment and adaptability.

Here the notion of "strategic *flexibility*" is invoked to capture the attributes of treating strategic risks with strategic options. Staying committed to an established and successful business is almost always a good idea. Compromising the power of existing commitments based on the possibility that they might be inappropriate at some point in the future is certainly a rational choice but is perhaps an unnecessary one. Devoting some resources—as a form of "strategic insurance policy"—to exploring alternative strategies that are tied to different innovation trajectories can create the option of shifting to a new strategy when and as relevant risks materialize.

It is by preserving the power of commitment with benefits of adaptability that strategic flexibility breaks the long-standing tradeoff between the two and is, just maybe, an innovation in the management of strategic risk.

Notes

1. The details on Blockbuster and, for the purposes of this chapter, its relevant competitors Redbox and Netflix, are taken from the Wikipedia entries for each company. The sources cited in these entries for the facts adduced here have been verified.
2. Michal E. Raynor and Mumtaz Ahmed, *The Three Rules: How Exceptional Companies Think* (New York: Portfolio, 2013).
3. This definition of "strategy" is extrapolated from Porter, Michael E. (1996), "What Is Strategy?" *Harvard Business Review*, and from Raynor, Michael E., *The Innovator's Manifesto* (New York: Currency/Doubleday, 2011).
4. Michael E. Raynor, *The Strategy Paradox: How Committing to Success Leads to Failure... and What to Do about It* (New York: Currency/Doubleday, 2007).
5. Pankaj Ghemawat, *Commitment: The Dynamic of Strategy* (New York: The Free Press, 1991).

Index

Note: Page numbers followed by "*b*," "*f*," and "*t*" refer to boxes, figures, and tables, respectively.